T0122210

Data Analytics

Series Editors

Longbing Cao, Advanced Analytics Institute, University of Technology, Sydney, Broadway, NSW, Australia

Philip S. Yu, University of Illinois, Chicago, IL, USA

Aims and Goals:

Building and promoting the field of data science and analytics in terms of publishing work on theoretical foundations, algorithms and models, evaluation and experiments, applications and systems, case studies, and applied analytics in specific domains or on specific issues.

Specific Topics:

This series encourages proposals on cutting-edge science, technology and best practices in the following topics (but not limited to):

- Data analytics, data science, knowledge discovery, machine learning, deep learning, big data, statistical and mathematical methods, exploratory and applied analytics,
- New scientific findings and progress ranging from data capture, creation, storage, search, computing, sharing, analysis, and visualization,
- Integration methods, best practices and typical applications across heterogeneous, multi-sources, domains and modals for data-driven real-world decision-making, and value creation.

Suggested Titles for Proposals:

- Introduction to data science
- Data science fundamentals
- Applied analytics
- Advanced analytics: concepts and applications
- Banking data analytics
- Behavior analytics
- Big data analytics
- Biomedical data analytics
- Business analytics
- Cloud analytics
- Computational intelligence methods for data science
- Data visualization
- Data optimization
- Data representation
- Distributed analytics and learning
- Educational data analytics
- Environmental data analytics
- Ethics in data science
- Feature selection and mining
- Financial data analytics and FinTech
- Government data analytics
- Health and medical data analytics
- Heterogeneous data analytics
- High performance analytics
- In-memory analytics
- Insurance data analytics
- Large-scale inference
- Learning analytics
- Large-scale learning
- Mobile analytics
- Model optimization
- Multimedia analytics
- Network analytics
- Non-IID learning
- Predictive analytics
- Prescriptive analytics
- Scientific data analytics
- Service analytics
- Smart cities, home and IoT
- Statistics for data science
- Social analytics
- Social security data analytics
- Smart city and analytics
- Spatial-temporal data analytics
- Telco data analytics
- Textual data analytics
- Time-series analysis
- Transport data analytics
- Web analytics
- Visual analytics

Chaocan Xiang • Panlong Yang • Fu Xiao •
Xiaochen Fan

Multi-dimensional Urban Sensing Using Crowdsensing Data

Chaocan Xiang 🆔
College of Computer Science
Chongqing University
Chongqing, China

Panlong Yang
Computer Science and Technology
University of Science and Technology of China
Hefei, Anhui, China

Fu Xiao 🆔
College of Computer Science
Nanjing University of Posts and
Telecommunications
Nanjing, Jiangsu, China

Xiaochen Fan 🆔
Faculty of Engineering and IT
University of Technology Sydney
Broadway, NSW, Australia

ISSN 2520-1859   ISSN 2520-1867   (electronic)
Data Analytics
ISBN 978-981-19-9008-3   ISBN 978-981-19-9006-9   (eBook)
https://doi.org/10.1007/978-981-19-9006-9

© The Editor(s) (if applicable) and The Author(s), under exclusive license to Springer Nature Singapore
Pte Ltd. 2023
This work is subject to copyright. All rights are solely and exclusively licensed by the Publisher, whether
the whole or part of the material is concerned, specifically the rights of translation, reprinting, reuse of
illustrations, recitation, broadcasting, reproduction on microfilms or in any other physical way, and
transmission or information storage and retrieval, electronic adaptation, computer software, or by
similar or dissimilar methodology now known or hereafter developed.
The use of general descriptive names, registered names, trademarks, service marks, etc. in this publication
does not imply, even in the absence of a specific statement, that such names are exempt from the relevant
protective laws and regulations and therefore free for general use.
The publisher, the authors, and the editors are safe to assume that the advice and information in this
book are believed to be true and accurate at the date of publication. Neither the publisher nor the authors or
the editors give a warranty, expressed or implied, with respect to the material contained herein or for any
errors or omissions that may have been made. The publisher remains neutral with regard to jurisdictional
claims in published maps and institutional affiliations.

This Springer imprint is published by the registered company Springer Nature Singapore Pte Ltd.
The registered company address is: 152 Beach Road, #21-01/04 Gateway East, Singapore 189721,
Singapore

Preface

In smart cities, the indispensable devices of people's daily life, such as smartphones, smartwatches, vehicles, and smart buildings, are equipped with more and more sensors. For example, most smartphones have cameras, GPS, acceleration, and light sensors. Also, the number of equipped sensors in many off-the-shelf vehicles is up to 100. Hence, these ubiquitous devices—equipped with plenty of on-board sensors as well as powerful computation and communication capabilities—produce numerous crowdsensing data. For example, the explosive volume of sensing data collected by global smart buildings was nearly 7.8 ZB and 37.2 ZB in 2015 and 2020, respectively. The CNN News in 2017 reported that the car's sensing data would be more valuable than the car itself. Leveraging the massive sensing data produced by the common devices of users for large-scale, fine-grained sensing in smart cities is referred to as urban crowdsensing. It can enable many urban applications that benefit different kinds of urban services, including traffic, wireless communication service (4 G/5 G), and environmental protection.

In this book, as shown in Fig. 1, we provide an overview of our recent research progress on urban crowdsensing, *i.e.*, multi-dimensional urban sensing using crowdsensing data. It focuses on multi-dimensional fundamental issues and applications, highly differing from existing literatures. Specifically, we first focus on how to utilize crowdsensing to see the smart city in terms of three-dimensional fundamental issues, including how to incentivize users' participation, how to recommend tasks, and how to transmit the massive sensing data. We propose a series of mechanisms and algorithm designs to address these important issues, which are key to leveraging the crowdsensing data for realizing urban applications. Second, we present how to exploit this available crowdsensing data to see the smart cities through three-dimensional applications, including urban pollution monitoring, traffic volume prediction, and urban airborne sensing. More importantly, this book explores using building sensing data for urban traffic sensing, thus establishing connections between smart buildings and intelligent transportation.

As shown in Fig. 1, the contents of this book are divided into three main parts as follows.

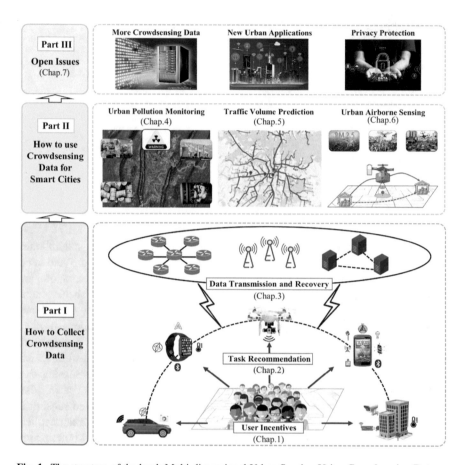

Fig. 1 The structure of the book Multi-dimensional Urban Sensing Using Crowdsensing Data

- Part I (Chaps. 1–3): We introduce how to collect the crowdsensing data, including user incentive mechanism, data transmission, and data calibration. Specifically, in Chap. 1, we specify how to incentivize users to participate in mobile crowdsensing. We present *Picasso*, a novel mechanism design for incentivizing platform–user interactions. It not only encourages more user's participation with personalized bidding but also reduces the crowdsensing platform owner's cost with efficient algorithm designs. In Chap. 2, based on a large-scale vehicle dataset analysis, we propose a new Long-Short-Term Profit-combined task recommendation model called *LSTRec*. It guarantees not only positive profits for drivers but also a near-optimal profit for the platform. In Chap. 3, we introduce how to transmit large amounts of crowdsensing data and propose an edge computing-empowered system named *GTR*. It leverages the decentralized computing power of edge nodes to process massive crowdsensing data for accurate and real-time data recovery.

- Part II (Chaps. 4–6): We introduce how to utilize crowdsensing data for multi-dimensional applications in smart cities, including urban pollution monitoring, traffic volume prediction, and urban airborne sensing. Specifically, in Chap. 4, we introduce how to use the crowdsensing data for identifying urban radiation sources in an accurate and robust way. We propose an iterative truthful-source identification algorithm. It iterates alternately between sensor efficiency estimation and truthful probability estimation, gradually improving the identification accuracy. In Chap. 5, we explore how to exploit the crowdsensing data from the buildings to predict the traffic of their nearby roads. We conduct a comprehensive building-traffic analysis based on multi-source datasets. Based on the analyzed results, we propose a novel Recurrent Neural Network (RNN) for traffic prediction, leveraging the cross-domain learning with two attention mechanisms. This work opens a new gate of using building sensing data for urban traffic sensing, thus establishing connections between smart buildings and intelligent transportation. In Chap. 6, we propose novel studies on the reutilization of delivery drone resources for large-scale and low-cost urban crowdsensing. We conduct real-world experiments to develop an energy cost model for delivery drones. Then, the route-time-weight joint optimization problem was formulated based on this model. Finally, the near-optimal algorithms were proposed when the delivery weight of each route was fixed and adjustable, respectively. This chapter uncovers that drone sharing, similar to ride sharing (such as Uber and DiDi), will become a promising force in the sharing economy.
- Part III (Chaps. 7–8): We discuss some of the open issues and possible applications involved in urban crowdsensing. Finally, we summarize the content of this monograph.

The contents of this book will be of particular interest to readers, *e.g.*, researchers, students, professionals, and urban planners. Furthermore, this book can serve as a primer for beginners to gain a big picture of mobile crowdsensing in smart cities. It could also help them understand how to collect and exploit the crowdsensing data for different kinds of urban applications. To understand this book easily, readers should be familiar with the concepts and common methods of Internet of Things (IoT), optimization theory, and machine learning.

Chongqing, China   Chaocan Xiang
Hefei, Anhui, China   Panlong Yang
Nanjing, Jiangsu, China   Fu Xiao
Broadway, NSW, Australia   Xiaochen Fan

Acknowledgments

Thanks to my students who help proofread the manuscript of this book carefully, including Lianghua Cheng, Wenhui Cheng, Ruixue Huang, and Hao Chen. We also want to express our appreciation to the staff at Springer, Mr. Zhu, for his guidance through our publication journey. This book was also partially supported by the National Natural Science Foundation of China under Grants No. 62172063 and No. 61872447.

Contents

Part I
How to Collect Crowdsensing Data
(Multi-dimensional Fundamental Issues)

Chapter 1
Incentivizing Platform-Users with Win-Win Effects

1.1 Introduction

Due to the potential of crowds and widespread mobile devices, crowdsensing has been gaining popularity and attractiveness, boosting numerous crowdsensing systems and platforms [1–3], such as Crowdsensing Map [4], Amazon Mechanical Turk, and Gigwalk.[1] The success of crowdsensing is subject to interactions between the platform (or the platform owner) and the crowdsensing participants [5]. Hence, it is crucial to incentivize the interactions of participants and platforms, as witnessed by various proposals [6–8].

Among existing incentive mechanisms, the auction model has been widely studied, as it boosts competitiveness among participants and enables better incentivization [9, 10]. After users bid for published tasks according to their preferences in describing bids, the platform applies certain criteria to assign task(s) to users. Practically, users are of diverse preferences in bidding for a combination of tasks due to the differences in in-situ context, location, available time, interest, etc. [11]. For instance, Lucy and Bob are two users interested in the same N tasks, but Lucy prefers only one of them as her time is limited, while Bob, whose time is sufficient, is in want of any subset of these N tasks.

Ensuring users' bidding is tailored to their personal preferences, called *personalized bidding* (PB) [12]. It is critical to incentivize crowdsensing with benefits for both the participants and the platform owner. According to a recent survey [13] which covers over 1500 users, more than 56% of them prefer personalized services. To sum up, PB is capable of motivating users to participate in crowdsensing by accommodating their personal preferences and increasing the intrinsic motivation of psychological factors [14, 15]. Additionally, it encourages users to bid for more tasks with higher utility, thereby boosting the competition among users and lowering the platform's cost/payment.

---

[1] http://www.gigwalk.com/

© The Author(s), under exclusive license to Springer Nature Singapore Pte Ltd. 2023
C. Xiang et al., *Multi-dimensional Urban Sensing Using Crowdsensing Data*, Data Analytics, https://doi.org/10.1007/978-981-19-9006-9_1

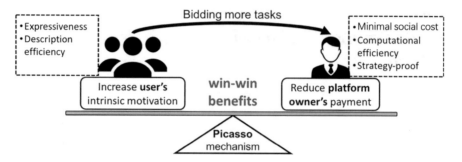

Fig. 1.1 Incentivization of platform–user interactions with win-win benefits using *Picasso*

Prior works focus on the design of task allocation at the lowest social cost, computational efficiency, and strategy-proof from the perspective of the platform, neglecting the users' diverse preferences [10]. Most studies [16–19] used single-minded bids, which are incapable of stating the users' diverse preferences [20]. For instance, the single-minded bids, which allow participants to bid for either the bundle of all tasks or nothing [18, 21], give no permission to Lucy to state her personal preference for a combination of tasks. Hence, the *expressiveness* of PB, *i.e.*, the ability that a mechanism allows users to express all possible task combinations in their bids, is not supported by them. Still, one thing that should be paid attention to is that a few researchers [20, 22, 23] have examined the users' expressiveness with the help of multi-minded bids. However, seeing from the user's perspective, the expressiveness or description efficiency of PB is still unsatisfactory.

To fill this gap, as illustrated in Fig. 1.1, we put forward a comprehensive incentive mechanism that achieves (a) *expressiveness* and (b) *description efficiency* of PB in describing users' bids; (c) *minimal social cost*, (d) *computational efficiency*, and (e) *strategy-proof* in the platform owner's assignment of tasks to the users [22, 23]. Nevertheless, it is difficult to realize all of them in concert, since there exist intrinsically clashing goals of the platform owner and participants as follows.

- **Chg1. Describing bids**: Owing to the rising number of task bids (*i.e.*, task bundles), PB's expressiveness makes it possible for a much broader space of candidate task allocation, at the expense of significantly higher computational complexity for the optimal task allocation. In addition, the bidding flexibility required via PB's expressiveness broadens the users' bid descriptions, causing incompetency in the application. Therefore, realizing expressiveness without degrading description efficiency stays a challenging task.
- **Chg2. Allocating tasks**: Countless bidding options add more complex constraints upon the allocation of different tasks to users, called *task dependency*. Such dependency makes it challenging to address the problem of task-allocation for lowering social costs as much as possible. It has been proved that this problem is NP-hard in Sect. 1.3.4. Additionally, such dependency might be inappropriately applied by users with the selfish intention to misreport and manipulate for higher utility, making the task allocation less strategy-proof.

To solve these two challenges, we propose a novel incentive mechanism for crowdsensing, called ***Picasso***.[2] As shown in Fig. 1.1, in contrast to prior work, *Picasso* realizes all five features (a)–(e) from the perspectives of both the platform and users with two key ideas as follows.

- To deal with Chg1, in Sect. 1.4.1, a formal framework of bid description in 3-D expressive space is established by putting three logical operations, *i.e.*, AND, XOR, and OR in combination. In addition, we propose a new PB description method based on this framework to realize a balance between expressiveness, computational complexity, and description efficiency.
- To address Chg2, in Sect. 1.4.2, firstly, we construct a task dependency graph to model the dependency of task allocations in a user's PB. After that, regarding the relationships in logical operations in a general manner, we decompose the complex graph of a user's PB into multiple subgraphs of independent single-minded bids for more tractable task allocation. In addition, these subgraphs of a user are recombined so as to put forward an adaptive critical-payment computation scheme, preventing users from strategically exploiting task dependencies for higher utility. At last, the aforementioned properties of *Picasso* are evaluated via theoretical analyses in Sect. 1.4 and trace-based Gigwalk case studies in Sect. 1.5.

To conclude, this chapter contributes mainly to three aspects:

1. Design a comprehensive framework for the description of users' bids and generalization prior to work. By applying this framework, we devise a new PB description method by employing a 3-D expression space with the orchestration of AND, XOR, and OR, which has realized a good trade-off between expressiveness, computational complexity, and description efficiency.
2. Design of a dependency-aware task allocation algorithm, realizing constant-factor approximation and strategy-proof in polynomial time with the decomposition and the subsequent recombination of the task dependency graph.
3. Extensive theoretical analyses and trace-driven Gigwalk case studies for evaluating the performance of *Picasso*. According to our trace-driven evaluations, unlike existing approaches [16, 22, 23], *Picasso* allows each user to bid for $9.7\times$ more tasks. In addition, it decreases the description length by 74%, inspiring more user participation. Consequently, the social cost is reduced, and the platform's payment is decreased by more than 60% and 61%, respectively. Therefore, *Picasso* makes a win-win solution to incentivize interactions between the users and the platform owner, advancing long-term crowdsensing.

The subsequent content of this chapter is arranged as follows. To start with, the related work in Sect. 1.2 will be discussed. And then, it will be the declaration of the system model and the formalization of the problem in Sect. 1.3. Also, we put forward an incentive mechanism called *Picasso* together with theoretical analyses in Sect.

---

[2]Like the Cubist painting pioneered by Pablo *Picasso*, we describe the bids in 3-D space by decomposing and recombining the graph.

1.4. Traces-driven evaluations will be conducted in Sect. 1.5. Finally, we discuss several influenced factors in Sect. 1.6 and conclude remarks in Sect. 1.7.

1.2   Related Work

There have been a large number of studies on incentivized crowdsensing [8, 24], most of which apply the reverse auction model [10, 25]. As *Picasso* falls into this category, the focus is placed on reviewing its related studies regarding users' bids, classified as single-minded and multi-minded bids [23, 26, 27]. Other orthogonal studies like the posted-pricing model [28, 29] can be referred to [8, 10].

Single-minded bids Seeing from the perspective of the platform, studies of the most exciting ones are based on single-minded bids (SMB), given the ease of design and priority of task allocation. For instance, many of them intend to maximize the platform's profit [17] or realize constant-factor approximation [16] subject to constraints, such as computational efficiency [19, 30], strategy-proof [18, 31], quality constraint [16], budget limitation [19], and social network [32–35]. Although they report promising results for the platform, they are all on the basis of single-minded bids, *i.e.*, each user is permitted to select one bundle of tasks in a 'win all or nothing' fashion [26]. Therefore, they fall flat in considering users' diverse preferences for task bundling [36]. In the absence of diversified bid design [26], the design goal of expressiveness is not satisfied, which deters users' participation by lessening intrinsic psychological motivations [14, 37]. In contrast, in the users' perspectives, *Picasso* operates in allowing the user's diverse bids with regard to their social and psychological diversity [15]. Being complementary to these state-of-the-arts, *Picasso* is capable of further incentivizing the users with both extrinsic and intrinsic motivations [14].

Multi-minded bids Some researchers [20, 22, 23, 26, 27] have considered multi-minded bids in the design of incentive mechanisms from the perspective of users. Han et al. [26] concentrated on the posted-pricing model, but it is bid-independent. Therefore, it is unsuitable for our scenarios based on the bid-dependent auction model [26]. The focus of Lin et al. [27] was on protecting user privacy and security attack, but that is orthogonal to our work.

One line of prior works [20, 22, 23] that are extremely related to this chapter investigates the design of incentive mechanisms with multi-minded bids in the auction model. Feng et al. [22] design the TRAC mechanism, with which every user can submit multiple disjoint bids and obtain any subset of them. It is generalized to the Single-OR-Bidding (SOB) model, which has been proved to be inexpressive (Sect. 1.4.1.2). Even though QoI-MRC [20] and IMC-SM [23] can be satisfied in the user's expressiveness, the impact of multi-minded bids on the allocation of tasks and payments are neglected by them. For instance, QoI-MRC is not competent for full trust of user for payment allocation, while IMC-SM cannot realize guaranteed near-optimal social cost in task allocation. Additionally, their designs [20, 23], being a special case of the Single-XOR-Bidding (SXB) model, are description-inefficient with exponential length, which has been proved. Conversely, we build a generic framework of bid description which accommodates these results [20, 22, 23] painlessly. With this framework being the basis, a new bid description scheme is designed, causing decrease in the description length to polynomial complexity. Moreover, a new task allocation algorithm is proposed, which has realized constant-factor sub-optimization and truthfulness in polynomial time.

Moreover, researchers [38–40] have studied the bidding language of combinatorial auctions. Based on that, bidders state their complicated preferences on bundles of expected tasks. They center on either the expressiveness to reveal user's preferences [40] or the description efficiency, which promotes user-friendliness and communication [39] thoroughly. We do not study the bidding language independently. Instead, we take into consideration the relationship between the bid design and task allocation in crowdsensing scenarios. It is fed back to make refinement of the bid description scheme so as to create a balance between the features of the platform and users.

Summary as summarized in Table 1.1, compared with existing approaches, *Picasso* is a new incentive mechanism designed from the perspectives of both the platform and users, faring well in all five important features. With the 'win-win' benefits, *Picasso* promotes the interaction between the platform and the user. Moreover, it incentivizes the entire crowdsensing, advancing the long-term development of the crowdsensing community [7].

1.3 System Model and Problem Formulation

Firstly, we introduce the system model of the auction-based incentive mechanism. It is followed by giving a toy example of personalized bidding in Gigwalk. Then the mechanism design problem is formulated, considering the perspectives of both users and platform owners simultaneously. At last, this problem is proved to be NP-hard in theory.

1.3.1 System Model

Figure 1.2 illustrates the general model for the incentive mechanism of crowdsensing, whose workflow consists of the following three phases.

Step 1 (Task publishing) The platform publishes sensing tasks to the crowd of potential users who may have an interest in this crowdsensing campaign. Let $\mathcal{T}$ be the set of tasks, *i.e.*, $\mathcal{T} = \{\tau_j | j \in \{1, \ldots, M\}\}$, where τ_j and M denote the j-th task

Table 1.1 Comparison between our work and existing works from the perspectives of the platform and users

References	Bid's type	User's perspective		Platform's perspective		
		Expressiveness	Description efficiency	Guaranteed near-minimal social cost	Computational efficiency	Strategy proof
Yang et al. [18, 21]	Single-mind	×	√	×	√	√
Jin et al. [16, 41]	Single-mind	×	√	√	×	√
Tang et al. [31, 42]	Single-mind	×	√	√	√	√
Feng et al. [22]	Multi-mind	×	√	√	√	√
Jin et al. [20]	Multi-mind	√	√	√	√	×
Zhang et al. [23]	Multi-mind	√	×	×	√	√
Our work	**Multi-mind**	√	√	√	√	√

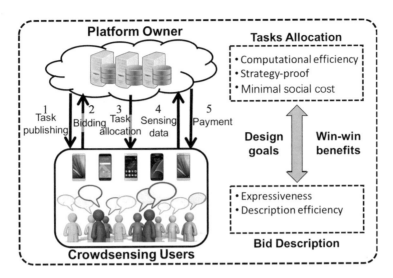

Fig. 1.2   System model of incentive mechanism with design goals

and the number of tasks, respectively. For each τ_j, there is a corresponding valuation $v_j > 0$. Assume there are N users interested in the tasks, and let $\mathcal{U} = \{u_i | i \in \{1, \ldots, N\}\}$ denote the set of users.

Step 2 (Task bidding)   As stated by the description method, each user u_i makes her/his PB for those tasks at their preference r_i, including the tasks they want to perform and the desired payments. We define the PB of u_i as $B_i = \{b_{i,k} | b_{i,k} = (T_{i,k}, a_{i,k}), k \in \{1, \ldots, \delta_i\}\}$, where $b_{i,k}$ and δ_i denote the atomic bid of u_i as Definition 1.1 and the number of atomic bids, respectively. Last, they send the PBs to the platform.

Definition 1.1   *Atomic bid, also called single-minded bid (SMB): a user can submit a bid $b_{i,k} = (T_{i,k}, a_{i,k})$, where $T_{i,k}$ is a subset of tasks (i.e., $T_{i,k} \subseteq T$) and $a_{i,k}$ is the desired payment for executing these tasks. The user may execute all the tasks in $T_{i,k}$ with the payment $a_{i,k}$, or not execute any task without payment. Such a bid is said to be atomic, i.e., the basic unit of bid description.*

Apart from the desired payment $a_{i,k}$, u_i incurs a real cost $c_{i,k}$ of executing $T_{i,k}$, which is in practice private information and is inclusively known to herself/himself. Since humans are complicated in being selfish and rational concurrently, users prefer not to ask for their real costs in the bids to earn more money. Hence $c_{i,k} \leq a_{i,k}$.

Steps 3, 4 and 5 (Allocation, execution, and payment of tasks)   based on their bids (i.e., $\{B_i | i = 1, \ldots, N\}$), the platform determines the set of allocated tasks S_i and the payment p_i for u_i, according to the task allocation and the payment rules (Step 3). Note that $S_i = \bigcup_{k=1}^{\delta_i} S_{i,k}$, where $S_{i,k}$ denotes the set of task allocation for $T_{i,k}$, i.e., $S_{i,k} \subseteq T_{i,k}$. Let $p_i = \sum_{k=1}^{\delta_i} p_{i,k}$, where $p_{i,k}$ denotes the payment of the task allocation $S_{i,k}$,

Table 1.2 Frequently used notations

Symbols	Definitions
$\tau_j, c_j, M, \mathcal{T}$	j-th task; its cost; its number; set of tasks
$u_i, N, \mathcal{U}$	i-th user; its number; set of users.
$B_i, b_{i,k}$	u_i's bid; k-th atomic bid of u_i, i.e., $b_{i,k} \in B_i$
$T_{i,k}, a_{i,k}, p_{i,k}$	Task set of $b_{i,k}$; its bidding price; its payment
$S_i, u_{i,k}^{\vee}$	Set of allocated tasks for u_i; k-th virtual user of u_i.
E, ξ	Expressive power; cost-efficiency.
λ, π	Description length; utility of user(platform).

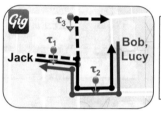

User's Preferences

- **Bob**: one of τ_1, τ_2 and $\{\tau_1,\tau_2\}$,
- **Lucy**: either τ_1 or τ_2,
- **Jack**: either $\{\tau_1,\tau_2\}$,

  or one of τ_1, τ_3 and $\{\tau_1,\tau_3\}$.

Fig. 1.3 Toy example of Gigwalk for user's personalized bidding, where τ_j denotes the j-th task

depending on its desired payment $a_{i,k}$. Each u_i then executes the tasks (i.e., S_i) assigned to her/him by sensing and reports the sensing results to the platform (Step 4), which then pays p_i to u_i (Step 5). We assume that all the tasks can be executed successfully due to a large number of potential users equipped with diverse skills in crowdsensing [22]. We also assume that the users can successfully finish their allocated tasks while discussing the users' unreliability in Sect. 1.6. Hence, the **utility of user** u_i is $\pi_i^{\mathrm{u}} = \sum_{k=1}^{\delta_i} \left(p_{i,k} - c_{i,k} \right)$. Furthermore, all the users finish the set of tasks as $S = \bigcup_{i=1}^{N} S_i$, and the **utility of platform** is $\pi^{\mathrm{p}} = \sum_{\forall \tau_j \in S} \left(v_j - c_j \right)$. Table 1.2 illustrates frequently used notations.

1.3.2   Example of Personalized Bidding Scenario

Take as an example to illustrate the PB in crowdsensing. Gigwalk is a crowdsensing app that is widely applied. The platform of Gigwalk enables mobile participants to visit shops at different places to collect real-time data on specific products, as shown in Fig. 1.3.

Suppose Gigwalk publishes three sensing tasks (i.e., τ_1, τ_2, and τ_3) at three different locations. Assume that there are three participants, e.g., Bob, Lucy, and

Jack. As they differ in interests, contexts, and availability, these three users have different preferences on task bidding. Specifically, both Bob and Lucy will go through the locations of τ_1 and τ_2 along with the purple line routine in Fig. 1.3, since Bob is sufficient in time and expects to do any subset of τ_1 and τ_2 with the prices of \$50 and \$10, respectively. Nonetheless, as Lucy's time is limited, she expects to bid either τ_1 or τ_2 with the prices of \$10 and \$30, respectively. There are two alternative routines for Jack as the black solid line and the black dashed line in Fig. 1.3. He wants to either do the bundle of τ_1 and τ_2 in one routine with prices \$15 and \$35 accordingly, or take either τ_1 or τ_3 for the price of \$15 or \$10, respectively.

Let u_1, u_2, and u_3 denote Jack, Bob, and Lucy, respectively. Then, as shown in the system model in Sect. 1.3.1, the personalized bids of Jack, Bob, and Lucy are formalized as $B_1 = \{(\tau_1), (\tau_3), (\tau_1, \tau_2), (\tau_1, \tau_3)\}$, $B_2 = \{(\tau_1), (\tau_2), (\tau_1, \tau_2)\}$, and $B_3 = \{(\tau_1), (\tau_2)\}$, respectively.

1.3.3 Problem Formalization

As shown in Fig. 1.2, the mechanism design problem for personalized bidding can be stated as:

1. from the perspective of the platform, how to design the *task allocation algorithm* $\Psi(\cdot)$ for the platform to allocate all the tasks $\mathcal{T}$ to the users $\mathcal{U}$ with the payments based on the users' PBs ($\mathbf{B} = \{B_1, \ldots, B_N\}$) as Eq. (1.3), so as to achieve (a) *minimal social cost*, (b) *strategy-proof*, and (c) *computational efficiency*.
2. from the perspective of users, how to design a *bid description method* $\Omega(\cdot)$ for u_i to describe PBs B_i based on her/his preferences r_i as Eq. (1.2), in order to satisfy (d) *expressiveness* and (e) *description efficiency*. Let $x_{i,j}$ be the indicator variable ($x_{i,j} \in \{0, 1\}$), i.e., $x_{i,j} = 1$ if task j is allocated to u_i, and $x_{i,j} = 0$ otherwise. $\mathbf{X}_i = \{x_{i,j} | j = 1, \cdots, M\}$. The problem is formulated as:

$$\mathbf{Min} \sum_{i=1}^{N} \sum_{j=1}^{M} x_{i,j} c_{i,j} \tag{1.1}$$

$$\text{s.t. } B_i = \Omega(r_i), i \in \{1, \ldots, N\}, \tag{1.2}$$

$$(\mathbf{X}_i, p_i) = \Psi(\mathbf{B}, \mathcal{T}, \mathcal{U}), i \in \{1, \ldots, N\}, \tag{1.3}$$

$$\sum_{j=1}^{M} \left(p_{i,j} - c_{i,j}\right) \geq 0, \forall i \in \{1, \ldots, N\}, \tag{1.4}$$

$$\pi_i^{\mathrm{u}}(c_i, a_{-i}) \geq \pi_i^{\mathrm{u}}(a_i, a_{-i}), \forall i \in \{1, \ldots, N\}, \tag{1.5}$$

$$\sum_{i=1}^{N} x_{i,j} = 1, \forall j \in \{1, \ldots, M\},$$

(1.6)

where the features of the platform owner and users are:

(a) **Minimal social cost**: from the perspective of the platform, it aims at maximizing the platform utility, *i.e.,*

$$\sum_{i=1}^{N} \sum_{j=1}^{M} x_{i,j}\left(v_j - c_{i,j}\right)$$

(1.7)

As shown in Eq. (1.6), each task is constrained to be allocated to at most one user, and all the tasks should be completed [18]. Therefore, $\sum_{i=1}^{N} \sum_{j=1}^{M} x_{i,j}v_j$ is a constant. The objective function can be equivalently represented as Eq. (1.1), *i.e.,* minimizing the social cost (or called social welfare [31]), which is the sum of the user's real costs of all tasks s/he finished [22].

(b) **Strategy-proof**: the mechanism should have *individual rationality* [16], *i.e.,* all the users receive non-negative utilities as Eq. (1.4). Also, it should satisfy *truthfulness* [19] as Eq. (1.5), which means that it is a main strategy in a Nash equilibrium for all the users to claim the real costs c_i in their bids, where a_i denotes the bidding price of u_i, and a_{-i} denotes those of the other users. Since users cannot improve her/his utility in misstating the costs individually, which makes the mechanism a plainer one. This is based on the assumption that each user is independent and will not be engaged in collusion with each other [43]. Additionally, only the tasks covered by bids of at least two users for truthfulness are under consideration, as there are a large number of potential users with various skills in crowdsensing [22].

(c) **Computational efficiency**: an algorithm is computationally efficient if and only if it can be completed in polynomial time [19]. In the PB formulation, the task allocation algorithm $\Psi(\cdot)$ should fare well in computation efficiency for real-time allocation, which is of great importance for incentivizing users in practice [26]. To streamline the formulation, as Eq. (1.1), we consider the additive cost/payments of tasks, where the total cost/payments of multiple tasks are the summation of that of each individual task [8, 23]. We will also have a discussion on the non-additive cost of tasks [44] in Sect. 1.6.

(d) **Expressiveness**: The description method $\Omega(\cdot)$ should be flexible enough so the users can express their diverse bidding preferences of task combinations [45]. The set of all possible task combinations in users' bids allowed by $\Omega(\cdot)$ is referred to as its *expressive space* [40]. Then the size of expressive space is defined as an *expressive power* (denoted as E), which quantifies the expressiveness of a description method [45]. The larger the expressive power is, the more diverse of preferences the users can express.

(e) **Description efficiency**: (also referred to as *Description succinctness*). The bid description method $\Omega(\cdot)$ should show efficiency for users to express their preferences [40]. The amount of atomic bids in a bid description is defined as its description length (λ) [12]. We also apply *average description length* (ADL) $\bar{\lambda}$ of all the descriptions to fulfill the quantification of the description efficiency of $\Omega(\cdot)$. To see in an intuitive way, a shorter ADL eases bidding description for participants, leading to higher description efficiency [12]. In addition, the computational complexity of $\Omega(\cdot)$ is dominated by the maximum description length (MDL) $\hat{\lambda}$ of all the descriptions.

1.3.4 Analysis of Problem Complexity

Considering the aforementioned comprehensive problem formalization for both the platform and users, the computational complexity of task allocation features personalized bidding is examined.

Theorem 1.1 *The optimal task allocation problem with PB is NP-hard.*

Proof Recall that Bi is the PB of u_i. Let $b_{i,\,k} := (T_{i,\,k}, a_{i,\,k})$ be a single-minded bid by u_i as Definition 1.1. Then, we have $b_{i,\,k} \in B_i$. If we replace B_i by $b_{i,\,k}$ for each $u_i \in \mathcal{U}$, the constraint in Eq. (1.2) can be relaxed, and the optimal task allocation problem with PB (called OTA-PB) becomes the one without PB (named OTA-NonPB).

Then we demonstrate the NP-hardness of OTA-PB by proving that OTA-NonPB is at least NP-hard. Let S_i be the set of sensing tasks assigned to u_i to execute and c_i be the corresponding total cost. Thus, in the problem OTA-NonPB, constraint in Eq. (1.3) is equal to a set cover constraint over task set $\mathcal{T}$, *i.e.,* $\underset{i=1,\,2,\,...,\,N}{\cup} S_i = \mathcal{T}$, meaning that all sensing tasks will be executed.

Furthermore, constraint in Eq. (1.6) implies that the intersection of any two different sets S_i and $S_j (\forall i, j \in \{1, 2, \ldots, N\}, i \neq j)$ is null, *i.e.,* $S_i \cap S_j = \varnothing$. As the strategy-proof is dependent on the task allocation instead of the payment, constraints in Eqs. (1.4) and (1.5) can be relaxed [10]. As a result, OTA-NonPB will become:

$$\text{Min} \ \sum_{i=1}^{N} c_i \tag{1.8}$$

$$\text{s.t.} \quad \underset{i \in \{1,\,...,\,N\}}{\cup} S_i = \mathcal{T}, \tag{1.9}$$

$$S_i \cap S_j = \varnothing, \forall i, j \in \{1, 2, \ldots, N\}, i \neq j. \tag{1.10}$$

The decision version of the above problem is a minimum weighted set cover (MWSC) problem with the mutual exclusiveness constraint as Eq. (1.10) [46]. Note that MWSC is a widely accepted NP-complete problem [47]. To examine whether an obtained solution is satisfactory to the mutual exclusiveness constraint in polynomial time, the decision problem is NP-hard [47]. Therefore, the problem OTA-NonPB is NP-hard, which proves the NP-hardness of OTA-PB.

1.4   Design of *Picasso*

To deal with the mechanism design problem with PB in Sect. 1.3.3, as shown in Fig. 1.4, we propose *Picasso*, which allocates the tasks with the truthful payment to the users according to their diverse preferences on the published tasks. Particularly, *Picasso* mainly includes the following two components:

1. **Bid description based on 3-D space** (Sect. 1.4.1): Firstly, we propose a formal framework of bid description on the basis of 3-D expressive space, which is created by the orchestration of AND, XOR, and OR in Sect. 1.4.1.1. Then, in Sect. 1.4.1.2, it has been proved theoretically to reach a balance among expressiveness, description efficiency, and computational complexity.
2. **Task allocation based on dependency graph** (Sect. 1.4.2): To start with, we build the task dependency graph model to represent the user's bid in Sect. 1.4.2.1. Then, in Sect. 1.4.2.2, the task allocation scheme is designed based on graph decomposition to solve the NP-hard problem, realizing a near-optimal solution with a guaranteed approximation ratio in polynomial time. Finally, in Sect. 1.4.2.3, we propose a novel payment method based on graph recombination. It applies the critical payment computation to design the strategy-proof payment scheme, which can deter users with selfish intentions from strategically exploiting the complex PB to improve their utilities.

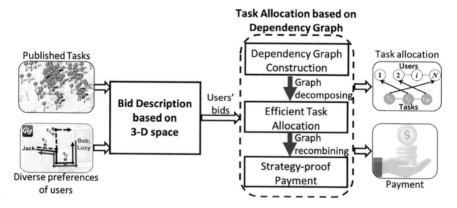

Fig. 1.4 Framework of *Picasso*, which incentivizes platform-user interactions

1.4.1 Bid Description in 3-D Space

PB Description in 3-D Space

We first build a formal framework for the bid description by leveraging 3-D expressive space. Then we propose a specific description method as well as a walk-through example.

Formal Framework of Bid Description Using 3-D Expressive Space

To ensure the expressiveness, description efficiency, and computational efficiency, we apply three basic logical operators, *i.e.*, AND, XOR, and OR, to describe users' bids as Definition 1.2.

Definition 1.2 *XOR-of-OR Bidding Description: it is constructed based on* AND, XOR, *and* OR*in three steps as follows.*

1. ***Construct atomic bids**: each u_i can submit an atomic bid, denoted by $b_{i,\,k}$, including an arbitrary number (e.g., $H_{i,\,k}$) of task pairs ($\tau_{i,\,k,\,h}, a_{i,\,k,\,h}$) by* AND *($\wedge$), $h \in \{1, \ldots, H_{i,\,k}\}$. The implication of that the user expects to be allocated all of the tasks $T_{i,\,k} = \{\tau_{i,\,k,\,h} | h \in \{1, \ldots, H_{i,\,k}\}\}$ with the total payment $a_{i,k} = \sum_{h=1}^{H_{i,k}} a_{i,k,h}$ or none of the tasks with no payment. Therefore, $b_{i,\,k} = (T_{i,\,k}, a_{i,\,k})$.*

2. ***Construct** OR **bids**: each u_i can submit an OR bid, denoted by b_i^O, including an arbitrary number (e.g., K_i) of disjoint atomic bids $b_{i,\,k}$ by the logical operator OR ($\cup$), i.e., $b_i^O = \bigcup_{k=1}^{K_i} b_{i,k}$. $\forall k_1, k_2 \in \{1, \ldots, K_i\}$ and $k_1 \neq k_2$ we have $T_{i,k_1} \cap T_{i,k_2} = \varnothing$*

   . It shows that the user expects to be allocated the tasks of any subset of these atomic bids with the sum of their respective payments.

3. ***Construct XOR-of-OR bids**: each u_i can submit an XOR-of-OR bid denoted by b_i^{XO}, which includes an arbitrary number (e.g.,L_i) of OR bids $b_{i,l}^O$ by the logical operator XOR($\bigoplus$), i.e., $b_i^{XO} = \bigoplus_{l=1}^{L_i} b_{i,l}^O = \bigoplus_{l=1}^{L_i} \bigcup_{k=1}^{K_{i,l}} b_{i,l,k}$. As it implies, the user expects allocation of at most one of these OR bids, e.g., $b_{i,l}^O$.*

Theorem 1.2 *XOR-of-ORbidding description in terms of x XOR and y OR operators has the expressive power $E^{XO}(x, y)$ as Eq. (1.11) with $\hat{\lambda} = O(x \cdot y)$. Additionally, it is capable of representing all the PBs with the largest number of XORs and ORs (i.e.,$x = 2^M$ and $y = M$).*

Fig. 1.5 PB description via
3-D space

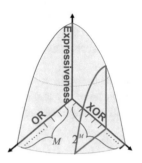

$$E^O(y) = \sum_{k=1}^{y} \sum_{i=1}^{k} \frac{(-1)^i (k-i)^M}{i!(k-i)!}, \tag{1.11}$$

where the expressive power $E^O(y)$ with y OR operators is $E^O(y) = \sum_{k=1}^{y} \sum_{i=1}^{k} \frac{(-1)^i (k-i)^M}{i!(k-i)!}$.
Note that $x \in \{1, \ldots, E^O(y)\}$, and $y \in \{1, \ldots, M\}$.

Proof This theorem is proved by applying dynamic programming and the Inclusion-Exclusion Principle theorem of combinatorics [46]. See Appendix for detailed proof.

As shown in Eq. (1.11), the increment of $E^{XO}(x, y)$ w.r.t. x is

$$\Delta_x E^{XO}(x, y) = \frac{E^O(y)!}{x! (E^O(y) - x)!}. \tag{1.12}$$

As shown in Eqs. (1.11) and (1.12), we can create a 3-D expressive space, as shown in Fig. 1.5. In this 3-D space, the x-axis and y-axis represent the number of XORs (*i.e.,* x) and ORs (*i.e.,* y), respectively. The z-axis represents the increase of expressive space by adding the x-th XORs with yORs as $\Delta_x E^{XO}(x, y)$. Therefore, the 3-D space can be applied to represent the expressiveness of XOR-*of*-OR bidding description method. Moreover, as Theorem 1.2 reveals, this 3-D expressive space with the largest number of XORs and ORs is equivalent to that of PB. Hence, we can leverage AND, OR, and XOR to perform the description of all PBs in a 3-D space.

PB Description Method

we use the aforementioned XOR-of-OR bidding framework to describe PBs. In order to trade-off between expressiveness and computational complexity, the 3-D expressive space is reduced by controlling the length of one dimension (*e.g.,* XOR or OR) with a constant R. As shown in Eq. (1.11), the dominant dimension of the entire expressive space for computational complexity is the number of XORs. Therefore, we further limit the number of XORs by a constant R, and the expressive power is given by Eq. (1.13) with $\hat{\lambda} = R \cdot M$.

$$E^{XO}(R) = \sum_{i=1}^{R} \frac{E^{O}(M)!}{i!\left(E^{O}(M) - i\right)!}, \quad R \in \left\{1, \ldots, E^{O}(M)\right\}. \tag{1.13}$$

Hence, the PB description method consists of the following steps.

1. *Describing a bundle of tasks:* if a user is in expectation to be allocated a bundle of tasks, s/he creates an atomic bid for this bundle of tasks. Otherwise, s/he creates an atomic bid for each task.
2. *Describing the union of tasks:* if the user expects to be allocated any subset of the tasks, s/he uses OR based on the atomic bids to design the plan.
3. *Generating R exclusive plans:* based on the above two steps, each user can create exclusive plans continuously with the maximum limit R. Each participant uses XOR to describe it and expects to be allocated tasks of at most one of these plans.

We consider the Gigwalk example in Sect. 1.3.2 to show how to describe the PB based on 3-D space. Having two exclusive plans, Jack uses XOR to describe his PB as Eq. (1.14). Similarly, the PBs of Bob and Lucy are given by Eqs. (1.15) and (1.16), respectively. Moreover, we discuss how to enable user-friendly PB description in Sect. 1.6.

$$\text{Jack} : \{(\tau_1 \wedge \tau_2, 50)\} \bigoplus \{(\tau_1, 15) \cup (\tau_3, 10)\}, \tag{1.14}$$

$$\text{Bob} : \{(\tau_1, 50) \cup (\tau_2, 10)\}, \tag{1.15}$$

$$\text{Lucy} : \{(\tau_1, 10) \bigoplus (\tau_2, 30)\}. \tag{1.16}$$

Theoretical Analysis

Based on the framework in Sect. 1.4.1.1, firstly, we present the models of *SOB* and *SXB* as Definitions 1.3 and 1.4, respectively, both of which give a generalization of the multi-minded bids [20, 22, 23]. Then, we compare ours with *SMB*, *SOB*, and *SXB* concerning the expressiveness and the description efficiency through theoretical analysis.

Definition 1.3 *SOB Bidding Description: it is constructed by using operators* AND *and* OR *in two steps:*

1. *construct atomic bids: same as in* Definition 1.2.
2. *construct* OR *bids: same as in* Definition 1.2.

Definition 1.4 *SXB Bidding Description: it is constructed using operators* AND *and* XOR *in two steps:*

1. *construct atomic bids: same as in* Definition 1.2.
2. *construct* XOR *bids: each* u_i *can submit an* XOR *bid denoted by* b_i^X, *which includes an arbitrary number (e.g.,* K_i*) of atomic* $b_{i,k}$ *by* XOR *operations* $(\bigoplus)$, *i.e.,* $b_i^X = \bigoplus_{k=1}^{K_i} b_{i,k}$. *It implies that the user expects allocation of at most one of these atomic bids, e.g., getting the set of tasks* $T_{i,k}$ *of* $b_{i,k}$ *with payment* $a_{i,k}$.

As shown in Definitions 1.3 and 1.4, we put forward the following propositions.

Proposition 1.1 *SOB bidding description has the expressive power* $E^O(x)$, *which is formally given by*

$$E^O(x) = \sum_{k=1}^{x} \sum_{i=1}^{k} \frac{(-1)^i (k-i)^M}{i!(k-i)!}, \quad x \in \{1, \ldots, M\}, \tag{1.17}$$

with the MDL $\widehat{\lambda} = x$, *when the number of* OR *operations is x. However, it fails to symbolize all the PBs with the largest number of ORs.*

Proof We prove that $E^O(x)$ equals to Eq. (1.17) by applying dynamic programming and the Inclusion-Exclusion Principle theorem of combinatorics. Then, we exploit the *reduction ad absurdum* method to prove the *SOB* bidding description cannot represent all PBs. In fact, it only represents one kind of bid with no substitutability [12]. A detailed proof is omitted due to page limit.

Proposition 1.2 *SXB bidding description has the expressive power* $E^X(x)$ *as Eq.* (1.18) *with the MDL* $\widehat{\lambda} = x$, *when the number of* XOR *operators is x. Moreover, SXB has the same expressive power as Picasso, and both of them can represent all the PBs with the largest number of* XORs.

$$E^X(x) = \sum_{i=1}^{x} \frac{(2^M)!}{i!(2^M - i)!}, \quad x \in \{1, \ldots, 2^M\}. \tag{1.18}$$

Proof The proofs are conducted by using Definition 1.4, and a detailed proof is omitted due to page limit.

Proposition 1.3 *Given M tasks, ADL of Picasso is* $O(M)$ *that is on the same scale as SMB and SOB, while that of SXB is* $O(2^M)$ *for the same expressive power.*

Proof We prove it based on Eqs. (1.11), (1.17), and (1.18). The detailed proof is omitted due to page limit.

Summary according to Propositions 1.1, 1.2, and 1.3, both *SMB* and *SOB* are inexpressive, which cannot accommodate all the expressive space of PB. Although *SXB* is satisfactory in the expressiveness, it is not description-efficient with ADL $O(2^M)$. In contrast, *Picasso* realizes a better balance between the expressiveness and description efficiency than XOR, *i.e.,* when achieving the same expressive power, *Picasso can* reduce ADL from $O(2^M)$ to $O(M)$.

1.4.2   Task Allocation Based on Dependency Graph

Construction of Task Dependency Graph

According to the formal framework of bid description in Sect. 1.4.1, u_i's PB can be formally described as

$$b_i^{\text{XO}} = \bigoplus_{l=1}^{L_i} \bigcup_{k=1}^{K_{i,l}} \wedge_{h=1}^{H_{i,l,k}} (\tau_{i,l,k,h}, a_{i,l,k,h}), \tag{1.19}$$

where $(\tau_{i,l,k,h}, a_{i,l,k,h})$ denotes a task. $\wedge$, $\cup$, and $\bigoplus$ represent three different dependencies between task allocation, *i.e.,* AND, OR, and XOR, respectively. For instance, in Jack's PB description as Eq. (1.14), τ_1 and τ_2 have AND dependency and should be jointly allocated. τ_1 and τ_3 have OR dependency, and any subset of them can be allocated. $(\tau_1 \wedge \tau_2)$ and $(\tau_1 \cup \tau_3)$ have XOR dependency, and at most one of them can be allocated. Therefore, the PB description of a user consists of various complex task dependencies. As illustrated in Fig. 1.6b, we use a graph $G = (\mathcal{T}, \mathbf{e})$, called *task dependency graph*, to represent the PB description in Fig. 1.6a. Specifically, the vertices represent tasks $\tau_j, j \in \{1, \ldots, M\}$. The edge $e = (\tau_j, \tau_{j'}) \in \mathcal{T} \times \mathcal{T}$ represents the allocation dependency between τ_j and $\tau_{j'}$. They include AND, OR, and XOR dependencies, which are represented by the purple, green, and red edges respectively in Fig. 1.6b. With this task dependency graph, we put forward a dependency-aware task allocation and adaptive critical-payment computation method by *decomposing* and then *recombining* the task dependency graph of PB.

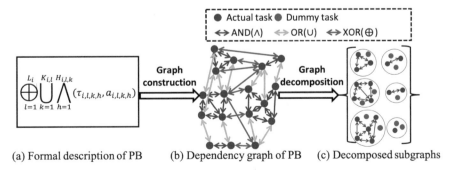

Fig. 1.6 Construction, decomposition, and recombination of task dependency graph based on PB model. (**a**) Formal description of PB. (**b**) Dependency graph of PB. (**c**) Decomposed subgraphs

PB Decomposition for Efficient Task Allocation

The task dependency graph is generally complex because of PB description, which makes the direct allocation rather challenging. In response to this challenge, we convert this complex problem with PB description into a simple problem with independent SMB ones by decomposing the task dependency graph. We then propose a greedy-based allocation algorithm to realize constant-factor approximation with polynomial time cost for this NP-hard problem.

Problem Transformation by Decomposing the Task Dependency Graph

We use the properties of the logical operators and their intrinsic relationships to decompose the XOR and OR dependencies for the problem transformation. First, as illustrated in the red circles in Fig. 1.6b, we use *dummy tasks d* with no intrinsic values and costs to express XOR constraints in an indirect way, thereby decomposing the XOR dependencies. The reason is that the XOR dependency between the task sets T_i and $T_{i'}$ is equivalent to the OR dependency by adding a dummy task $d_{i,i'}$ for each of them, i.e., $T_i \bigoplus T_{i'} \Leftrightarrow (T_i \wedge d_{i,i'}) \cup (T_{i'} \wedge d_{i,i'})$, where $d_{i,i'}$ represents the dummy task added for T_i and $T_{i'}$. Specifically, as shown in Lines 2–3 of Algorithm 1.1, for $b_{i, l, k}$ in u_i's PB, we add a dummy task $b_{l,k,l',k'}$ for each $b_{i,l',k'}$ inside different OR bids with $b_{i, l, k}$, i.e., $l' \neq l$.

Therefore, according to Fig. 1.6b, by adding the dummy tasks to decompose these XOR dependencies, the XOR-of-OR bidding description in Eq. (1.19) is transformed into that with *SOB* bidding description as
$$\overset{K_{i,l}}{\underset{k=1}{\cup}} \wedge_{h=1}^{H_{i,l,k}} (\tau_{i,l,k,h} \wedge d_{i,l,k,h}, a_{i,l,k,h}).$$

Additionally, the PB description with OR is transformed to that with independent SMBs in decomposing OR dependencies. Also, *virtual users* with SMBs are added to represent OR dependency. Particularly, according to Line 4 of Algorithm 1.1, for each $b_{i, l, k}$ of u_i, we create a virtual user $u_{i,l,k}^v$ with an SMB $b_{i, l, k}$, where $b_{i,l,k} = \wedge_{h=1}^{H_{i,l,k}} (\tau_{i,l,k,h} \wedge d_{i,l,k,h}, a_{i,l,k,h})$.

Let δ_i be the number of virtual users for u_i, i.e., $\delta_i = K_{i, l}$. Such transformation is to leverage the similarity of properties between the OR dependency and the task allocation. According to Definition 1.2, atomic bids of an OR bid have disjunction and independent properties.

To sum up, on the basis of the above decomposition of XOR and OR dependencies, the task allocation problem with a complex PB description as Eq. (1.19) is equivalently transformed to the simple problem only with SMBs.

Proposition 1.4 *A user's PB description of length λ can be equivalently transformed to λ independent SMB bids of λ virtual users by adding at most λ^2 dummy tasks.*

Task Allocation with Constant-Factor Approximation

based on the above transformation, the optimal task allocation problem with PB is transformed to the one with SMB bids. This problem has been proved to be NP-hard in Sect. 1.3.4. Therefore, an approximate task allocation scheme is put forward by greedily selecting the virtual users u_{i^*,k^*}^{v} who are the most cost-efficient as

$$u_{i^*,k^*}^{\text{v}} = \arg\max_{\forall u_{i,k}^{\text{v}} \in \mathcal{U}^{\text{v}}} \left(\xi_{i,k} | T_{i,k} \cap \mathcal{S} = \varnothing \right), \qquad (1.20)$$

where $T_{i,\,k}$ denotes the task set of the virtual user $u_{i,k}^{\text{v}}$. $\mathcal{U}^{\text{v}}$ denotes the set of un-selected virtual users. $\mathcal{S}$ represents the set of selected tasks. $\xi_{i,\,k}$ denotes the cost efficiency of $u_{i,k}^{\text{v}}$ with SMB bid $(T_{i,\,k}, a_{i,\,k})$, i.e., $\xi_{i,k} = \frac{\sqrt{|T_{i,k}|}}{a_{i,k}}$, where $|T_{i,\,k}|$ is the number of tasks in $T_{i,\,k}$, and the dummy tasks (e.g., $d_{i,\,k}$) contribute 0.

Specifically, as in Line 7 of Algorithm 1.1, we first sort all the virtual users (e.g., $u_{i,k}^{\text{v}}$) according to the decreasing cost-efficiency $\xi_{i,\,k}$. Then, we iteratively select the most *cost-effective* virtual user $u_{i,k}^{\text{v}}$ whose bidding task set $T_{i,\,k}$ is disjoint with the set of the allocated tasks $\mathcal{S}$, until all the task allocation is finished, as illustrated in Lines 8–15 of Algorithm 1.1. Note that $\mathbf{B}^{\text{s}}$ in Line 11 of Algorithm 1.1 denotes the set of selected atomic bids.

Algorithm 1.1 Task and Payment Allocation in Picasso

Input: Task set: $\mathcal{T} = \{\tau_1, \tau_2 \cdots, \tau_M\}$; Bid set of users: $\left\{ b_i^{\text{XO}} \mid b_i^{\text{XO}} = \bigoplus_{l=1}^{L_i} \bigcup_{k=1}^{K_{i,l}} \wedge_{h=1}^{H_{i,l,k}} (\tau_{i,l,k,h}, a_{i,l,k,h}), i \in [1, N] \right\}$;

Output: Task & payment allocation of users: $\{(\mathcal{S}_i, p_i), i \in [1, N]\}$;
1: %*Equivalent Decomposing of Task Dependency Graph*
2: while $(\forall i \in \{1, \ldots, N\}, \forall b_{i,\,l,\,k} \in B_i)$ **do**
3: $\forall b_{i,l',k'} \in B_i$ and $l' \neq l$, Create $d_{l,k,l',k'}, T_{i,l,k} = T_{i,l,k} \wedge \{d_{l,k,l',k'}\}$;
4: Create $u_{i,l,k}^{\text{v}}$ with $b_{i,\,l,\,k} = (T_{i,\,l,\,k}, a_{i,\,l,\,k})$;
5: end while
6: %*Greedy Allocation of Tasks based on Cost Efficiency*
7: With $\xi_{i,\,k}$, sort $u_{i,k}^{\text{v}}$ $(\forall i \in \{1, \ldots, N\}, \forall k \in \{1, \ldots, \delta_i\})$ in descending order as $\mathcal{U}^{\text{v}}$. Let $\mathcal{S} = \varnothing, \mathbf{B}^{\text{s}} = \varnothing$;
8: while$((\mathcal{T} \backslash \mathcal{S} \neq \varnothing))$ **do**
9: Let u_{i^*,k^*}^{v} denote the first user of $\mathcal{U}^{\text{v}}$;
10: **if**$((T_{i^*,k^*} \cap \mathcal{S} \neq \varnothing))$ **then**
11: $\mathcal{U}^{\text{v}} = \mathcal{U}^{\text{v}} \backslash \{u_{i^*,k^*}^{\text{v}}\}$;
12: **else**
13: $\mathcal{S} = \mathcal{S} \cup T_{i^*,k^*}, \mathbf{B}^{\text{s}} = \mathbf{B}^{\text{s}} \cup b_{i^*,k^*}$;

Algorithm 1.1 (continued)
  14:   **end if**
  15:**end while**
  16:*%Strategy-proof Payment Allocation*
  17:**while** ($\forall i \in \{1, \ldots, N\}, \forall k \in \{1, \ldots, \delta_i\}$) **do**
  18:   **if** ($b_{i, k} \in \mathbf{B}^s$) **then**
  19:      Compute $p_{i, k}$ according to Eqs. (1.23) and (1.24);
  20:   **else**
  21:      $p_{i, k} = 0$
  22:   **end if**
  23:**end while**

  24:**return** $S_i = \underset{\forall b_{i,k} \in \mathbf{B}^s}{\cup} T_{i,k}, p_i = \sum_{k=1}^{\delta_i} p_{i,k}, \forall i \in \{1, \ldots, N\}.$

Theoretical Analysis

We analyze the proposed task allocation scheme with regard to the approximation ratio and the computing complexity as follows.

Lemma 1.1 *Algorithm 1.1 solves the problem with a constant factor $\sqrt{M}$ of the optimal solution, given M tasks.*

Proof Let $\mathbf{B}^s$ and $\mathbf{B}^*$ be the set of selected atomic bids for *Picasso* and the optimal solutions, respectively. For $\forall b_k \in \mathbf{B}^*$, we create $\mathbf{B}_k^s = \{b_i \in \mathbf{B}^s | \xi_i \geq \xi_k, T_i \cap T_k \neq \varnothing\}$. As $c_i \leq c_k \cdot \sqrt{|T_i|}/\sqrt{|T_k|}$, we have $\sum_{b_i \in \mathbf{B}_k^s} c_i \leq \frac{c_k}{\sqrt{|T_k|}} \sum_{b_i \in \mathbf{B}_k^s} \sqrt{|T_i|}$. Using the Cauchy-Schwarz inequality, we have $\sum_{b_i \in \mathbf{B}_k^s} \sqrt{|T_i|} \leq \sqrt{|\mathbf{B}_k^s|} \sqrt{\sum_{b_i \in \mathbf{B}_k^s} |T_i|}$. As $\forall b_i \in \mathbf{B}_k^s$, $T_i \cap T_k \neq \varnothing$ and $\forall b_{i_1}, b_{i_2} \in \mathbf{B}_k^s, T_{i_1} \cap T_{i_2} = \varnothing$, $|\mathbf{B}_k^s| \leq |T_k|$. Moreover, $\sum_{b_i \in \mathbf{B}_k^s} |T_i| \leq M$. Hence, based on the above derivations, we have

$$\sum_{b_i \in \mathbf{B}_k^s} c_i \leq \sqrt{M} \cdot c_k. \tag{1.21}$$

We define $\mathbf{B}^{s*} = \cup_{\forall b_k \in \mathbf{B}^*} \mathbf{B}_k^s$. Then, according to Eq. (1.21), $\sum_{b_i \in \mathbf{B}^{s*}} c_i \leq \sqrt{M} \cdot \sum_{b_k \in \mathbf{B}^*} c_k$. Since $\mathbf{B}^s \subseteq \mathbf{B}^{s*}$, $\sum_{b_i \in \mathbf{B}^s} c_i \leq \sum_{b_i \in \mathbf{B}^{s*}} c_i$. Finally, we have

$$\sum_{b_i \in \mathbf{B}^s} c_i \leq \sqrt{M} \cdot \sum_{b_k \in \mathbf{B}^*} c_k, \tag{1.22}$$

where $\sum_{b_i \in \mathbf{B}^s} c_i$ and $\sum_{b_k \in \mathbf{B}^*} c_k$ denote the social cost realized by *Picasso* and the optimal solution in a respective manner. Hence, Lemma 1.1 holds.

Lemma 1.2 *Given M tasks and N users, the time complexity of Algorithm 1.1 is* $O(M^2N^2)$, *while those of SMB, SOB, and SXB are* $O(N^2)$, $O(M^2N^2)$, *and* $O(N^2)$, *respectively.*

Based on Lemmas 1.1 and 1.2, we finally have Theorem 1.3.

Theorem 1.3 *Picasso achieves computational efficiency and approximates the optimal solution with a constant factor* $\sqrt{M}$.

PB Recombination for Strategy-Proof Payment

In Sect. 1.4.2.2, by decomposing the complex PB into independent SMBs, we transform the problem into a form with efficient task allocation. Considering this transformation, firstly we design the truthful payment scheme on the ground of the critical value for independent SMBs without considering PB, *i.e.,* non-PB. Then, we show that the PBs change the user's bids into more complex ones, causing the untruthfulness problem for the payment scheme. In response to this newly emerged problem, we also design the payment scheme for PB based on graph recombination, which is proved to have truthfulness and individual rationality in the end.

Truthful Payment Scheme for Non-PB Based on Critical Prices

As shown in the Truthful Theorem [12], the auction-based mechanisms on a single parameter domain are truthful if and only if the following two conditions hold:

- **monotonicity**: the task allocation scheme is monotone. Particularly, for u_i, if the bid $b_i = (T_i, a_i)$ is selected for task allocation, then her/his bid $b_i = (T_i, a_i - \delta)$ is still selected when $\delta > 0$.
- **critical price**: users should be paid the critical price for the selected bid. The critical price p_i is the minimum one for u_i, such that her/his bid (T_i, a_i) would not be selected if $a_i > p_i$. With the use of the task allocation scheme based on the greedy selection in Sect. 1.4.2.2, the monotone condition for truthfulness is satisfied. Therefore, in order to hold truthful property, we leverage the critical payment to compute remittance of virtual users for her/his SMB.

Particularly, as shown in Lines 17–23 of Algorithm 1.1, the virtual users with no task allocation get no payment. However, according to the bid $\left(T_{\hat{i}^*, \hat{k}^*}, a_{\hat{i}^*, \hat{k}^*}\right)$ of the critical user $u^{\text{v}}_{\hat{i}^*, \hat{k}^*}$, the selected virtual user $u^{\text{v}}_{i,k}$ with $b_{i,\ k} = (T_{i,\ k}, a_{i,\ k})$ gets the payment as

$$p_{i,k} = a_{\hat{i}^*,\hat{k}^*} \cdot \frac{\sqrt{|T_{i,k}|}}{\sqrt{|T_{\hat{i}^*,\hat{k}^*}|}}, \tag{1.23}$$

where $u^{\text{v}}_{\hat{i}^*,\hat{k}^*} = \arg\max\limits_{u^{\text{v}}_{\hat{i},\hat{k}}} \left\{ \xi_{\hat{i},\hat{k}} | T_{\hat{i},\hat{k}} \cap T_{i,k} \neq \varnothing, \xi_{\hat{i},\hat{k}} \neq \xi_{i,k} \right\}$.

Truthful Payment Scheme for PB Based on Graph Recombination

Although the above mechanism based on the critical payment guarantees the users to be truthful in terms of the SMB bidding, it is inapplicable for users' PBs. Take Jack in Fig. 1.3 as an example. We assume that $u^{\text{v}}_{1,2}$ is selected and $u^{\text{v}}_{1,1}$ is the critical user of $u^{\text{v}}_{1,2}$. According to Eq. (1.23), the payment of Jack is $a_{1,1} \cdot \sqrt{|T_{1,2}|}/\sqrt{|T_{1,1}|}$. Thus, Jack may strategically misreport $a_{1,1}$ to improve his own total utility. The reasons are as follows. Users with PB can be decomposed into several virtual users with SMB bids. Individual virtual users cannot directly improve utility (*i.e.*, earnings) by misreporting. They may otherwise strategically help other virtual users improve their respective utilities, promoting the total utility of that actual user as a result. In the end, *the PB can be strategically utilized by selfish users to improve their utilities, hence inducing untruthfulness.*

In response to untruthfulness, we recombine the task dependency graph of PB and design an adaptive critical payment computation. Specifically, for selected users, we find a critical user from the group of different actual users who have intersecting (common) tasks with the selected one. Formally, for the k-th virtual user of u_i, *i.e.*, $u^{\text{v}}_{i,k}$, we find the critical user $u^{\text{v}}_{\hat{i}^*,\hat{k}^*}$ as

$$u^{\text{v}}_{\hat{i}^*,\hat{k}^*} = \arg\max\limits_{u^{\text{v}}_{\hat{i},\hat{k}}} \left\{ \xi_{\hat{i},\hat{k}} | \hat{i} \neq i, T_{\hat{i},\hat{k}} \cap T_{i,k} \neq \varnothing \right\}. \tag{1.24}$$

Based on Eq. (1.24), recombining the task dependency graph of PB won't select Jack's $u^{\text{v}}_{1,1}$ as the critical user. Therefore, Jack cannot improve his utility strategically.

Theoretical Analysis

We analyze the strategy-proof of the above payment design and have Theorem 1.4.

Theorem 1.4 *Picasso is individually rational and truthful, both of which are called strategy-proof.*

Proof In the following content, we will prove the individual rationality and the truthfulness accordingly.

Proof of individual rationality for each u_i, if $u_{i,k}^v$ is not selected, according to Algorithm 1.1, $p_{i,k} = 0$, $c_{i,k} = 0$. Otherwise, $p_{i,k} = a_{i^*,k^*} \cdot \sqrt{|T_{i,k}|}/\sqrt{|T_{i^*,k^*}|}$. As $\sqrt{|T_{i,k}|}/a_{i,k} \geq \sqrt{|T_{i^*,k^*}|}/a_{i^*,k^*}$, $p_{i,k} \geq a_{i,k}$. Since $a_{i,k} \geq c_{i,k}$, u_i's utility $\sum_{k=1}^{N_i}(p_{i,k} - c_{i,k}) \geq 0$. Thus, *Picasso* is individually rational.

Proof of truthfulness we prove it in terms of (a) independent SMBs which are proved truthful in copious studies [19, 21, 22], and (b) dependent SMBs. Next, we prove that *Picasso* stays truthful even with dependent SMBs in applying the *reduction ad absurdum* method.

We assume the original proposition is not true, *i.e.*, there exists a user (say u_i) who can raise his utility by unilaterally misreporting his costs. Specifically, u_i promotes his utility by changing the bids of his virtual users $u_{i,k}^v(k = 1 \ldots N_i)$ from $B_i = \{(T_{i,k}, c_{i,k})|k = 1, \ldots, \delta_i\}$ to $B_i = \{(T_{i,k}, a_{i,k})|k = 1, \ldots, \delta_i\}$, where $(c_{i,1}, \ldots, c_{i,\delta_i}) \neq (a_{i,1}, \ldots, a_{i,\delta_i})$. We prove this theorem according to two different cases, *i.e.*, u_i is un-selected/selected with B_i. The detailed proofs are omitted due to page limit.

To sum up, even if users strategically use the task dependencies, *Picasso* achieves truthfulness and individual rationality by bringing the task dependency graph of PB in recombination.

1.5 Performance Evaluation of *Picasso*

Firstly, we conduct extensive simulations to evaluate the performance of *Picasso*, which is further tested by carrying out a real case study of Gigwalk based on real traces.

1.5.1 Simulations

Simulation Methodology and Settings

There are N users to provide PBs for M tasks. The number L of OR bids for one PB and the number K of atomic bids in one OR bid are uniformly distributed, *i.e.*, $L{\sim}U(1, R)(R = 5)$ and $K{\sim}U(1, 0.6M)$. The real cost of users in executing a task is normally distributed as $N(\mu, \sigma^2)$, where $\mu{\sim}U(20, 40)$ and $\sigma{\sim}U(5, 15)$. Each data point is obtained by averaging 20 execution results. Our simulation was conducted on a PC with 2.3 GHz dual-core Intel Core i5 CPU and 8 GB RAM. *Picasso* is compared to the four baseline methods mentioned before, **SMB** [21], **SOB** [22], **SXB** [20, 23], and **OPT**. SMB, SOB, and SXB use the greedy algorithm and the critical payment in task allocation and payment computation which are similar to *Picasso*. OPT utilizes brute-force search and Vickrey Clarke Groves mechanism [12] for the optimal solution using the same description method as *Picasso*. We leverage four performance metrics, *i.e., social cost, total payment, time cost,* and *ADL*.

Results

Firstly, we compare *Picasso* with SMB and SOB in terms of social cost and total payment for different numbers of users. We set $M = 30$ and vary N from 100 to 300. According to Fig. 1.7a, b, the social cost and total payment of *Picasso* are less than those of SMB and SOB by a large margin. In social cost and total payment, *Picasso* surpasses SMB and SOB by over 32.6% for a varying number of users. We also vary M from 10 to 50 and set $N = 200$. As shown in Fig. 1.8a, b, the social cost and total payment of *Picasso* are always smaller than those of SMB and SOB. *Picasso*

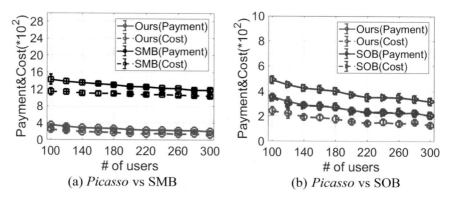

Fig. 1.7 Comparison of the social cost and the total payment for different numbers of users. **(a)** *Picasso* vs. SMB. **(b)** *Picasso* vs. SOB

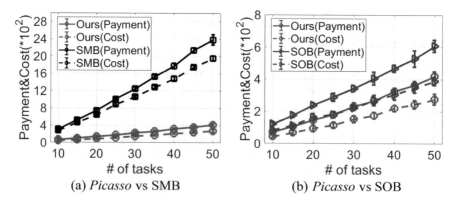

Fig. 1.8 Comparison of the social cost and the total payment for different numbers of tasks. **(a)** *Picasso* vs. SMB. **(b)** *Picasso* vs. SOB

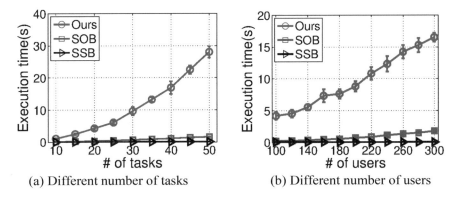

Fig. 1.9 Comparison of time cost with different numbers of users and tasks by comparing SSB and SOB. (**a**) Different number of tasks. (**b**) Different number of users

surpasses SMB and SOB in both social cost and total payment by over 34.9% for different numbers of tasks.

We evaluate the computation time for different numbers of users. Figure 1.9a, b show that despite the higher time cost of *Picasso* compared with SMB and SOB, it increases roughly quadratically with N and M. Specifically, *Picasso* costs only 16.5 s in the worst case and 9.8 s on average when the number of users varies from 100 to 300. It also costs 28.1 s in the worst case and 11.6 s on average when the number of tasks is changed from 10 to 50. We also compare the execution times of *Picasso* and OPT in Fig. 1.11a. Since the problem is NP-hard, OPT takes highly much time (the time complexity is $O(M^M N^M)$), *e.g.*, running for more than 68,859 s (about 19 h) only when $M = 8$ and $N = 12$, while *Picasso* completes within 0.6 s, which can be insignificant in practice. Moreover, its execution time tremendously extends with the number of tasks and users, making it much less applicable to large-scale systems. These results are consistent with the theoretical analysis in Lemma 1.2.

We use the ADL in Fig. 1.10a, b to evaluate the description efficiency of *Picasso* in comparison with SOB and SXB. Since SMB has much worse performance in expressiveness when compared with SOB and its ADL is always 1, it is not included here. As the ADL of SXB is extremely large, we show its logarithm for ease of presentation. Figure 1.10a shows that ADL increases linearly with the number of tasks for both *Picasso* and SOB, while it increases exponentially with the number of tasks for SXB. ADL of SOB and *Picasso* are 9.1 and 23.7 on average, respectively, while SXB increases dramatically up to $2^{16.9}$. As shown in Fig. 1.10b, it is also observed that ADL changes slightly with the number of users for all of these three methods. ADL of SOB and *Picasso* are 9.1 and 23.8 on average, respectively, while SXB explodes to $2^{11.2}$. These results are consistent with the theoretical analysis in Sect. 1.4.1.2. To conclude, *Picasso* is more description-efficient than SXB, realizing a good trade-off between expressiveness, description efficiency, and computational complexity.

Finally, we evaluate the individual rationality of our method. We plot the CDF for the ratio of the user's extra payment to her/his real cost, called the *overpayment*

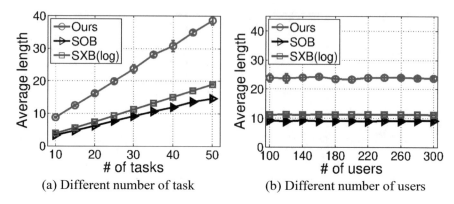

(a) Different number of task   (b) Different number of users

Fig. 1.10 Comparison of average description length (ADL) for different numbers of users and tasks. (**a**) Different number of task. (**b**) Different number of users

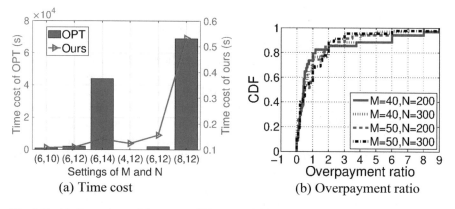

(a) Time cost   (b) Overpayment ratio

Fig. 1.11 (**a**) Comparison of time costs of Picasso and OPT. (**b**) CDF of overpayment ratio

ratio, for four different settings (*i.e.,* user and task number). As shown in Fig. 1.11b, the overpayment ratio is above 0 for 100%, below 1 for 60%, and below 2 for 80%. The results show that all of the payments for each user are more than their real cost. Moreover, the overpayment, *i.e.,* within double of the real cost for 80%, is reasonable. Therefore, individual rationality is realized in our method.

1.5.2 Trace-Driven Case Study of Gigwalk

Evaluation Methodology and Settings

To enhance the evaluation, we conduct a case study that emulates Gigwalk based on the real traces of drivers with the following setup.

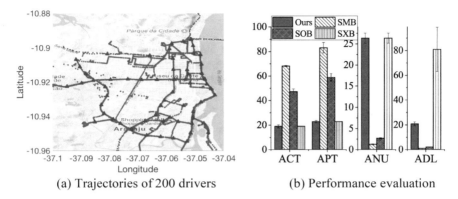

(a) Trajectories of 200 drivers   (b) Performance evaluation

Fig. 1.12   Trace-based Gigwalk case studies: (**a**) Trajectories of 200 driver's. (**b**) Performance evaluation

Traces and Participants as illustrated in Fig. 1.12a, we apply the real trajectories of 200 drivers to mimic the mobility of users and choose 20 locations (represented by the blue triangles) in a random manner in these trajectories. Each location has a random amount of tasks, following the distribution $U(1, 5)$. For instance, there are multiple different tasks at a shop or in its neighborhoods. We emulate 500 crowdsourcing participants expecting the Gigwalk tasks on their driving paths. Participants randomly choose a starting point, such as her/his home or work location. We leverage the real driving paths within 3 km from the participant's starting point as her/his potential paths, along only one of which will she/he drive.

Time and Price it takes time for participants to perform the tasks, as one needs to find a parking lot [48] before picking up the task. We set 10 min per location on average as her/his dwelling time according to the report in [48]. Additionally, users vary in available time limits following $\mathcal{U}(10, 120)$ (min). Each user randomly selects a limited number of locations up to her/his time limit on her/his path and fulfills the tasks at any subset of these locations. At each location, participants choose a random number of tasks and are expected to do either all of them after parking there or none without stopping, owing to their own rationality. The bidding price for each task is initiated considering the user, driving paths, and locations within a distribution $\mathcal{U}(1, 100)$, and its actual price according to the task type, platform, and area. For instance, if the platform sets the maximum price at $10, the bidding price will randomly change from $0.10 to $10.

Metrics besides **ADL** for description efficiency, we apply the **A**verage bidding task **N**umber per **U**ser (**ANU**) to evaluate the user's expressiveness. The more tasks users can bid for, the more user's expressiveness this mechanism enables. In addition, we exploit the **A**verage social **C**ost per executed **T**ask (**ACT**) and **A**verage platform **P**ayment per executed **T**ask (**APT**) to represent platform utility.

Results

First, we evaluate the influences made by the settings of XOR-OR limits on the performance of *Picasso's performance*. As the maximum available time of users is set at 120 min and the dwelling time 10 min, the number of OR operations is no more than 12. Therefore, we change the settings of XOR-OR limits (R_{XOR}, R_{OR}) as $(1,1)$, $(1,4)$, $(1,8)$, $(1,12)$, $(4,12)$, and $(8,12)$, where R_{XOR} and R_{OR} denote the limits of XOR and OR operations, respectively. As shown in Fig. 1.13a, b, the ACT and APT of the platform decline gradually with the limits of XOR and OR operations, while both ANU and ADL are rising with them. Moreover, as illustrated in Fig. 1.14a, b, the high XOR-OR limits diminish the utility of users and the execution time of the proposed algorithm increases. According to the result, the higher XOR-OR limits bring more bidding freedom, inspiring users to bid on more tasks, which in return increases the description length and the computation time. However, the growth of

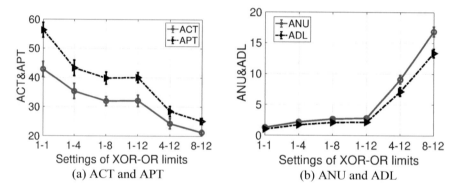

Fig. 1.13 Performance evaluation for different settings of XOR and OR limits, including (**a**) ACT, APT, (**b**) ANU, and ADL

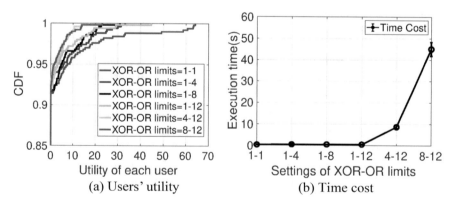

Fig. 1.14 Evaluation of users' utility and system's time cost with different settings of the XOR-OR limits. (**a**) Users' utility. (**b**) Time cost

the ADL and the time cost of *Picasso* is slow with the XOR-OR limits, which is a polynomial increase, as shown in Figs. 1.13b and 1.14b. The interesting thing is that more bidding freedom causes competition among users for the allocation of limited tasks, diminishing the utility of each user and causing much lower social costs (and platform payment). Similarly, in economic freedom, people are empowered and their powerful forces of choice unleashed; thus, the market competition and overall economy [49] are promoted.

In addition, we compare *Picasso* with existing schemes, *i.e.,* SMB, SOB, and SXB. The presented means are out of 20 emulations. According to Fig. 1.12b, compared to SMB and SOB, *Picasso* reduces ACT and APT by more than 60% and 61%, respectively, while increasing ANU by at least 9.7×. So, *Picasso* effectively enables the user's expressiveness and significantly reduces the social cost as well as the platform payment. On the other hand, compared to SXB, *Picasso* cuts ADL by more than 74%, despite the similar ACT, APT, and ANU. Therefore, *Picasso* realizes powerful expressiveness without compromising description efficiency.

To sum up, *Picasso* is shown to benefit not only the platform owner by considerably decreasing its payment, but also the participants by increasing their intrinsic motivation with more expressiveness and description efficiency. That is, *these Gigwalk case studies confirmed the effectiveness of Picasso in incentivizing both the platform owner and the participants.*

1.6 Discussion and Future Work

Task execution unreliability After task bidding and allocation, users might have a problem in executing the allocated tasks due to users' unreliability and their mobility's uncertainty [50]. In addressing this issue of task execution unreliability, *Picasso* give rewards only to the users who successfully executed the tasks, such as uploading the sensed data. Moreover, to avoid bidding misbehavior of users (*i.e.,* bidding as many tasks as possible), we can introduce a penalty to the user whose allocated tasks are not completed, such as stopping allocating tasks to them in the future. Moreover, we can extract the users' reliability from their historical behaviors by applying deep learning methods [51], which are fed back to design the task allocation scheme. In the future, we would like to explore the allocation of tasks based on the users' task execution probability model.

Non-additive cost of tasks due to the law of diminishing return in economics [44], users may pay cost less while conducting multiple tasks together compared with that conducted individually. For instance, in the application of Gigwalk, if multiple tasks are located close to each other, some users with enough time might pay a discounted cost while executing all the tasks. However, with mild modification, *Picasso* can be easily extended to the case of non-additive cost. Particularly, it happens only when the user wants to fulfill multiple tasks together, which is represented by the atomic bid in *Picasso*. Therefore, for this atomic bid, users can set a minimal cost and the desired payment according to their actual cost, taking into account the decreasing cost. Moreover, the diminishing-cost property of the task cost can be further exploited to strengthen the total utility of the platform owner [18], which is part of our future work.

User-friendly preference expression   In practice, based on the formal bid description in Sect. 1.4.1, a user-friendly preference expression system should be designed when the underlying applications are considered. In what follows, the practical personalized bidding in Gigwalk is taken as an example. First, a user inputs the source and destination locations as well as her/his available time slots. Then, similar to Google navigation, the system returns multiple candidate routes from the source to the destination. Each route consists of several Gigwalk tasks. In addition, users express their preferences by applying user-friendly interfaces, such as binding the tasks expected to be done together. Moreover, we can utilize machine learning [52] to automatically extract the users' preferences based on their behavior datasets [53], further facilitating the users' input. Finally, the system automatically creates the formal bid description using *Picasso*.

1.7   Conclusion

We have designed and evaluated a novel PB-based incentive mechanism called *Picasso*. It consists of two main components. Firstly, we have proposed a PB description method in 3-D expressive space with AND, XOR, and OR, achieving a good trade-off among expressiveness, computational complexity, and description efficiency. Secondly, we have designed schemes for constant-factor approximation in optimal task allocation and strategy-proof in payment with computational efficiency by decomposing and recombining task dependency graph of PB. Both the theoretical analysis and trace-based Gigwalk case studies have validated the aforementioned essential properties of *Picasso*.

References

1. S. He, K.G. Shin, (Re)configuring bike station network via crowdsourced information fusion and joint optimization. Paper presented at the Eighteenth ACM International Symposium on Mobile Ad Hoc Networking and Computing, 26–29 June 2018
2. J. Wang, Y. Wang, D. Zhang, et al., Multi-task allocation in mobile crowd sensing with individual task quality assurance. IEEE Trans. Mobile Comput. **17**(9), 2101–2113 (2018)
3. C. Xiang, P. Yang, C. Tian, et al., Calibrate without calibrating: an iterative approach in participatory sensing network. IEEE Trans. Parallel Distrib. Syst. **26**(2), 351–361 (2014)
4. C. Xiang, P. Yang, C. Tian, et al., CARM: crowd-sensing accurate outdoor RSS maps with error-prone smartphone measurements. IEEE Trans. Mobile Comput. **15**(11), 2669–2681 (2015)

5. J. Wang, F. Wang, Y. Wang, et al., HyTasker: hybrid task allocation in mobile crowd sensing. IEEE Trans. Mobile Comput. **19**(3), 598–611 (2019)
6. S. He, K.G. Shin, Steering crowdsourced signal map construction via Bayesian compressive sensing. Paper presented at the IEEE INFOCOM 2018—IEEE Conference on Computer Communication, 16–19 April 2018
7. J. Xu, S. Wang, N. Zhang, et al., Reward or penalty: aligning incentives of stakeholders in crowdsourcing. IEEE Trans. Mobile Comput. **18**(4), 974–985 (2018)
8. X. Zhang, Z. Yang, W. Sun, et al., Incentives for mobile crowd sensing: a survey. IEEE Commun. Surv. Tutorials **18**(1), 54–67 (2015)
9. Z. Duan, W. Li, Z. Cai, Distributed auctions for task assignment and scheduling in mobile crowdsensing systems. Paper presented at the 2017 IEEE 37th International Conference on Distributed Computing Systems (ICDCS), 5–8 June 2017
10. F. Restuccia, S.K. Das, J. Payton, Incentive mechanisms for participatory sensing: survey and research challenges. ACM Trans. Sens. Netw. (TOSN) **12**(2), 1–40 (2016)
11. L. Duan, L. Huang, C. Langbort, et al., Human-in-the-loop mobile networks: a survey of recent advancements. IEEE J. Select. Areas Commun. **35**(4), 813–831 (2017)
12. N. Nisan, T. Roughgarden, E. Tardos, V.V. Vazirani (eds.), *Algorithmic Game Theory* (Cambridge University Press, Cambridge, 2007)
13. Personalization pulse check 2016. Accenture interactive (report), 2016
14. Y. Chen, B. Li, Q. Zhang, Incentivizing crowdsourcing systems with network effects. Paper presented at the IEEE INFOCOM 2016—the 35th Annual IEEE International Conference on Computer Communications, 10–14 April 2016
15. R.M. Ryan, E.L. Deci, Intrinsic and extrinsic motivations: classic definitions and new directions. Contemp. Educ. Psychol. **25**(1), 54–67 (2000)
16. I. Koutsopoulos, Optimal incentive-driven design of participatory sensing systems. Paper presented at the 2013 Proceedings IEEE INFOCOM, 14–19 April 2013
17. T. Luo, H.P. Tan, L. Xia, Profit-maximizing incentive for participatory sensing. Paper presented at the IEEE INFOCOM 2014—IEEE Conference on Computer Communications, 27 April 2014–2 May 2014
18. D. Yang, G. Xue, X. Fang, et al., Crowdsourcing to smartphones: incentive mechanism design for mobile phone sensing. Paper presented at the 18th Annual International Conference on Mobile Computing and Networking, 22–26 August 2012
19. Z. Zheng, F. Wu, X. Gao, et al., A budget feasible incentive mechanism for weighted coverage maximization in mobile crowdsensing. IEEE Trans. Mobile Comput. **16**(9), 2392–2407 (2016)
20. H. Jin, L. Su, D. Chen, et al., Thanos: incentive mechanism with quality awareness for mobile crowd sensing. IEEE Trans. Mobile Comput. **18**(8), 1951–1964 (2018)
21. H. Jin, L. Su, K. Nahrstedt, CENTURION: incentivizing multi-requester mobile crowd sensing. Paper presented at the IEEE INFOCOM 2017—IEEE Conference on Computer Communications, 1–4 May 2017
22. Z. Feng, Y. Zhu, Q. Zhang, et al., TRAC: truthful auction for location-aware collaborative sensing in mobile crowdsourcing. Paper presented at the IEEE INFOCOM 2014—IEEE Conference on Computer Communications, 27 April 2014–2 May 2014
23. X. Zhang, G. Xue, R. Yu, et al., Truthful incentive mechanisms for crowdsourcing. Paper presented at the 2015 IEEE Conference on Computer Communications (INFOCOM), 26 April 2015–1 May 2015
24. J. Xu, Z. Rao, L. Xu, et al., Incentive mechanism for multiple cooperative tasks with compatible users in mobile crowd sensing via online communities. IEEE Trans. Mobile Comput. **19**(7), 1618–1633 (2019)
25. Z. Duan, W. Li, X. Zheng, et al., Mutual-preference driven truthful auction mechanism in mobile crowdsensing. Paper presented at the 2019 IEEE 39th International Conference on Distributed Computing Systems (ICDCS), 7–10 July 2019

26. K. Han, Y. He, H. Tan, et al., Online pricing for mobile crowdsourcing with multi-minded users. Paper presented at the Eighteenth ACM International Symposium on Mobile Ad Hoc Networking and Computing, 10–14 July 2017
27. J. Lin, M. Li, D. Yang, et al., Sybil-proof incentive mechanisms for crowdsensing. Paper presented at the IEEE INFOCOM 2017—IEEE Conference on Computer Communications, 1–4 May 2017
28. K. Han, H. Huang, J. Luo, Quality-aware pricing for mobile crowdsensing. IEEE/ACM Trans. Netw. **26**(4), 1728–1741 (2018)
29. Y. Qu, S. Tang, C. Dong, et al., Posted pricing for chance constrained robust crowdsensing. IEEE Trans. Mobile Comput. **19**(1), 188–199 (2019)
30. Z. Cai, Z. Duan, W. Li, Exploiting multi-dimensional task diversity in distributed auctions for mobile crowdsensing. IEEE Trans. Mobile Comput. **20**(8), 2576–2591 (2020)
31. M. Tang, H. Pang, S. Wang, et al., Multi-dimensional auction mechanisms for crowdsourced mobile video streaming. IEEE/ACM Trans. Netw. **26**(5), 2062–2075 (2018)
32. J.L.Z. Cai, M. Yan, Y. Li, Using crowdsourced data in location-based social networks to explore influence maximization. Paper presented at the IEEE INFOCOM 2016—the 35th Annual IEEE International Conference on Computer Communications, 10–14 April 2016
33. Y. Lin, Z. Cai, X. Wang, et al., Incentive mechanisms for crowdblocking rumors in mobile social networks. IEEE Trans. Veh. Technol. **68**(9), 9220–9232 (2019)
34. J. Wang, F. Wang, Y. Wang, et al., Social-network-assisted worker recruitment in mobile crowd sensing. IEEE Trans. Mobile Comput. **18**(7), 1661–1673 (2018)
35. J. Xu, C. Guan, H. Wu, et al., Online incentive mechanism for mobile crowdsourcing based on two-tiered social crowdsourcing architecture. Paper presented at the 2018 15th Annual IEEE International Conference on Sensing, Communication, and Networking (SECON), 11–13 June 2018
36. Z. Wang, J. Hu, R. Lv, et al., Personalized privacy-preserving task allocation for mobile crowdsensing. IEEE Trans. Mobile Comput. **18**(6), 1330–1341 (2018)
37. D. Geiger, M. Schader, Personalized task recommendation in crowdsourcing information systems—current state of the art. Decis. Support Syst. **65**, 3–16 (2014)
38. C. Boutilier, Solving concisely expressed combinatorial auction problems. Paper presented at the Eighteenth National Conference on Artificial Intelligence, 28 July 2002–1 August 2002
39. C. Boutilier, H.H. Hoos, Bidding languages for combinatorial auctions. Paper presented at the 17th International Joint Conference on Artificial Intelligence, vol 2, 4–10 August 2001
40. S. Lahaie, D.C. Parkes, D.M. Pennock, An expressive auction design for online display advertising. Paper presented at the 23rd National Conference on Artificial Intelligence—Volume 1, 13–17 July 2008
41. X. Jin, Y. Zhang, Privacy-preserving crowdsourced spectrum sensing. IEEE/ACM Trans. Netw. **26**(3), 1236–1249 (2018)
42. H. Jin, L. Su, H. Xiao, et al., Incentive mechanism for privacy-aware data aggregation in mobile crowd sensing systems. IEEE/ACM Trans. Netw. **26**(5), 2019–2032 (2018)
43. D. Zhao, X.Y. Li, H. Ma, Budget-feasible online incentive mechanisms for crowdsourcing tasks truthfully. IEEE/ACM Trans. Netw. **24**(2), 647–661 (2014)
44. H.H. Chou, H.C. Chiu, N.F. Delaney, et al., Diminishing returns epistasis among beneficial mutations decelerates adaptation. Science **332**(6034), 1190–1192 (2011)
45. N. Nisan, Bidding and allocation in combinatorial auctions. Paper presented at the 2nd ACM Conference on Electronic Commerce, 17–20 October 2000
46. R.L. Graham, M. Grötschel, L. Lovász (eds.), *Handbook of Combinatorics*, vol 1 (Elsevier, Amsterdam, 1995)
47. S. Arora, B. Barak, *Computational Complexity: a Modern Approach* (Cambridge University Press, Cambridge, 2009)
48. Stop wasting time searching for parking, https://blog.spothero.com/park-smarter-parking-search-time/
49. N. Berggren, The benefits of economic freedom: a survey. Indep. Rev. **8**(2), 193–211 (2003)

50. G. Gao, M. Xiao, J. Wu, et al., Truthful incentive mechanism for nondeterministic crowdsensing with vehicles. IEEE Trans. Mobile Comput. **17**(12), 2982–2997 (2018)
51. X. Fan, C. Xiang, C. Chen, et al., BuildSenSys: reusing building sensing data for traffic prediction with cross-domain learning. IEEE Trans. Mobile Comput. **20**(6), 2154–2171 (2020)
52. C. Xiang, Z. Zhang, Y. Qu, et al., Edge computing-empowered large-scale traffic data recovery leveraging low-rank theory. IEEE Trans. Netw. Sci. Eng. **7**(4), 2205–2218 (2020)
53. C. Chen, D. Zhang, X. Ma, et al., Crowddeliver: planning city-wide package delivery paths leveraging the crowd of taxis. IEEE Trans. Intell. Transp. Syst. **18**(6), 1478–1496 (2016)

Chapter 2
Task Recommendation Based on Big Data Analysis

2.1 Introduction

The Mobility-on-Demand (MOD) vehicle market has been prospering in recent years, which can be seen from Uber, Lyft, DiDi, etc. [1]. By December 2020, Uber and Lyft had each employed over one million drivers in the U.S. [2], and the size of the global market is expected to reach \$228 billion by 2022 [3]. But at the same time, we take note of the decreased income of many MOD drivers year by year from 2013 to 2020 [4], possibly thanks to rising competition among drivers. The circumstance has worsened over the past 2 years due to the COVID-19 pandemic [5]. Therefore, a new market invented by the Payver platform called MOD-Vehicular-Crowdsensing (MOVE-CS) was launched in 2017 [6]. Payver pays the drivers to collect road data when driving, primarily according to the length and the specific segments of the roads, usually at \$0.01–0.05 per mile.

Once gathering road data collected by the drivers, Payver usually sold them to fastidious companies like digital map construction corporations (*e.g.*, Google Maps [7] and lvl5 [8]). Therefore, the results seemed to be a win-win situation for both the platform and the drivers. In just 3 months of operation, Payver had enrolled almost 2000 Uber and Lyft drivers to collect data on more than 500K-mile roads, while increasing their income by 5–15% [9]. However, after only 2 years of operation, the number of participating drivers remained low, so Payver had to declare bankruptcy in April 2019 [10].

To investigate the fundamental cause of the dilemma mentioned above, we surveyed 581 MOD drivers (see Sect. 2.3.1 for details) through a well-known crowdsourcing platform (*i.e.*, Amazon Mechanical Turk [11]). They include 41.2% of women and 58.8% of men, ranging in age from 20 to 60; 43.6%, 77.3%, and 90.2% of them drive at least once a day, a week, and a month, respectively. The findings revealed that the withdrawal of MOVE-CS drivers' has a lot to do with Payver's simple operation model based on blindly competitive rewards. To be Specific, since each driver collects data for certain road segments without knowing

© The Author(s), under exclusive license to Springer Nature Singapore Pte Ltd. 2023
C. Xiang et al., *Multi-dimensional Urban Sensing Using Crowdsensing Data*, Data Analytics, https://doi.org/10.1007/978-981-19-9006-9_2

about others, they tend to end up with low-value collected data for duplicate road segments. Therefore, this model results in little or even negative benefits for most drivers (*e.g.*, when the sensing task is performed when the vehicle is idle), triggering them to withdraw from the MOVE-CS market.

In contrast to MOVE-CS, we found that a similar market termed MOD-Human-Crowdsensing (MOMAN-CS), led by Gigwalk [12], has been successful since 2010. It employs people to collect data on goods (*e.g.*, the location, price, and sales) for specific vendors, and has attracted 1.7 million participants by 2021 [12]. Behind the success of Gigwalk, is a complex operation model with exclusively customized rewards. To be specific, Gigwalk posts an initial reward for one task and allows only one person to take it; if no one takes it up for a long time, the reward increases. Since the operation model of MOMAN-CS is effective in motivating humans, and humans drive the vehicles, we want to know if this model could be applied to vehicle incentivization with a view to resurrect the MOVE-CS market.

Due to the plenty of similarities between the two markets, most mechanisms in MOMAN-CS can be borrowed to enhance MOVE-CS. For instance, road data collection in MOVE-CS can be divided into exclusive sensing tasks for that drivers can choose. Besides, more rewards would be assigned to those road segments seldom chosen. That being said, a major obstacle we identified during the application process is that the drivers also care about the passenger tasks which usually decide their income. Hence, the task selection strategy in MOVE-CS should be very different from that in MOMAN-CS.

To tackle this problem, we analyze a large-scale dataset[1] of 12,493 MOD vehicles' service records for 1 month (03/01/2017–03/31/2017) in a 4400 km^2 metropolitan area with 10.3 million residents, including each passenger mission's pick-up/drop-off locations, time-variant occupied/vacant statuses, and fine-grained vehicle trajectories (explicated in Sect. 2.3.2). The results indicate two findings as follows.

1. On a daily basis, we find that the majority (88.2%) of drivers drive from low-yield areas to high-yield areas to pick up passengers, indicating their *explicit preference* for *short-term, immediate gains*.
2. On a monthly basis, however, we notice that a significant portion (30%) of drivers still drive from high-yield areas to low-yield areas to pick up passengers, with a high incidence of 21.1%. To our surprise, we find their hourly earnings to be 17.5% higher than the average level ($126.6 monthly raise), revealing their *implicit rationality* in their quest for *long-term, stable profits*.

Inspired by these findings, we propose Long-Short-Term Profit-combined Task Recommendation (*LSTRec*), a new operation model for MOVE-CS, whose main goal is to meet both drivers' explicit preference for short-term gains and their implicit need of long-term profits. For this purpose, *LSTRec* actively recommends tasks to intelligently-balanced drivers in order to attract more participants while also generating sufficient profits to regular drivers. At the same time, *LSTRec* should also

---

[1] We collected all the data (excluding user-sensitive information) under a well-organized IRB with informed consent of involved drivers and passengers.

take into consideration the platform's profit. In practice, the interests of drivers and the platform are aligned in some cases. For example, when the platform recommends a task that takes a driver from a low-yield area to a high-yield area, this driver is likely to accept it even if the reward is relatively low. In other cases, their interests might conflict. For example, for an unpopular road segment whose information is valuable to the platform, the platform must offer a relatively high reward to incentivize drivers.

To address the above challenges, we design a spatial-temporal differentiation-aware task recommendation scheme empowered by submodular optimization. Specifically, based on the historical MOD vehicle dataset, we first construct a two-dimensional pick-up profit heatmap. We then predict the evolution of the profit heatmap by exploiting Recurrent Neural Networks (RNN). Using the above information, we formulate a task recommendation problem, taking into account concerns of both new and regular drivers', as well as the profit of the platform. However, it is NP-hard to find the optimal solution to the problem (the computation cost increases exponentially with the number of drivers). To solve this problem, following the methodology of submodular optimization, we design a near-optimal algorithm that uses greedy local-search to achieve an acceptable approximation ratio $(1 - e^{-2})/2$ with polynomial time complexity.

Using the large-scale MOD vehicle dataset described above, we simulate the operation of the original MOVE-CS model and *LSTRec,* respectively, on a common commodity server. Results indicate that in *LSTRec*, 87.3% of the recommended tasks cater to drivers' explicit preference of short-term gains; at the same time, all the drivers are expected to receive positive income, with 50% of them making 3.2× more income (than with the original MOVE-CS model), satisfying their implicit need of long-term returns. In addition to benefiting the drivers, *LSTRec* brings 34.3% more profit to the platform. Therefore, we feel that the new model we proposed has the potential to revive the MOVE-CS market.

2.2 Related Work

There have recently been quite a few studies of incentivized mobile crowdsensing [13–17]; most of them focus on human mobility [14–16], which do not take the special impacts of vehicle mobility into consideration. Since this chapter belongs to the category of incentivizing vehicular crowdsensing [18, 19], we pay attention to reviewing its related studies, while other orthogonal studies can be found in [19–21].

To be specific, He et al. [22] designed a participant recruitment strategy as one of the earliest works, which jointly exploits both the current location and vehicles' predictable mobility pattern. And then, Wang et al. [23] investigated both the deterministic and probabilistic trajectory models and proposed two efficient vehicle recruitment algorithms. Zhu et al. [24] exploited RNN to predict vehicle mobility in the future for selecting vehicles, maximizing their coverage with a limited budget. In addition, Fan et al. [25] proposed Hector, a novel joint scheduling and incentive mechanism for crowdsensing of vehicular. The above works are mainly for common vehicles and do not involve the special MOD vehicles. Instead, a latest work called iLOCuS [26], which is highly related to this chapter, takes into account MOD vehicles. It proposes a hybrid incentive that combines the monetary rewards and the non-monetary hidden incentives (*i.e.*, the passenger's requests in the task's zone). However, iLOCuS ignores the deep needs for short-term and long-term profits of MOD drivers, ineffective in encouraging them. Xiang et al. [27] propose a deep reinforcement learning-based sensing task allocation scheme, achieving a near-optimal solution with a coefficient that depends on the maximum and minimal costs of all the sensing tasks. Instead, this work leverages the greedy local search to achieve an approximation ratio of $(1 - e^{-2})/2$, which is more robust to practical applications in different settings. Unlike existing works, we conduct user studies and in-depth dataset analysis to uncover both MOD drivers' explicit and implicit needs. Results are then fed back into designing a novel LSTRec model that benefits both drivers and the platform.

Furthermore, many efficient recommendation systems [28, 29] have been proposed, like web service recommendation [30] and social network recommendation [31, 32]. Furthermore, many good works about allocation/recommendation of passenger tasks for MOD drivers have been proposed. For instance, Xu et al. [33] designed an effective order dispatching algorithm that takes into account both the instant satisfaction of passengers and the expected income of drivers in the future. However, all of the works mainly focus on either passenger tasks or item recommendations, which are orthogonal to our work.

2.3 Motivation

In this section, we leverage user studies and large-scale data analysis to figure out the causes of the downturn of the MOVE-CS market and explore a potential resurrection approach with reference to the booming MOMAN-CS market.

2.3.1 *Crowdsourcing-Based User Studies*

Methodology To figure out why the two markets face completely different fortunes, we conduct a user study [34] of 581 MOD drivers via Amazon Mechanical Turk. The study is limited to qualified drivers. The participants consist of 41.2% of women and 58.8% of men, including North Americans (34.4%), Europeans (12.7%), Asians (38.6%), and others (14.3%, such as Australians and Africans), ranging in age from 20 to 60; 43.6%, 77.3%. 90.2% of them drive at least once a day, a week, and a month, respectively.

We use the USE questionnaire methodology [35] and a 5-point Likert scale (from Strongly Disagree to Strongly Agree) to assess the participants' perspectives. The results are divided into two groups, *i.e.,* 4 and 5 indicating agreement; 1, 2, and

3 indicating disagreement. These questionnaires are designed to address key questions, namely, why does the MOVE-CS model fail to encourage MOD drivers? why is the MOMAN-CS model effective in motivating users?

Results We first investigate the willingness of the MOD drivers to perform sensing tasks. The survey results show that *92.6% of the participants are willing to perform sensing tasks on the move.* If we Dig deeper, it seems to be related to the fact that the majority (63.8%) of drivers expect additional income when performing sensing tasks, which is in line with common sense.

A further survey of both models indicates that the blind competition model used by Payver is not welcomed by 63.3% of the participants; 94.3% cited duplicate data collection—which can lead to a lower or even negative profit—as a major defect. Thus, it is reasonable to infer that the blind competition model induces uncertainty in drivers' profits and seriously affects their motivation to participate in the mission. Conversely, 95.2% of participants prefer MOMAN-CS since it not only has transparent rewards (70.2% agreement) but also gives more choices on the tasks (81.3% agreement). All in all, the failure of MOVE-CS *may be due to the fact that the blind competition model fails to provide drivers with stable profits*, while MOMAN-CS *successfully motivates participants with its exclusive task selection and transparent reward.*

2.3.2 Large-Scale Dataset Collection and Analysis

Dataset collection Cooperating with a MOD company, we acquired a large-scale MOD vehicular dataset. All the user-sensitive information is deleted based on the local IRB protocols. This dataset comprises 92 GB of service records of 12,493 MOD vehicles for 1 month (03/01/2017–03/31/2017) in a 4400 km^2 metropolitan area with 10.3 million residents. Each record contains an anonymized vehicle ID, the trajectory time series with 15-s intervals, and an occupied/vacant state indicator. In addition, the trajectory series allow us to calculate the pick-up profits based on the existing MOD vehicle fare policy [36].

Pick-up profit analysis The pick-up profit refers to the average profit of MOD drivers picking up passengers in a certain zone during a certain time period (*e.g.*, 1 h). It depends to a large extent on the probability of picking up passengers and the per-trip earnings in this zone. Therefore, we randomly select an area (about 256 km^2) of the city and divide it into 14 × 18 uniform zones. And then, we analyze the spatial-temporal variation in pick-up profits in each zone and time period, in terms of the pick-up probability and the per-trip earnings.

We firstly analyze the temporary variety of pick-up probability and per-trip earnings in a randomly selected zone in different time periods. According to Fig. 2.1a, both the pick-up probability (top) and the per-trip earnings (bottom) differ significantly over time. Particularly, the pick-up probability and per-trip earnings are distributed

Fig. 2.1 Variations of pick-up probability (top) and per-trip earnings (bottom) in different time periods for the same zone. (**a**) Temporal differentiation analysis

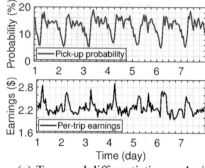

(a) Temporal differentiation analysis

between 5.0% and 19.1%, $1.96 and $2.91, respectively. Besides, both pick-up probability and per-trip earnings roughly follow cyclical patterns. For example, Fig. 2.1a shows that the pick-up probability from midnight to 6 a.m. is always smaller than the probability at other times of a day when most citizens are sleeping. And then, we analyze their spatial diversities over time (*e.g.,* 6 p.m. to 7 p.m.) in different zones, as shown in Fig. 2.3a, b. Similarly, both the pick-up probability and the per-trip earnings are found to vary by zones over the same period. Particularly, the pick-up probability and per-trip earnings fluctuate between 0% and 39%, $1.55 and $5.41, respectively. To sum up, the pick-up profits of MOD drivers have huge spatial-temporal differences in different zones and time periods.

MOD drivers' behavior analysis MOD drivers' behavior patterns have a common goal (making money) but different individual preferences based on driving experiences (like how to make more money). To gain a full grasp of their behavior patterns, we conduct a comprehensive analysis of the large-scale dataset—in terms of short-term and long-term profits—and segment on a daily basis and an individual basis, respectively.

First, we slice the dataset on a daily basis to study drivers' daily short-term preferences. And then, we randomly select ten low-yield zones. For each zone, we calculate the corresponding percentage of drivers who enter directly (from this low-yield zone) into a high-yield zone to pick up passengers. As demonstrated in Fig. 2.2a, the 1-month average percentage for all selected zones is 88.2%. It shows that most drivers in low-yield zones have a tendency to move outward (towards higher-yield zones), which is strong evidence of drivers' explicit preference for immediate gains.

Second, in order to understand drivers' long-term pursuits, we slice the dataset into individual slices, each with the driver's entire 1-month driving records. Next, we arbitrarily select 300 drivers. For each driver's behavior pattern, we calculate the incidence of her/his picking up passengers from a high-yield zone into a low-yield zone over the course of the month. After ranking drivers, as shown in Fig. 2.2b, we find that 30% of them (90 drivers) have an incidence of more than 21.1%, which seems to be abnormal at first. If we compare the hourly pick-up profits of these

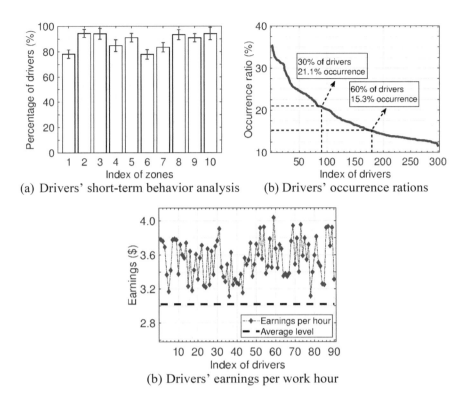

(a) Drivers' short-term behavior analysis   (b) Drivers' occurrence rations

(b) Drivers' earnings per work hour

Fig. 2.2 In-depth analysis of drivers' behavior patterns via 2D slicing. (**a**) Drivers' short-term preference on a daily basis, *i.e.*, the percentage of drivers moving from low-yield zone to high-yield zone. (**b, c**) Drivers' long-term pursuit on an individual basis, including their occurrence ratios of driving from high-yield zone to low-yield zone, and their average earnings in a month

90 drivers with the average profits of all 12,493 drivers, we surprisingly find that these drivers make 17.5% more profits every work hour than the average level (about $126.6 monthly raise considering 8 working hours in each day), as demonstrated in Fig. 2.2c. After thoroughly analyzing these findings, we find that regular drivers can sometimes predict the dynamic profit and rationally choose where to go based on this knowledge to pursue long-term, stable profits rather than blindly pursue the immediate gains.

2.4   LSTRec Design for MOVE-CS

Inspired by the findings in Sect. 2.3, we design a new model called Long-Short-Term Profit-combined Task Recommendation model (*LSTRec*) to resurrect the MOVE-CS market and further address the crucial research problem.

2.4.1   Model Design

Logic behind the design *LSTRec* utilizes the *active task recommendation of the platform* to meet drivers' explicit and implicit needs for short-term and long-term profits at the same time. The logic behind this model design is as follows:

1. The dataset analysis in Sect. 2.3.2 demonstrates that MOD drivers have an explicit preference for both short-term, immediate gains and implicit rationality when they pursue long-term, stable profits. Hence, the model design should satisfy drivers' demands to motivate them to participate.
2. Nevertheless, the short-term and long-term profits can only be predicted with a wide knowledge of the pick-up profits at any time and place, which is unlikely to happen for regular drivers, not to mention those new registrants. Hence, it is unrealistic for drivers to actively select from all the tasks and gain acceptable profits in a short period of time.
3. Therefore, instead of driving selecting tasks as in the MOMAN-CS model, we adopt the task recommendation scheme, *i.e.,* the professional platform which has enough spatial-temporal knowledge predicts the pick-up profits of the drivers, so it can actively recommend tasks comprehensively in view of their short-term and long-term profits.

All in all, the LSTRec model prevents drivers from the rather complex computation of profit prediction and thus reduces the response time of each driver while they still have enough wiggle room for options. Simultaneously, the platform can also pursue its own interest in this process.

***LSTRec* model design** First of all, our *LSTRec* model includes three major steps as follows:

1. *Task publishing*: The new MOVE-CS platform discretizes the required road data collection into S exclusive sensing tasks, according to the road topology and length, as well as the specified applications. We denote the set of these published tasks by S, *i.e.,* $S = \{1, \ldots, S\}$. The zone $j (j \in S)$ and the platform profit of each task are denoted by z_j and u_j, respectively.
2. *Task requesting and recommendation*: There are many MOD drivers picking up passengers in the city, willing to use MOVE-CS. $\mathcal{M}$ denotes the set of these MOD drivers, *i.e.,* $\mathcal{M} = \{1, \ldots, M\}$. Every driver $k (k \in \mathcal{M})$ reports her/his current zone z_k. And then, the platform recommends one task for each driver, as well as its location and reward, and the driver's expected profit. x_{kj} denotes whether task j is recommended to driver k, *i.e.,* $x_{kj} = 1$ if yes, and $x_{kj} = 0$ otherwise. The recommendation set is then denoted by $\mathbf{x} = \{x_{kj}\}$.
3. *Task acceptance and execution*: Once a driver k is recommended task j, s/he has a probability ρ_{kj} of accepting and performing it. Each driver's probability of accepting is decided by her/his preference and reliability, as well as the recommended task that can be learned from abundant MOD vehicle data [18]. To guarantee a high task execution probability, one task might be

recommended to multiple drivers. Therefore, the execution probability of each task j can be calculated by $1 - \prod_{k=1}^{M} \left(1 - \rho_{kj} x_{kj}\right)$. Similar to [37, 38], the total platform profit, *i.e.*, the expected executed of all the performed sensing tasks for the platform, is denoted as

$$U(\mathbf{x}) = \sum_{j=1}^{S} u_j \left(1 - \prod_{k=1}^{M} \left(1 - \rho_{kj} x_{kj}\right) \right). \tag{2.1}$$

At last, after the road data of task j is uploaded to the MOVE-CS platform, driver k gets a reward c_{kj}; then, the rewards of all drivers form a set $\mathbf{c} = \{c_{kj}\}$. Thus, the driver's total revenue is equal to the sum of the reward for performing the sensing task and the pick-up profit for delivering passengers.

2.4.2   Research Problem and Challenge Analysis

The key problem in the LSTRec model design is how to recommend tasks to drivers with proper rewards, by studying and predicting the spatial-temporal differences, which is presented below.

Long-short-term profit-aware optimal task recommendation problem (*LSTO*) *considering the historical MOD vehicle dataset, how to recommend each task j to a MOD driver k with the sensing reward $\{c_{kj}\}$, so the total platform profit $U(\mathbf{x})$ can be maximized under the constraint of budget B, while satisfying both drivers' explicit preference for short-term profits and implicit demand for long-term profits.*

In order to address the above problem, there are the following three main challenges:

1. *Due to their spatial-temporal dynamics, it is difficult to predict the global distribution of the pick-up profits.* The pick-up profits exhibit spatial-temporal dynamics, as shown in Figs. 2.1a and 2.3a, b. In addition, the highly complex movement of both passengers and MOD vehicles between different zones and time complicates such dynamics, therefore making it particularly difficult to accurately predict the global distribution of pick-up profits.
2. *It is challenging to meet the requirements of both drivers and the platform, which are consistent in some cases but conflicting in others.* In some cases, a task may require sensing in a high-yield zone to which drivers are eager to move towards, so that they may accept a relatively low reward, consistent with the platform's interests. In other cases, a task valuable to the platform may relate to an unwelcome zone, where drivers are reluctant to go. The two parties do not share mutual interests so that drivers will only take on the task if the reward is high enough to meet their expectations, increasing the cost of the platform.

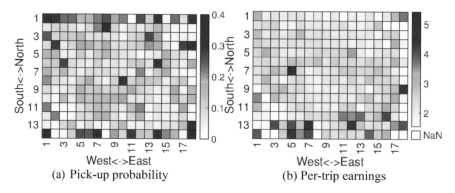

Fig. 2.3 Pick-up profits in different zones during the same time period, in terms of (**a**) pick-up probability and (**b**) per-trip earnings ($)

3. *The optimal task recommendation subproblem of LSTO is NP-hard.* This problem can be simplified from the classical 0–1 knapsack problem [39]: Given a capacity B and a group of items $\{(k,j)|\forall k \in \mathcal{M}, \forall j \in \mathcal{S}\}$, each of which has a value c_{kj} and a weight ρ_{kj}, a collection of items are selected to maximize the total value $U(\mathbf{x})$ subject to the capacity constraint of weights (the detailed proofs are omitted due to the page limit). Therefore, achieving optimal recommendations with computational efficiency is extremely challenging, especially for the large-scale MOVE-CS market with a large number of drivers (*e.g.*, 12,493 drivers in our dataset).

2.5 Key Algorithm Design for LSTRec

To address the three above challenges, we propose a spatial-temporal differentiation-aware task recommendation scheme empowered by submodular optimization. As shown in Fig. 2.4, it mainly consists of three parts:

1. *Construction of Pick-up profit heatmap* (Sect. 2.5.1): we first construct the two-dimensional pick-up profit heatmaps by utilizing the historical MOD vehicle dataset. The pick-up profit heatmaps are used to predict the future heatmaps by exploiting dual-attention-based RNN.
2. *Differentiation-aware sensing reward design* (Sect. 2.5.2): Based on the global understanding of the pick-up profit heatmaps, we learn the spatial-temporal dynamics of pick-up profits, and feed it back into devising the sensing rewards to meet the driver's explicit and implicit demands of the short-term and long-term profits, respectively.
3. *Submodularity-based task recommendation* (Sect. 2.5.3): considering the sensing reward design, we first analyze the characteristics of the optimal task

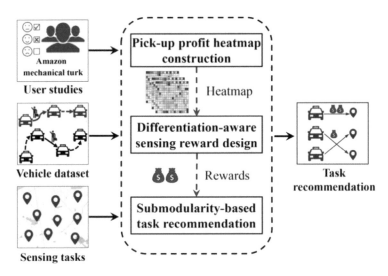

Fig. 2.4   Overview of our algorithm

recommendation problem by reformulating it. Based on the analysis results, we propose an approximation algorithm to solve this NP-hard problem, utilizing the methodology of submodular optimization.

2.5.1   Pick-Up Profit Heatmap Construction

Two-dimensional pick-up profit heatmap model   The pick-up profit is highly dependent on the pick-up probability and the per-trip earnings in each zone. In addition, the dataset analysis in Sect. 2.3.2 shows that there are spatial-temporal dynamics in both the pick-up probability and the per-trip earnings across different zones and time periods. Therefore, we use the two-dimensional heatmaps, which is called *pick-up profit heatmaps*, to represent the dynamic spatial-temporal pick-up profits.

Particularly, we categorize the map of an entire city into Z non-overlapping zones, based on the shape and the specified spatial granularity of the area. Let z_i and $\mathcal{Z}$ denote each zone i and the set of zones, respectively, such that $z_i \in \mathcal{Z}$. Similarly, the time is evenly classified into T time slots, and the set of time slots is denoted as $\mathcal{T}$. Each time slot t is also called period t. Let p_i^t and r_i^t denote the pick-up probability and the per-trip earnings in zone i at period t. Therefore, the pick-up profit heatmaps $\mathbf{H}^T$ during the periods $[1, T]$ are denoted as

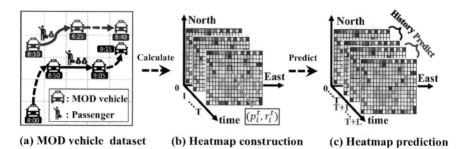

(a) MOD vehicle dataset   **(b) Heatmap construction**   **(c) Heatmap prediction**

Fig. 2.5 Illustration of pick-up profit heatmap construction based on the MOD vehicle dataset using dual-attention-based RNN. (**a**) MOD vehicle dataset. (**b**) Heatmap construction. (**c**) Heatmap prediction

$$\mathbf{H}^T = \{\mathbf{h}^t | 1 \leq t \leq T\}, \qquad (2.2)$$

$$\mathbf{h}^t = \{(p_i^t, r_i^t) | \forall i \in \mathcal{Z}\}, \qquad (2.3)$$

where $\mathbf{h}^t$ denotes the t-th frame of the heatmaps, representing the pick-up profits of all the zones at period t. Besides, each pixel of the heatmap frame (*i.e.*, $(p_i^t, r_i^t) \in \mathbf{h}^t$) represents the pick-up probability and the per-trip earnings in zone i at period t. In the heatmaps, intuitively, the warmer the color, the more the pick-up profits drivers are expected to earn (with higher pick-up probability and more per-trip earnings), as demonstrated in Fig. 2.3a, b.

Heatmap construction based on MOD vehicle dataset We use the historical MOD vehicle dataset to construct the pick-up profit heatmap, including their trajectories, occupied/vacant statuses, and pick-up earnings of each trip, as shown in Fig. 2.5a. To be specific, as shown in Fig. 2.5b, according to the trajectories of MOD vehicles and the information of their occupied/vacant status, we calculate the ratio of the vehicles delivering passengers to all the vacant vehicles in zone i across period t as the pick-up probability p_i^t. Furthermore, we use the average income to compute the per-trip earnings r_i^t of all the vehicles that deliver passengers from zone i at period t. Therefore, we use the historical MOD vehicle dataset for the periods [1, T] to construct the corresponding pick-up profit heatmaps, *i.e.*, $\mathbf{H}^T = \{(p_i^t, r_i^t) | \forall i \in \mathcal{Z}, 1 \leq t \leq T\}$.

Heatmap prediction based on RNN As illustrated in Fig. 2.5c, we accurately predict the future L periods by utilizing the pick-up profit heatmaps $\mathbf{H}^T$ of periods [1, T]. Note that, the prediction length L is dependent on the time interval of each task proposed in Sect. 2.5.2. In particular, the dual-attention based RNN [40, 41] is exploited to accurately predict several future profit heatmaps based on historical ones. Its main idea is to utilize an LSTM-based encoder-decoder architecture with dual-attention mechanisms, which include spatial attention and temporal attention. The spatial attention is used to acquire the complex spatial correlations in different zones; the temporal attention is exploited to learn the time-varying correlations between different time periods. In conclusion, we construct and predict the global pick-up profit heatmaps over the periods by using the MOD vehicle dataset [1, $T + L$], $i.e.\mathbf{H}^{T+L} = \left\{ \left(p_i^t, r_i^t \right) | \forall i \in Z, 1 \leq t \leq T + L \right\}$.

2.5.2   Differentiation-Aware Sensing Reward Design

According to the global pick-up profit heatmaps, we first calculate the spatial-temporal differences of pick-up profits for designing the sensing rewards of drivers. The pick-up profit difference represents the expected pick-up profit increase for a vacant vehicle traveling from one zone to another to perform the sensing task. Formally, we make $I_{kj}(t_0)$ represent the pick-up profit difference for driver k, as she/he moves from her/his original zone z_k to the task's zone z_j at t_0. Then, $I_{kj}(t_0)$ is given by

$$I_{kj}(t_0) = \mathbb{E}_{t_0} \left[p_j^t \cdot r_j^t \right] - \mathbb{E}_{t_0} \left[p_k^t \cdot r_k^t \right], \tag{2.4}$$

where $\mathbb{E}_{t_0}[\cdot]$ denotes the mathematical expectation concerning t_0. $\mathbb{E}_{t_0} \left[p_k^t \cdot r_k^t \right]$ denotes the expected pick-up profit of driver k at her/his original zone z_k. $\mathbb{E}_{t_0} \left[p_j^t \cdot r_j^t \right]$ represents that of driver k at the new zone z_j. Both of them depend on the probability p_k^t (p_j^t) that drivers pick up passengers in $z_k(z_j)$ at period t; the probability $\overline{p}_k^t$ ($\overline{p}_j^t$) that drivers cannot do it in $z_k(z_j)$ before t. Hence, both $\mathbb{E}_{t_0} \left[p_k^t \cdot r_k^t \right]$ and $\mathbb{E}_{t_0} \left[p_j^t \cdot r_j^t \right]$ can be calculated based on the global pick-up profit heatmaps $\mathbf{H}^{T+L} = \left\{ \left(p_i^t, r_i^t \right) | \forall i \in Z, 1 \leq t \leq T + L \right\}$, utilizing the expectation model [27].

Knowing each driver's pick-up profit difference, we design a sensing reward model, which is subtracted from her/his expected earnings. Specifically, let $b_{kj}(t_0)$ denote driver k's expected income from passenger tasks, when driving from z_k to z_j. Therefore, according to Eq. (2.4), the sensing reward $c_{kj}(t_0)$ for performing task j by driver k at t_0 is denoted as

$$c_{kj}(t_0) = b_{kj}(t_0) - \left(\mathbb{E}_{t_0} \left[p_j^t \cdot r_j^t \right] - \mathbb{E}_{t_0} \left[p_k^t \cdot r_k^t \right] \right). \tag{2.5}$$

Note that $b_{kj}(t_0)$ can be computed according to the driving time and distance [25, 26], as well as the pricing policies of MOD vehicles [36]. With reference to the drivers' actual hourly wage, the platform gives each driver a reward called the expected profit, which makes drivers willing to spend time on the sensing tasks. A driver's expected profit is combined by her/his explicit reward $c_{kj}(t_0)$ that is directly given by the platform, and implicit reward $\mathbb{E}_{t_0} \left[p_j^t \cdot r_j^t \right] - \mathbb{E}_{t_0} \left[p_k^t \cdot r_k^t \right]$ that is subtly received by relocation to a higher-yield zone for task j. Therefore, as shown in Eq. (2.5), if the implicit reward is sufficient, the platform can reduce the explicit reward. If it is insufficient, the platform should provide a higher explicit compensation reward. Thus, all drivers receive more profits than the rewards from passenger-only tasks, which is called positive profits. In summary, *the design of sensing reward based on the pick-up profit differentiation learning can guarantee positive profits by balancing the explicit and implicit rewards of all the drivers.*

2.5.3 Submodularity-Based Task Recommendation Algorithm

Problem analysis based on equivalent transformation First of all, given the sensing reward design $\{c_{kj}\}$, we can equivalently transform the LSTO problem into a set function optimization problem to facilitate the analysis of the problem. Particularly, we define the ground set $\mathcal{V} := \{v = (k,j) | \forall k \in \mathcal{M}, \forall j \in \mathcal{S}\}$. Let $\mathcal{A}$ denote the set of the recommended driver-task pairs, *i.e.,* $\mathcal{A} := \{v = (k,j) | x_{kj} = 1, \forall k \in \mathcal{M}, \forall j \in \mathcal{S}\}$, and $\mathcal{A} \subseteq \mathcal{V}$. Moreover, $\forall \mathcal{A} \subseteq \mathcal{V}$, $U(\mathcal{A}) := \{U(\mathbf{x}) | \forall (k,j) \in \mathcal{A}, x_{kj} = 1; \forall (k,j) \notin \mathcal{A}, x_{kj} = 0\}$. It is worth noting that $U(\mathcal{A})$ and $U(\mathbf{x})$ are different functions, but for simplification, we adopt the same symbol $U(\cdot)$. According to the above definitions, the optimal task recommendation subproblem of *LSTO* can be equivalently transformed to

$$\underset{\mathcal{A} \subseteq \mathcal{V}}{\text{Max}} U(\mathcal{A}) = \sum_{j \in \mathcal{S}} u_j \left(1 - \prod_{k \in \mathcal{M}} \left(1 - \rho_{kj} x_{kj} \right) \right), \tag{2.6}$$

$$\text{s.t.} \sum_{j:(k,j) \in \mathcal{A}} \mathbf{1}_{(k,j) \in \mathcal{A}} \leq 1, \tag{2.7}$$

$$\sum_{(k,j) \in \mathcal{A}} c_{kj} \rho_{kj} \leq B, \tag{2.8}$$

where $\mathbf{1}$ denotes the indicator function. Equation (2.7) restricts each driver is recommended at most one task in each recommendation period, similar to [42, 43]. Equation (2.8) illustrates that the drivers' expected sensing rewards are less than the platform's budget.

Furthermore, based on the set function optimization problem, we theoretically analyze the characteristics of the problem. First of all, we notice that the objective function of this problem is *submodular*. Particularly, let $\mathcal{A}_1 \subseteq \mathcal{A}_2$; $\mathcal{A}_1^0 := \{(k, j_0) | \forall k, (k, j_0) \in \mathcal{A}_1\}$; $\mathcal{A}_2^0 := \{(k, j_0) | \forall k, (k, j_0) \in \mathcal{A}_2\}$. Hence, $U(\mathcal{A}_1 \cup \{v_0\}) - U(\mathcal{A}_1) = u_{j_0} \rho_{k_0 j_0} \prod_{k:(k,j) \in \mathcal{A}_1^0} \left(1 - \rho_{kj} \right)$, and $U(\mathcal{A}_2 \cup \{v_0\}) - U(\mathcal{A}_2) = u_{j_0} \rho_{k_0 j_0} \prod_{k:(k,j) \in \mathcal{A}_2^0} \left(1 - \rho_{kj} \right)$. Since $\prod_{k:(k,j) \in \mathcal{A}_1^0} \left(1 - \rho_{kj} \right) \geq \prod_{k:(k,j) \in \mathcal{A}_2^0} \left(1 - \rho_{kj} \right)$, according to the definition of submodularity [44], the objective function is submodular. In addition, it is easy to prove that the objective function is also non-negative and monotone [44]. Furthermore, based on the definitions of the matroid constraint and the knapsack constraint [45], we find that constraints (2.7) and (2.8) are a matroid constraint and a knapsack constraint, respectively. Detailed proofs are omitted because of the page limit. In short, we obtain the following results: *The optimal task recommendation subproblem of LSTO is to maximize non-negative, monotone, and submodular objective function with a matroid constraint and a knapsack constraint.*

Algorithm design Following the submodular optimization approach [46], we propose *a near-optimal task recommendation algorithm based on greedy local search*, exploiting two key ideas: (1) Since this problem is the maximization of a monotone and submodular objective function, we leverage the *greedy strategy* to iteratively explore the local optimal solution that has the *largest marginal profit-cost ratio*. (2) In each iteration, we leverage *local search* to swap a non-recommended driver-task pair with a recommended one, to maximize profit under the matroid constraint (2.7). If the marginal profit-cost ratio of this swap is greater than the lower bound $\frac{\epsilon}{M^2 S^2}$, then a swap is applied.

Specifically, the detailed design of the algorithm is illustrated in Algorithm 2.1. $\mathcal{A}_n$ denotes the set of recommended driver-task pairs in the n-th iteration. Let(v_+, v_-) and $\mathcal{V}_s$ represent a swap and the swap set, respectively, where v_+ represents a non-recommended pair, *i.e.*, $v_+ = (k_+, j_+) \in \mathcal{V} \backslash \mathcal{A}_n$; v_- represents a recommended one, *i.e.*, $v_- = (k_-, j_-) \in \mathcal{A}_n \cup \{\varnothing\}$; $\mathcal{V}_s = \{(v_+, v_-)\}$. Note that $\varnothing$ represents a dummy element. Swapping v_+ with $\varnothing$ is equivalent to adding v_+ directly into $\mathcal{A}_n$. Therefore, the marginal profit-cost ratio of this swap (v_+, v_-), *i.e.*, the ratio of the platform profit increased by the swap to the sensing reward of v_+, is denoted by

$$\pi(v_+, v_-) = \frac{U(\mathcal{A} \backslash \{v_-\} \cup \{v_+\}) - U(\mathcal{A})}{c_{k_+ j_+}}. \tag{2.9}$$

According to Algorithm 2.1, we analyze the algorithm design's theoretical performance. To be more specific, since the profit increase by swap in each iteration should be at least $\frac{\epsilon}{M^2 S^2}$, the number of its iterations is no more than $\frac{M^2 S^2}{\epsilon} \log(MS)$. In addition, the time complexity of each iteration in lines 3–12 is $O(M^2 S^2)$. And the time complexity of Algorithm 2.1 is $O(M^4 S^4 \log (MS))$, since ϵ is a constant. Based on the analysis aforementioned, this problem is a monotone, submodular maximization problem with a matroid constraint and a knapsack constraint. Therefore, referring to [46], Algorithm 2.1 can achieve an approximation ratio of $(1 - e^{-2})/2$-approximation ratio. In summary, *Algorithm 2.1 can achieve a near-optimal solution of $(1 - e^{-2})/2$-approximation with the polynomial time complexity $O(M^4 S^4 \log (MS))$, where M and S represent the numbers of drivers and tasks, respectively.*

Algorithm 2.1. Greedy Local Search-Based Near-Optimal Task Recommendation Algorithm

Input: Task set S; MOD driver set $\mathcal{M}$;

    Sensing rewards set $\{c_{kj}\}$;

    Set of drivers' acceptance probability $\{\rho_{kj}\}$;

    Set of tasks' profits to the platform $\{u_j\}$; Budget B;

    Output: Recommended task set $\{x_{kj}\}$; Platform profit U;

    1: Initialize $\quad \mathcal{A}_0 = \{v_0, v_1\}\quad$, where $\quad v_0 = \arg\max\limits_{v \in \mathcal{V}} U(\{v\})\quad$, $\quad v_1 =$

$\arg\max\limits_{v \in \mathcal{V} \backslash \{v_0\}} U(\{v, v_0\}) - U(\{v_0\})$;

    2: Initialize $n = 0$, and *swap* = *true*;

    3: while *swap* **do**

    4:   *swap* $\leftarrow$ *false*;

    5: $\mathcal{V}_s := \{(v_+, v_-) | \forall v_+ \in \mathcal{V} \backslash \mathcal{A}_n, \forall v_- \in \mathcal{A}_n \cup \{\emptyset\}\}$;

    6:   **While**$\{(swap \neq true)$ && $(\mathcal{V}_s \neq \emptyset)$ **do**

    7: $\left(v_+^*, v_-^*\right) = \arg\max\limits_{(v_+, v_-) \in \mathcal{V}_s} \pi(v_+, v_-)$;

    8:   **if** $\mathcal{A}_n \backslash \{v_-^*\} \cup \{v_+^*\}$ satisfies constraints (2.7) (2.8) and $\pi\left(v_+^*, v_-^*\right) \geq$

$\frac{\epsilon}{M^2 S^2}$ **then**

    9: $\mathcal{A}_{n+1} \leftarrow \mathcal{A}_n \backslash \{v_-^*\} \cup \{v_+^*\}$;

    10: $n \leftarrow n + 1$;

    11:   *swap* $\leftarrow$ *true* ;

    12: $\mathcal{V}_s \leftarrow \mathcal{V}_s \backslash \{(v_+, v_-)\}$

    13: Set $\mathbf{x} \leftarrow \{x_{kj} = 1 | \forall k, \forall j, (k, j) \in \mathcal{A}_n\}$;

    14: Compute $U(\mathbf{x})$ based on $\mathbf{x}$, $\{u_j\}$, and $\{\rho_{kj}\}$, according to Eq. (2.6);

    15: return $\mathbf{x}$ and $U(\mathbf{x})$

2.6 Evaluation

We leverage the dataset of large-scale MOD vehicles to simulate the operation of the original MOVE-CS model and the LSTRec model, respectively. Therefore, we comprehensively compare the proposed algorithm's performance with five baseline algorithms.

2.6.1 Emulation Methodology and Settings

The simulation of the proposed LSTRec model and the original MOVE-CS model is in accordance with the large-scale MOD vehicle dataset (specified in Sect. 2.3.2) below. First of all, the platform of MOVE-CS requires of 878 road segments' road data with a total length of 191.1 miles across an area of 32 km². Therefore, each road needs to be sensed k times with decreasing profit u to the platform ($k = 3$, $u = \$2.5$, 1.5, and 0.5 per mile for the three times, respectively) for higher accuracy. There are M MOD drivers ($M = 1000$), randomly selected participants who are willing to collect the road data for the MOVE-CS market. Next up, we run the simulation for 5 days, which may end early if the budget is exhausted.

For the MOVE-CS model, drivers collect road data when driving at any time during her/his work hours. Drivers spend an average of $0.06 per mile on fuels [47]; their data collection costs are only induced in an unmanned state on additional trips to perform tasks. Each driver gets a reward after the data is uploaded. The original settings used by Payver ($0.01–0.05per mile) are so unreasonable that most participants would only get little or negative profits. To make a fair comparison in contrast, in the emulation, we make a portion ($1/a$) of the platform profit u be the reward, *e.g.*, $k = 3$, $1/a = 0.2$, and the rewards are $0.5, 0.3, 0.1 per mile respectively, in accordance with the economic theory [48]. For the LSTRec model, there are N rounds of task recommendations. As described in Sect. 2.4.1, in each round, the platform issues sensing tasks; each corresponds to a set of road segments. Then the platform predicts drivers' pick-up profits and recommends sensing tasks to them. The probability of each driver accepting and completing the task follows a random uniform distribution $\mathcal{U}(0, 1)$. Once the task is completed, s/he receives the reward provided by the proposed algorithm. We implement the simulation on a commodity server with 3.00 GHz dual-core Intel Core Xeon Gold 6561 CPU and 192 GB RAM.

2.6.2   Results of Model Evaluation

Drivers' profits   We first evaluate drivers' profits for the two models. As shown in Fig. 2.6a, for the MOVE-CS model, 14.5% of drivers get negative profits from sensing tasks, since they may spend a lot on collecting repeated road data, resulting

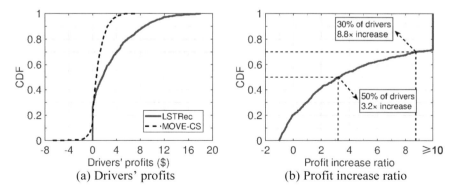

Fig. 2.6 Drivers' profits in the two models (**a**), and the profit increase ratio of LSTRec compared with the original MOVE-CS model (**b**)

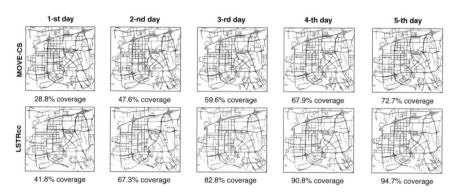

Fig. 2.7 Road coverage heatmaps in the two models; black, orange, red, and crimson represent collected times of 0, 1, 2, and 3, respectively

in rewards that are much lower than the driving cost.In comparison, all the drivers in the LSTRec model earn positive profits, because of the sensing reward design based on the spatial-temporal differentiation in pick-up profits. Furthermore, we analyze all the LSTRec task recommendation results. Results indicate that 87.3% of the recommended tasks move drivers from low-yield zones to high-yield zones, in accordance with their desires for immediate earnings.

In addition, we calculate the drivers' profit increase ratios in LSTRec to those in MOVE-CS to compare the drivers' profits in the two models. As shown in Fig. 2.6b, we find that in our model, 50% of the drivers increased their profits by 320%, and 30% increased their profits by 880%, compared to MOVE-CS. Further analysis shows that its effectiveness depends on the proactive task recommendation scheme, *i.e.*, motivating drivers to complete the tasks that are appropriate for them. In addition, Fig. 2.6b shows that 20% of drivers' profits decreased (compared to the MOVE-CS model) due to the lack of tasks recommended to them, which can be addressed by prior recommendation to drivers in the next round.

Platform's profits We evaluate the platform profit of both models. We first visualize the coverage heatmap of the road segments collected over a 5-day period. As indicated in Fig. 2.7, the coverage ratio of roads collected each day is consistently higher than that of MOVE-CS. Our coverage ratio increases day by day, reaching 94.7% on the last day, 22.0% higher than that of MOVE-CS. At the same time, our platform profit increases by 34.3%, which is also attributed to the proactive task recommendation scheme, *i.e.*, encouraging drivers to unwelcome roads, and increasing the road coverage ratio, and also the platform profit.

Impacts of parameters We evaluate the impacts of the number of drivers on the performance of the model, both in terms of drivers' profits and the platform profit. As demonstrated in Fig. 2.8a, we show the box-plot of the drivers' profits in both models. The results show that LSTRec can ensure positive profits of all the drivers, while 14.6% of drivers in MOVE-CS model have negative profits. Additionally, the drivers' profits from both models decrease with the increasing number of drivers, as

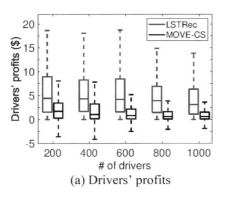 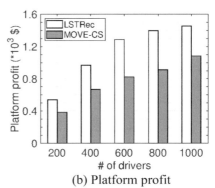

(a) Drivers' profits (b) Platform profit

Fig. 2.8 Impacts of different numbers of drivers on the performance of two models, in terms of (**a**) drivers' profits and (**b**) platform profit

more opt-in drivers lead to more intense competition for income. Nevertheless, the drop rate in MOVE-CS is on average 32.2% higher than that of LSTRec. Furthermore, Fig. 2.8b shows that the platform profits of both models increase with the increasing number of drivers. The platform profit of LSTRec is on average 45.8% higher than that of MOVE-CS. Other parameters (*e.g.*, budget) have similar effects on results, so we do not show them due to the page limit.

2.6.3 Results of Algorithm Evaluation

Baseline algorithms To evaluate the performance of the key algorithm of LSTRec from all respects, we utilize the following five baselines:

1. Hector [25] greedily recommends to the drivers sensing tasks with maximum marginal profit-cost efficiency, while making their basic driving costs as the rewards.
2. GA [22] utilizes the Genetic algorithm to maximize the platform profit, assuming that the sensing rewards have been given.
3. iLOCuS [26] greedily recommends the sensing tasks to minimize the task distribution divergence, while exploiting the high pick-up probability in the region as a hidden incentive.
4. RAD randomly recommends tasks with uniformly distributed pick-up profits.
5. OPT utilizes the brutal-force search method to achieve the optimal solution at an exponential time cost. In the rest of the content, for simplification, we also refer to the proposed algorithm as LSTRec.

Comparison of algorithms We first compare LSTRec with five baselines to evaluate the platform profit across different numbers of drivers and tasks. As shown in Fig. 2.9a, b, the platform profit of LSTRec is 466.8%, 103.2%, 61.7%,

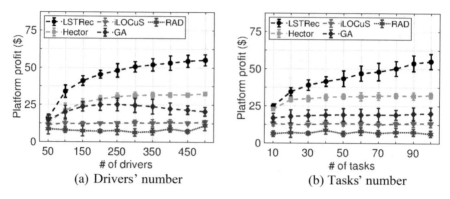

Fig. 2.9 Comparison of the LSTRec algorithm and four baselines in terms of the platform profit in different numbers of drivers (**a**) and tasks (**b**)

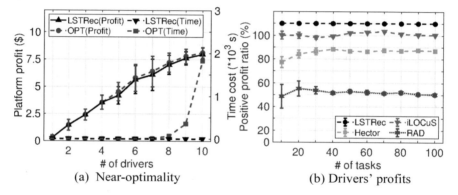

Fig. 2.10 Comparison of the LSTRec algorithm and four baselines in terms of (**a**) the near-optimality and (**b**) the drivers' profits

and 257.1% higher than those of RAD, GA, Hector, and iLOCus, in different numbers of drivers, respectively, and is 516.5%, 132.7%, 44.4%, and 237.8% higher in different numbers of tasks, respectively. Additionally, we compare the near-optimality of LSTRec with OPT in a small-scale scenario to evaluate it (*i.e.*, $M = 10$, $S = 6$). As shown in Fig. 2.10a, LSTRec can achieve 97.2% of the optimal platform profit on average with a time cost of only 0.004% of OPT across different numbers of drivers. As for drivers' profits, there is a wide gap between LSTRec and baselines. As demonstrated in Fig. 2.10b, LSTRec ensures a 100% positive profit ratio (*i.e.*, the percentage of MOD drivers with positive profits after participating in MOVE-CS), which is 24.2%, 9.2%, and 58.1% higher than that of Hector, iLOCus, and RAD. Therefore, unlike the three baselines, LSTRec ensures positive profits for all the drivers by taking into account both the driver's long-term and short-term profits.

2.7 Conclusion

In this chapter, motivated by the results in user studies and the analysis of large-scale vehicle dataset, we propose LSTRec, a new task recommendation model that combines long and short-term profits, trying to resurrect the MOVE-CS market. Behind it is a spatial-temporal differentiation-aware task recommendation scheme empowered by submodular optimization. Such scheme involves RNN-based pick-up heatmap prediction, the differentiation-aware sensing reward design, and the submodularity-based task recommendation algorithm. Simulation results show that LSTRec ensures not only positive profits for drivers, but also a near-optimal profit for the platform, thus potentially reviving MOVE-CS. In the future, we will explore the possible deployment of our LSTRec model by collaborating with MOD companies.

References

1. X. Tang, Z. Qin, F. Zhang, et al., A deep value-network based approach for multi-driver order dispatching. Paper presented at the 25th ACM SIGKDD International Conference on Knowledge Discovery & Data Mining, 4–8 August 2019
2. How many uber drivers are there? (2021), https://therideshareguy.com/how-many-uber-drivers-are-there/
3. Global mobility on demand market forecast & opportunities by 2022 (2017), https://www.techsciresearch.com/report/global-mobility-on-demand-market/1254.html
4. Drivers for uber, lyft are earning less than half of what they did four years ago, study finds (2019), https://www.marketwatch.com/story/drivers-for-uber-lyft-are-earning-less-than-half-of-what-they-/did-four-years-ago-study-finds-2018-09-24
5. Uber and lyft have a driver shortage problem, and it's costing them a lot of money (2021), https://www.theverge.com/2021/4/7/22371850/uber-lyft-driver-shortage-covid-bonus-stimulus
6. Payver (2019), https://www.lazymoneyguy.com/payver/
7. Google maps (2021), https://www.google.com/maps
8. Lvl5 (2020), https://www.crunchbase.com/organization/lvl5
9. Thanks to a dashcam, crafty uber drivers are boosting their pay (2017), http://money.cnn.com/2017/07/19/technology/business/rideshare-drivers-camera/index.html
10. Doordash acquires autonomous driving startup scotty labs (2019), https://techcrunch.com/2019/08/20/doordash-acquires-autonomous-driving-startup-scotty-labs/
11. Amazon mechanical turk (2021), https://www.mturk.com/
12. Gigwalk (2021), https://www.gigwalk.com/
13. Y. Chen, B. Li, Q. Zhang, Incentivizing crowdsourcing systems with network effects. Paper presented at the IEEE INFOCOM 2016—the 35th Annual IEEE International Conference on Computer Communications, 10–14 April 2016
14. H. Jin, H. Guo, L. Su, et al., Dynamic task pricing in multi-requester mobile crowd sensing with Markov correlated equilibrium. Paper presented at the IEEE INFOCOM 2019—IEEE Conference on Computer Communications, 29 April 2019–2 May 2019
15. J. Lin, M. Li, D. Yang, et al., Sybil-proof online incentive mechanisms for crowdsensing. Paper presented at the IEEE INFOCOM 2018—IEEE Conference on Computer Communications, 16–19 April 2018

16. H. Zhang, B. Liu, H. Susanto, et al., Incentive mechanism for proximity-based mobile crowd service systems. Paper presented at the IEEE INFOCOM 2016—the 35th Annual IEEE International Conference on Computer Communications, 10–14 April 2016
17. Z. Cai, Z. Duan, W. Li, Exploiting multi-dimensional task diversity in distributed auctions for mobile crowdsensing. IEEE Trans. Mobile Comput. **20**(8), 2576–2591 (2020)
18. G. Gao, M. Xiao, J. Wu, et al., Truthful incentive mechanism for nondeterministic crowdsensing with vehicles. IEEE Trans. Mobile Comput. **17**(12), 2982–2997 (2018)
19. M. Xiao, G. Gao, J. Wu, et al., Privacy-preserving user recruitment protocol for mobile crowdsensing. IEEE/ACM Trans. Netw. **28**(2), 519–532 (2020)
20. X. Zhang, Z. Yang, W. Sun, et al., Incentives for mobile crowd sensing: a survey. IEEE Commun. Surv. Tutor. **18**(1), 54–67 (2015)
21. X. Ji, Y. He, J. Wang, et al., Walking down the stairs: efficient collision resolution for wireless sensor networks. Paper presented at the IEEE INFOCOM 2014—IEEE Conference on Computer Communications, 27 April 2014–2 May 2014
22. Z. He, J. Cao, X. Liu, High quality participant recruitment in vehicle-based crowdsourcing using predictable mobility. Paper presented at the 2015 IEEE Conference on Computer Communications (INFOCOM), 26 April 2015–1 May 2015
23. X. Wang, W. Wu, D. Qi, Mobility-aware participant recruitment for vehicle-based mobile crowdsensing. IEEE Trans. Veh. Technol. **67**(5), 4415–4426 (2017)
24. X. Zhu, Y. Luo, A. Liu, et al., A deep learning-based mobile crowdsensing scheme by predicting vehicle mobility. IEEE Trans. Intell. Transp. Syst. **22**(7), 4648–4659 (2020)
25. G. Fan, H. Jin, Q. Liu, et al., Joint scheduling and incentive mechanism for spatio-temporal vehicular crowd sensing. IEEE Trans. Mobile Comput. **20**(4), 1449–1464 (2014)
26. S. Xu, X. Chen, X. Pi, et al., ilocus: incentivizing vehicle mobility to optimize sensing distribution in crowd sensing. IEEE Trans. Mobile Comput. **19**(8), 1831–1847 (2019)
27. C. Xiang, Y. Li, L. Feng, et al., Near-optimal vehicular crowdsensing task allocation empowered by deep reinforcement learning. Chin. J. Comput. **45**(5), 918–934 (2022)
28. X. He, K. Deng, X. Wang, et al., Lightgcn: simplifying and powering graph convolution network for recommendation. Paper presented at the 43rd International ACM SIGIR Conference on Research and Development in Information Retrieval, 25–30 July 2020
29. Z. Duan, W. Li, X. Zheng, et al., Mutual-preference driven truthful auction mechanism in mobile crowdsensing. Paper presented at the 2019 IEEE 39th International Conference on Distributed Computing Systems (ICDCS), 7–10 July 2019
30. D. Liu, Z. Cao, M. Hou, et al., Pushing the limits of transmission concurrency for low power wireless networks. ACM Trans. Sens. Netw. (TOSN) **16**(4), 1–29 (2020)
31. Z. Wang, Y. Zhang, H. Chen, et al., Deep user modeling for content-based event recommendation in event-based social networks. Paper presented at the IEEE INFOCOM 2018—IEEE Conference on Computer Communications, 16–19 April 2018
32. J.L.Z. Cai, M. Yan, Y. Li, Using crowdsourced data in location-based social networks to explore influence maximization. Paper presented at the IEEE INFOCOM 2016—the 35th Annual IEEE International Conference on Computer Communications, 10–14 April 2016
33. Z. Xu, Z. Li, Q. Guan, et al., Large-scale order dispatch in on-demand ride-hailing platforms: a learning and planning approach. Paper presented at the 24th ACM SIGKDD International Conference on Knowledge Discovery & Data Mining, 19–23 August 2018
34. User study form (2021), https://forms.gle/f6rSLextsfaXy8JS9
35. A.M. Lund, Measuring usability with the use questionnaire. Usab. Interface **8**(2), 3–6 (2001)
36. How much does a ride with the uber app cost? (2020), https://www.uber.com/global/en/price-estimate/
37. X. Zhang, G. Xue, R. Yu, et al., Truthful incentive mechanisms for crowdsourcing. Paper presented at the 2015 IEEE Conference on Computer Communications (INFOCOM), 26 April 2015–1 May 2015
38. D. Zhang, H. Xiong, L. Wang, et al., CrowdRecruiter: selecting participants for piggyback crowdsensing under probabilistic coverage constraint. Paper presented at the 2014 ACM

International Joint Conference on Pervasive and Ubiquitous Computing, 13–17 September 2014

39. S. Martello, P. Toth, *Knapsack Problems: Algorithms and Computer Implementations* (Wiley, Hoboken, 1990)
40. X. Fan, C. Xiang, C. Chen, et al., BuildSenSys: reusing building sensing data for traffic prediction with cross-domain learning. IEEE Trans. Mobile Comput. **20**(6), 2154–2171 (2020)
41. J. Zhang, S. Liang, Z. Deng, et al., Spatial-temporal attention network for temporal knowledge graph completion. Paper presented at the International Conference on Database Systems for Advanced Applications, 11–14 April 2021
42. Z. Zhou, J. Feng, B. Gu, et al., When mobile crowd sensing meets UAV: energy-efficient task assignment and route planning. IEEE Trans. Commun. **66**(11), 5526–5538 (2018)
43. K. Dorling, J. Heinrichs, G.G. Messier, et al., Vehicle routing problems for drone delivery. IEEE Trans. Syst. Man Cybern. Syst. **47**(1), 70–85 (2016)
44. G.L. Nemhauser, L.A. Wolsey, M.L. Fisher, An analysis of approximations for maximizing submodular set functions—I. Math. Program. **14**(1), 265–294 (1978)
45. J.G. Oxley, *Matroid Theory* (Oxford University Press, Oxford, 1992)
46. K.K. Sarpatwar, B. Schieber, H. Shachnai, Constrained submodular maximization via greedy local search. Oper. Res. Lett. **47**(1), 1–6 (2019)
47. Driving cost of mod vehicles (2019), https://www.greencarreports.com/news/1123364nyc-taxi-mpg-requirements-also-cut-pollution-study-confirms
48. G.S. Becker, G. Michael, R.T. Michael, *Economic Theory* (Routledge, London, 2017)

Chapter 3
Data Transmission Empowered by Edge Computing

3.1 Introduction

With the speedy urbanization, cities with the expanding populations and vehicles are confronted with various challenges, especially in transportation [1, 2]. Therefore, large amount of Intelligent Transportation Systems (ITSs)—such as Advanced Traffic Management System and Adaptive Traffic Control System—have been developed in recent years in order to handle the transportation issues [3]. For instance, as shown in Fig. 3.1, the transportation agency of New South Wale (NSW), Australia, built a Traffic Volume Viewer System (TVVS) [4]. Over 600 traffic collection stations are deployed in TVVS to monitor real-time traffic volume on most of the main roads in NSW [5]. However, as shown in the experimental observations on the TVVS in Sect. 3.3.1, this system is subject to a highly serious problem of missing traffic data. Indeed, this issue is widely seen in many existing ITSs [6]. Therefore, accurate and real-time recovery of traffic data in large-scale ITSs plays a key role in realizing the intelligent transportation in smart cities.

To deal with traffic data recovery, the experimental explorations are conducted based on a large-scale traffic volume dataset of TVVS in Sect. 3.3.2. According to the results, traffic data has both temporal and spatial correlations at different time and stations. Therefore, it provides a promising opportunity for traffic data recovery. Hence, it is auspicious to exploit a large amount of traffic data from multiple stations for accurate real-time recovery. However, it also leads to a complex dilemma of practical implementation with the three reasons as follows. First, it needs a large overhead of computation and storage for resource-intensive traffic data, such as real-time traffic videos [7]. Second, considering the massive deployment and the limited budget, few individual stations have enough capabilities of computation and storage to perform such a heavy responsibility [8]. At last, if all the traffic data is offloaded to the powerful remote cloud as a result of long-distance communication and huge traffic volume, the incurred latency would be intolerable in large-scale ITSs [9].

© The Author(s), under exclusive license to Springer Nature Singapore Pte Ltd. 2023
C. Xiang et al., *Multi-dimensional Urban Sensing Using Crowdsensing Data*, Data
Analytics, https://doi.org/10.1007/978-981-19-9006-9_3

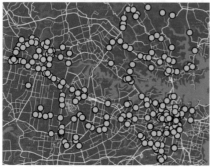
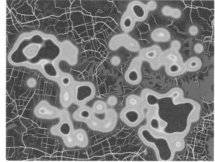

(a) Locations of traffic stations   (b) Heat map of distribution

Fig. 3.1 Illustrations of the traffic volume viewer system with 600 traffic collection stations deployed in New South Wale. (**a**) Locations of traffic stations. (**b**) Heat map of distribution

To solve this dilemma, we propose an edge computing-empowered large-scale traffic data recovery system by deploying edge nodes in physical proximity to traffic stations for real-time recovery [9]. With the appliance of the decentralized computing power of edge nodes, it deals with the insufficient capability issue in the process of recovering traffic on the individual station as well as the high latency for centralized computation on the cloud server [8]. However, it is of significant meaning to realize this system with two following challenges.

- **Optimal deployment of edge nodes for ITSs**: The edge node deployment should be jointly optimized with the traffic data collection in ITSs, while the cost of edge deployment and traffic collection should be minimized. It is a Mixed Integer Linear Program (MILP) problem which is proven to be NP-hard in Sect. 3.5.1.
- **Accurate traffic recovery with spatio-temporal dynamic correlations**: Although the experimental observations illustrate traffic data has spatio-temporal correlations, such relationships are non-linear and space-time varying, therefore rendering accurate recovery extremely tough even under the condition of optimal edge deployment.

In response to the two challenges, an ed**G**e computing-empowered large-scale **T**raffic data recovery system is put forward, leveraging low-**R**ank theory, called **GTR**.[1] It consists of two key modules as follows. (1) *Sub-optimal deployment of edge nodes with a performance guarantee*. According to our findings, given any fixed edge node deployment, the traffic data collection is a linear program problem (LP). Hence, the optimal deployment problem is reformulated as a set function optimization one, subject to only the variable of edge node deployment. Secondly,

---

[1] Similar to the Nissan GT-R vehicle with a powerful engine and high reliability, our system can provide powerful computing capability empowered by edge computing, while achieving highly accurate data recovery based on lowrank theory in ITSs.

although the expression of the objective function in this set function optimization is implicit, we theoretically prove it is non-negative super-modular. Finally, we put forward a local search-based edge node deployment algorithm, deploying the super-modularity theory to obtain a guaranteed sub-optimal solution. (2) *Accurate traffic data recovery based on low-rank theory.* We conduct Singular Value Decomposition (SVD) based on experiments to examine whether the matrix of traffic data is approximately low-rank in terms of the spatio-temporal dimensions. In addition, based on the positive result, the intractable problem of traffic data recovery is transformed into a low-rank minimization one in an equivalent manner. Then, we transform it into a convex optimization problem. In the end, we deploy the Fixed Point Continuation (FPC) iterative scheme to realize accurate recovery with minimal rank. We conduct both theoretical analyses and trace-based evaluations to evaluate the performance of GTR.

In summary, this chapter makes contributions in four main aspects:

1. We make the experimental explorations based on a large-scale traffic dataset of massive traffic stations. We propose a traffic data recovery system empowered by edge computing based on the inspiration of the observations of spatio-temporal correlations, thereby solving the dilemma between traffic stations and the cloud in large-scale ITSs.
2. We present a sub-optimal edge node deployment scheme with a theoretical performance guarantee, applying the equivalent reformulation and the super-modularity to decouple the joint optimization of the NP-hard problem efficiently.
3. We propose a low rank-based traffic data recovery algorithm based on the experimental observations of SVD, deploying the rank minimization to deal with the spatio-temporal dynamic of correlations.
4. We perform extensive experiments based on a large-scale traffic dataset with 100 traffic stations. The results indicate that GTR needs at most 5.7% extra total cost only in comparison with the optimal deployment. It outperforms four baseline methods by 63.8% regarding traffic data recovery accuracy.

The rest of this chapter is organized as follows. The motivations based on experimental explorations are introduced in Sect. 3.3. Then, we state the system model and formalize the problem in Sect. 3.4. We also propose an edge computing-based large-scale traffic volume recovery system called GTR as well as theoretical analyses in Sect. 3.5. In Sect. 3.6, traces-driven evaluations is performed, and we discuss practical factors in Sect. 3.7. Finally, the related work is reviewed in Sect. 3.2, and this work is concluded in Sect. 3.8.

3.2 Related Work

Traffic Data Recovery in ITSs With the pervasive deployment of large-scale intelligent transportation systems, missing data has become a common and serious issue that directly impacts the performance and integrity of ITSs. Hence, numerous research works have been devoted to realizing the recovery of traffic data that is accurate and complete, applying different methods [10, 11]. For example, Tak et al. [12] presented a modified k-Nearest- Neighbor method to impute the missing data in sectional units of road links. Moreover, Tang et al. [13] put forward a joint modeling framework to infer citywide traffic volume with GPS trajectory data and traffic counting data generated by surveillance cameras. By the same token, Chen et al. [14] employed a parallel data paradigm (applying real data and synthetic data) with Generative Adversarial Networks (GANs) to promote traffic data mining and recovery. Since traffic data has the spatio-temporal correlation across transportation networks in nature, the spatio-temporal patterns have been further employed for data recovery. As an illustration, Wang et al. [15] reconstructed the missing traffic data with low-rank matrix factorization. Furthermore, it added a Laplacian regularization constraint to capture the spatio-temporal characteristics in the traffic data. In addition, Chen et al. [16] formulated the traffic data recovery issue as a high-dimensional problem of tensor completion. Moreover, so as to realize robust recovery, they adopted singular value decomposition to capture latent features. Recently, multi-view learning methods have been put forward to fuse different data-driven algorithms and multiple data sources for traffic data estimation [17, 18].

Differing from the aforementioned works, we are devoted to delivering a real-time city-wide traffic data recovery system, thereby integrating the edge computing technique for traffic data processing. In brief, our solution solves the recovery accuracy of traffic data and targets the optimal deployment of edge nodes for high-efficiency data processing.

Nodes Deployment in Edge Computing Generally, our proposed system examines the problem of deploying the edge nodes in the edge computing environment for traffic data management and recovery. Among existing studies, the most relevant studies concern cost minimization for edge node deployment in Mobile Edge Computing (MEC) [19, 20]. Ceselli et al. [19] consider the way of deploying edge nodes for mobile networks to minimize the overall deployment cost. To realize this goal, edge node placement and routing schedule are optimized in combination. Additionally, Mondal et al. [20] concentrates on minimizing the edge node deployment cost given the constraints of capacity and latency. Nevertheless, most of the existing studies account for the edge node deployment cost only, neglecting the communication cost in ITSs. In our work, the incurred communication cost is non-negligible, as the traffic data collection in ITSs might consume amounts of communication resource, such as the bandwidth. Hence, the existing works cannot be leveraged to address our problem.

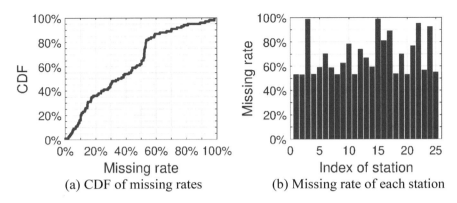

(a) CDF of missing rates   (b) Missing rate of each station

Fig. 3.2 Analysis of missing traffic data in 100 stations of TVVS. The missing rate is more than 25% for 60% of stations. (**a**) CDF of missing rates. (**b**) Missing rate of each station

3.3 Motivation

In this section, firstly, we perform extensive experiments to explore the issue of missing traffic data. Then, we investigate the spatio-temporal correlations. Finally, we analyze an implementation dilemma of traffic data recovery in large-scale ITSs.

3.3.1 Uncovering Missing Data Issue in Large-Scale ITSs

Traffic volume monitoring plays a fundamental role in ITSs, for it's essential for road navigation, congestion management, and vehicle emission monitoring [21, 22]. A number of real systems are developed to monitor traffic volume, such as TVVS [4]. Most of them are plagued by the severe issue of missing data, which may be caused by detector malfunction, data loss in transmission, power outage, *etc.* [23]. For instance, we choose 100 traffic stations of TVVS randomly and conduct statistics based on their traffic volume data. As shown in Fig. 3.2a, 90% of traffic stations have a missing rate that is over 5%. For more than 60% of stations, the missing rate is beyond 25%. Even worse, over 70% of stations are confronted with a missing rate of over 10%. Moreover, Fig. 3.2b shows the missing rate of 25 traffic stations. The results show that the missing rate of several stations is up to 98%. Also, missing traffic data is quite common in real ITSs, such as the 10% missing rate in the ITSs of Beijing city [6].

In summary, traffic volume data is of fundamental importance for ITSs, while many existing systems suffer from missing traffic data, which is rather serious. Therefore, accurate real-time traffic data recovery in large-scale ITSs is essential to the realization of intelligent transportation.

3.3.2 Experimental Explorations of Spatio-Temporal Correlations on Traffic Data

To overcome the issue of missing traffic data in ITSs, we conduct extensive experiments to analyze spatio-temporal correlations on traffic volume data. Particularly, we collect a traffic volume dataset from TVVS [4] in 25 traffic stations of Sydney for 1 year (*i.e.*, Jan.-Dec., 2018). The sampling interval is 1 h.

1. **Analysis of Temporal Correlation**: We analyze the correlation of traffic volume data in regard to the temporal dimension on a traffic station. Specifically, we divide 1 year into 52 weeks and analyze the correlations among the traffic volume of different weeks in one station. As shown in Fig. 3.3a, we only plot the traffic volume data of 4 weeks owing to similar results for other weeks. According to the experimental results, the traffic volume exhibits a similar pattern each week. Moreover, the patterns of weekends are different from those of weekdays, as the commuting activities of most citizens on weekdays (such as working) are distinguished from the ones on weekends (*e.g.*, shopping) [24]. The above results indicate that the traffic volume data has a temporal correlation during a day instead of a week.

   Furthermore, by employing the Pearson correlation coefficient, we quantify the correlations of traffic volume data between any 2 of these 52 weeks. As illustrated in Fig. 3.3b, their temporal correlations are over 0.6 for 100% of weeks, and above 0.95 for that of 80%. As a result, the traffic volume data has a strong temporal correlation on each week for one traffic station. Nevertheless, as illustrated in Fig. 3.3a, there exist abnormal patterns in some days, such as the Tuesday of the first week in April. That is because this Tuesday is a special holiday in Australia (*i.e.*, the Anzac Day of 2018), and the citizens are off duty on the weekday [25]. Therefore, the periodicity of traffic volume data on the

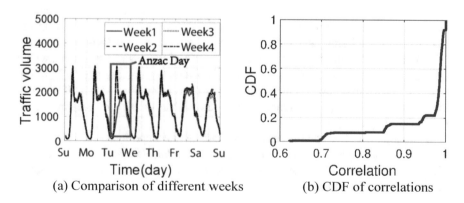

Fig. 3.3 Analysis of temporal correlation on traffic volume data in different weeks for the same traffic station. (**a**) Comparison of different weeks. (**b**) CDF of correlations

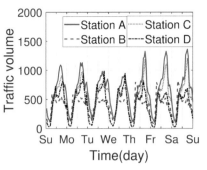
(a) Comparison of various stations

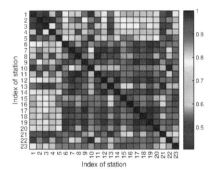
(b) Confusion matrix of correlations

Fig. 3.4 Analysis of spatial correlation on traffic volume data in different traffic stations. (**a**) Comparison of various stations. (**b**) Confusion matrix of correlations

temporal dimension is under the influence of social events, holidays and extreme weather conditions, etc.

2. **Analysis of Spatial Correlation**: We analyze the spatial correlations of traffic volume data in different traffic stations. Firstly, we compare the traffic volume data in different traffic stations. As shown in Fig. 3.4a, we only show the data of four stations on the first week due to similar results in other weeks. It indicates that the traffic volume of different stations is approximately similar in pattern even on special holidays (*e.g.*, Tuesday).

In addition, we employ the Pearson correlation coefficient to quantify the spatial correlations of traffic data among different stations. As illustrated in Fig. 3.4b, we leverage the confusion matrix to represent the correlations between any 2 of the 23 traffic stations. According to the experimental results, the correlations among most stations are more than 0.8. As a result, the traffic volume data has spatial correlations among different traffic stations. The reason is that the traffic stations in the city are interconnected by the roads. Therefore, the traffic volume of different stations suffers from the same influences, including the rush hours, holidays, social events, weather, etc. Nevertheless, Fig. 3.4b demonstrates that a few stations (*e.g.*, stations 1, 2, 3, and 4) have lower correlations with others. The reason is that the correlation between the two stations is undermined by the long-distance road network [24].

To sum up, the traffic volume data has both the temporal correlation in the period of 1 week and the spatial correlations among different traffic stations.

3.3.3 Implementation Dilemmas for Large-Scale Traffic Recovery

The experimental explorations in Sect. 3.3.2 show that the traffic volume data has the temporal and spatial correlations on different time and stations. Therefore, we can jointly leverage the traffic data of massive stations across the same time to recover missing data. However, the implementation of the traffic data recovery in large-scale ITSs is confronted with a dilemma due to the following reasons.

1. **Large overhead of computation** and **storage for resource-intensive traffic data**. Many ITSs deploy traffic cameras to monitor the traffic volume on the roads in real-time [26]. Therefore, the real-time and resource-intensive traffic video data causes numerous overheads on its computation and storage.
2. **Limited capability of computation** and **storage in an individual station**. Since the ITSs should cover a large-scale area, such as a big city, a large amount of traffic stations are supposed to be deployed at different roads, *e.g.*, more than 600 stations in TVVS [5]. Therefore, most stations are limited in capability of computation and storage due to large-scale deployments as well as a limited budget.
3. **High latency of data transmission in large-scale ITSs**. The transmission delay is very long because of the resource-intensive traffic data (such as videos) and the limited bandwidth of communication networks (*e.g.*, wireless network and cellular one). Even worse, as a result of the highly long communication distance from the traffic stations to the central server, this issue will be significantly aggravated in the large-scale ITSs.

In summary, recovering missing traffic data in an individual station stays a hard task, owing to the large overhead of computation, storage for resource-intensive traffic data, and the insufficient capacity of a single station. On the other hand, it is also challenging to recover on the cloud server due to the conflict between high transmission latency and real-time requirements in ITSs. Therefore, in terms of the computation, storage, and transmission, it is tremendously difficult to realize accurate, real-time traffic data recovery on both the individual station and the central server in large-scale ITSs.

3.4 System Model and Problem Formulation

3.4.1 System Model of Edge Computing

According to the experimental observations in Sect. 3.3.1, as the ITSs have a large amount of missing traffic data, its accurate recovery is essentially critical for the ITSs. What's more, according to the experimental explorations in Sect. 3.3.2, the traffic volume data has strong temporal-spatial correlations, which can be leveraged

Fig. 3.5 The framework of edge computing-based traffic data recovery system in large-scale ITSs

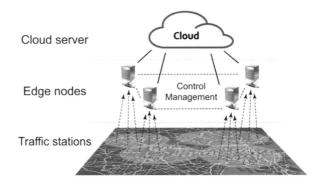

in pursuit of accurate recovery of traffic data. Accordingly, we utilize the traffic data of massive roads across time for accurate data recovery. Nevertheless, it requires numerous latency for transmission and computation because of large-scale coverage and a large volume of traffic data (*e.g.*, real-time traffic videos) in the ITSs. Therefore, as illustrated in Fig. 3.5, we put forward a traffic volume recovery framework based on edge computing to realize low-delay and highly accurate recovery in large-scale ITSs. Particularly, this framework is mainly comprised of traffic stations, edge nodes, and a central server as follows.

- **Traffic Stations**: In the ITSs, traffic monitoring systems are deployed on each traffic station for traffic sensing of one road segment, such as traffic cameras [1, 21]. Let r_i denote the i-th traffic station, *i.e.*, $i \in \{1, \ldots, N\}$. We assume the sensing interval is $[1,T]$, and the vector of sensing time is represented as $\mathbf{T} = \{1, \ldots, T\}$. In addition, we use $v_i(t)$ to denote the traffic data of r_i at time t, *i.e.*, $t \in \mathbf{T}$. Accordingly, $\mathbf{v}_i = \{v_i(t) | 1 \leq t \leq T\}$ denotes the set of traffic data on r_i, while its data size is represented by w_i. Let $\mathbf{V} = \{\mathbf{v}_i | 1 \leq i \leq N\}$ denote the set of the traffic data from all the traffic stations (*i.e.*, r_i, $\forall i \in \{1, \ldots, N\}$) within T.
- **Edge Nodes**: the traffic data is transmitted into nearby edge nodes deployed on certain traffic stations for real-time recovery. We assume that there are S edge nodes, and let e_s denote the s-th edge node, *i.e.*, $s \in [1, \ldots, S]$. Additionally, x_{js} indicates whether e_s is deployed on r_j, *i.e.*, $x_{js} = 1$ if yes, otherwise, $x_{js} = 0$. The different edge nodes vary in capacities of computation and storage because of device diversity. Therefore, we let c_s denote the capacity of e_s. Also, the deployment cost of edge nodes changes with the deployed traffic stations. Let d_{js} denote the cost of e_s deployed on r_j. y_{ij} denotes the proportion of the traffic data of r_i allocated to the edge node deployed at r_j, *i.e.*, $\forall i, j \in [1, \ldots, N]$, $y_{ij} \in [0, 1]$. We can adjust y_{ij} to react to the dynamic change of the traffic pattern in the stations r_i and r_j in an adaptive way. Given the different cost caused by communication in different paths, we let b_{ij} denote the communication cost of the unit traffic data transmitted from r_i to r_j.
- **Cloud Server**: It performs two functions in this edge computing-based system as follows. First, it is connected to all traffic stations and sets up control management, ensuring flexibility and efficiency in communications, which include traffic

data and control information among multiple traffic stations as well as edge nodes
[9]. Secondly, after the recovery of traffic data, it can provide further non-real-
time large-scale computation, which requires a more powerful capacity of computation and storage than the edge nodes, such as the comprehensive traffic
analysis of the overall city [8, 27].

3.4.2   Problem Formalization

Based on the aforementioned system model of edge computing-based traffic data
recovery, the research problem is mainly composed of the following two
sub-problems.

1. **Sub-Problem A: (Optimal deployment of edge nodes)** Given the capacities of
   the edge nodes (e.g., c_s), (a) how to place these S edge nodes (e.g., e_s) on the
   traffic stations (e.g., r_j), i.e., $\mathbf{x} = \{x_{js}| 1 \leq N, 1 \leq s \leq S\}$; and (b) how to assign
   traffic data of r_i into the edge nodes deployed at r_j, i.e., $\mathbf{y} = \{y_{ij}| \forall i,j \in \{1, \ldots,$
   $N\}\}$, so as to serve all the traffic data (i.e., $\mathbf{V}$) as well as minimizing the overall
   cost $\Omega(\mathbf{x}, \mathbf{y})$ of data communication and edge deployment. Formally,

$$\min_{\mathbf{x}, \mathbf{y}} \Omega(\mathbf{x}, \mathbf{y}) = (1-\alpha) \sum_{i=1}^{N} \sum_{j=1}^{N} w_i y_{ij} b_{ij} + \alpha \sum_{s=1}^{S} \sum_{j=1}^{N} x_{js} d_{js}, \tag{3.1}$$

$$\text{s.t.} \quad \sum_{j=1}^{N} y_{ij} = 1, \forall i \in \{1, \ldots, N\}, \tag{3.2}$$

$$\sum_{j=1}^{N} x_{js} \leq 1, \forall s \in \{1, \ldots, S\}, \tag{3.3}$$

$$\sum_{i=1}^{N} w_i y_{ij} \leq \sum_{s=1}^{S} x_{js} c_s, \forall j \in N, \tag{3.4}$$

$$y_{ij} \leq l_{ij}, \forall i,j \in \{1, \ldots, N\}, \tag{3.5}$$

$$x_{js} \in \{0,1\}, y_{ij} \in [0,1], \forall i,j \in \{1, \ldots, N\}, \tag{3.6}$$

where $\sum_{i=1}^{N} \sum_{j=1}^{N} w_i p_{ij} b_{ij}$ in Eq. (3.1) denotes the communication cost for the
transmission of all the data from $r_i (\forall i \in [1, \ldots, N])$ to the edge nodes deployed
on $r_j (\forall j \in [1, \ldots, N])$. $\sum_{s=1}^{S} \sum_{j=1}^{N} x_{js} d_{js}$ represents the deployment cost of all the edge
nodes, a represents the trade-off weight between the communication cost and the
deployment cost, which is dependent on the specific applications, i.e., $0 < \alpha < 1$.

Equation (3.2) shows that all the traffic data of r_i is completely served by the edge nodes. Equation (3.3) constrains that an edge server is deployed on at most one traffic station. Eq. (3.4) makes certain that the capacity of computation and storage is satisfying in recovering of traffic data in the s-th edge node, therefore ensuring the real-time traffic recovery. Note that, as the weak spatial correlation of the traffic data when the traffic stations are far from each other [24], the data of these traffic stations is not in help for data recovery. As a result, we only deploy the data of the traffic stations within coverage. Particularly, l_{ij} in Eq. (3.5) denotes whether r_i is within the coverage of r_j if it is, $l_{ij} = 1$. Otherwise, $l_{ij} = 0$.

2. **Sub-Problem B**: (**Accurate traffic recovery based on edge computing**) Considering the optimal deployment of edge nodes in sub-problem A, we examine the way to recover the missing traffic data of a traffic station accurately, utilizing the remaining data based on temporal correlation and the data of its nearby traffic stations based on spatial correlation. Formally, we assume the traffic station with incomplete traffic data is r_i, $i \in \{1, \ldots, N\}$. Let $\mathbf{T}^m = \{t_1, t_2, \ldots, t_n\}$ denote the time vector of missing data points with no traffic records, while $\mathbf{T}^s$ represents those with traffic data, *i.e.*, $\mathbf{T}^s = \mathbf{T}/\mathbf{T}^m$. The recovery value of $v_i(t)$ is represented by $\widehat{v}_i(t)$. Let $\mathbf{r}_i^c$ denote the set of traffic stations within the coverage of r_i, *i.e.*, $\mathbf{r}_i^c = \{r_j | \forall j \in \{1, \ldots, N\}, l_{ij} = 1\}$. Hence, the problem is formalized as:

$$\min_{\Phi} \frac{1}{T} \sum_{t=1}^{T} | v_i(t) - \widehat{v}_i(t) |, \tag{3.7}$$

$$\text{s.t.} \quad \widehat{v}_i(t) = \Phi(\mathbf{v}_i^s, \mathbf{v}_i^c), \forall t \in \mathbf{T}^m, \tag{3.8}$$

$$\widehat{v}_i(t) = v_i(t), \forall t \in \mathbf{T}^s, \tag{3.9}$$

$$\mathbf{v}_i^s = \{v_i(t) | \forall t \in \mathbf{T}^s\}, \tag{3.10}$$

$$\mathbf{v}_i^c = \{\mathbf{v}_j | \forall j \in \mathbf{r}_i^c\}, \tag{3.11}$$

where Eq. (3.7) represents the error measurement between the recovery value and the ground truth, *e.g.*, Mean Absolute Error [28]. $\mathbf{v}_i^s$ in Eq. (3.10) and $\mathbf{v}_i^c$ in Eq. (3.11) denote the set of sensing traffic data on r_i and that from all the traffic stations within r_i's coverage, respectively. In Eq. (3.8), the missing traffic data of r_i is estimated based on $\mathbf{v}_i^s$ and $\mathbf{v}_i^c$, exploiting the recovery function $\Phi(\cdot)$. Meanwhile, as Eq. (3.9), the recovery values (*e.g.*, $\widehat{v}_i(t)$) at the sensing time $t \in \mathbf{T}^s$ are required to be the same as the ground truth $v_i(t)$.

3.5 System Design

To solve the sub-problems A and B in Sect. 3.4.2, we present *GTR*, a large-scale
traffic data recovery system. It leverages edge computing and low-rank theory to
realize accurate, real-time traffic data recovery in large-scale ITSs. As illustrated in
Fig. 3.6, as the inputs of *GTR*, the ITSs provide large-scale traffic data of massive
stations with spatio-temporal dynamic workload and numerous missing data. Moreover, they offer the topology of the communication network among these traffic
stations in ITSs. Finally, the accurate traffic data is yielded from GTR for large
numbers of traffic stations in real-time. In particular, GTR is composed of three main
components as follows.

1. **Experimental Explorations** (Sect. 3.3). We first conduct experiments to examine missing traffic data based on large-scale traffic datasets in Sect. 3.3.1. The
   results show that this issue is greatly serious because of the high missing rate and
   its pervasiveness. Further, extensive experiments are carried out to investigate the
   spatio-temporal correlations of traffic data in Sect. 3.3.2. These experimental
   observations are fed back to design the edge nodes deployment scheme and
   traffic data recovery algorithm in the following components.
2. **Sub-optimal Deployment of Edge Nodes** (Sect. 3.5.1). To address the incom-
   pleteness of data, large-scale coverage, and resource-intensive traffic data, we
   present the edge computing-empowered large-scale traffic data recovery system.
   Particularly, we focus on the optimal deployment problem of edge nodes, which
   is an intractable NP-hard problem. Therefore, we employ the problem

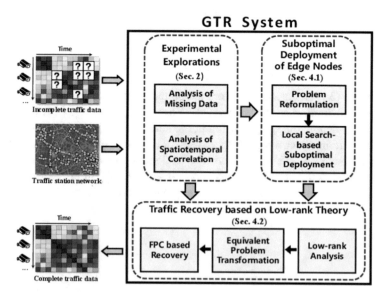

Fig. 3.6 Overview of GTR, an edge computing-based large-scale traffic data recovery system
leveraging low-rank theory

reformulation and the super-modular theory to achieve a sub-optimal solution with a performance guarantee.

3. **Traffic Recovery Based on Low-Rank Theory** (Sect. 3.5.2). Based on the experimental analysis of low rank by SVD, we propose an accurate traffic data recovery algorithm by employing the low-rank theory. It employs both the temporal and spatial correlations of traffic data at different time and stations to realize accurate data recovery.

3.5.1   Sub-optimal Deployment of Edge Nodes

In this subsection, we study the way to address the sub-problem A for the optimal edge node deployment, employing the sub-modularity/super-modularity. Meanwhile, the key ideas are as follows. According to our findings, at first, in the sub-problem A, given any edge node placement scheme $\mathbf{x}$, the traffic data allocation problem is a simple linear programming (LP) problem, whose optimal solution $\mathbf{y}^*(\mathbf{x})$ can be gained with efficiency. By substituting $\mathbf{y}$ with $\mathbf{y}^*(\mathbf{x})$ in the sub-problem A, it is equivalent to a Binary Integer Programming (BIP) problem for the edge node placement variable $\mathbf{x}$ only. Secondly, the aforementioned BIP problem is reformulated as a set function optimization problem. Despite the difficulty in obtaining the explicit form of the objective function, we prove that it is a problem with a super-modular objective function and a matroid constraint. Ultimately, we put forward a sub-optimal algorithm for the sub-problem A with a theoretical performance guarantee.

Problem Reformulation

For the sub-problem A, it has the following properties about the traffic data allocation optimization.

Lemma 3.1   In the sub-problem A, given any fixed edge node placement scheme, the optimal traffic data allocation can be gained in polynomial time.

Proof   Given any edge node placement $\mathbf{x^0} = \left\{ x_{ij}^0 \right\}$, the sub-problem A turns into a traffic data allocation assignment problem concerning $\mathbf{y}$ only in the following:

$$(\textbf{P0}) \quad \min_{\textbf{y}} \quad \sum_{i=1}^{N} \sum_{j=1}^{N} w_i y_{ij} b_{ij}$$

$$\text{s.t.} \quad (3.2), (3.5), (3.6), \tag{3.12}$$

$$\sum_{i=1}^{N} w_i y_{ij} \leq \sum_{s=1}^{S} x_{js}^0 c_s, \forall j \in \mathcal{N},$$

it is a simple LP problem and can be addressed in polynomial time by many classical LP methods [29].

Based on Lemma 3.1, we reformulate the sub-problem A as a set function optimization problem. Formally, let $\Omega(\textbf{x}, \textbf{y})$ denote the objective function of the sub-problem A. First, Lemma 3.1 shows that, given any $\textbf{x}$, we can obtain the optimal value of $\textbf{y}$, denoted as $\textbf{y}^*(\textbf{x})$. Though the explicit expression of $\textbf{y}^*(\textbf{x})$ is hard to obtain, it indicates that addressing the sub-problem A is equivalent to solving the problem concerning $\textbf{x}$ only by substituting $\textbf{y}$ with $\textbf{y}^*(\textbf{x})$. Therefore, the objective function can be transformed into $\Omega(\textbf{x}, \textbf{y}^*(\textbf{x}))$.

Second, let $\mathcal{G} := \{(j, s) | \forall j \in \mathcal{N}, s \in \mathcal{S}\}$, which establishes a one-one mapping between an edge node placement variable x_{js} and the element $e = (j, s) \in \mathcal{G}$. Particularly, $x_{js} = 1$ implies choosing element (j, s) from $\mathcal{G}$, while $x_{js} = 0$ means not choosing element (j, s) from $\mathcal{G}$. Let $\mathcal{A} \subseteq \mathcal{G}$ represent the set of selected pairs of edge node and traffic station, that is, $\mathcal{A} = \{(j, s) | x_{js} = 1, j \in \mathcal{N}, s \in \mathcal{S}\}$. For a feasible set $\mathcal{A} \subseteq \mathcal{G}$, we define $f(\mathcal{A}) := \Omega(\textbf{x}, \textbf{y}^*(\textbf{x}))$. For each x_{js} in $\textbf{x}$, $x_{js} = 1$ if $(j, s) \in \mathcal{A}$. Then, by introducing $\mathbb{1}$ as the indicator function, the sub-problem A is reformulated as follows:

$$(\textbf{P0}') \quad \min_{\mathcal{A} \subseteq \mathcal{G}} \quad f(\mathcal{A})$$

$$\text{s.t.} \quad \sum_{j:(j, s) \in \mathcal{A}} \mathbb{1}_{(j,s) \in \mathcal{A}} \leq 1, \forall s \in \mathcal{S}. \tag{3.13}$$

Next, we reveal some desirable properties of the problem $\textbf{P0}'$. Firstly we present the basic definitions of the non-negativity, monotonicity, submodularity, and matroid as follows.

Definition 3.1 (Non-negativity, Monotonicity, Submodularity [30]): A set function $f : 2^{\mathcal{G}} \rightarrow \mathbb{R}$ ($\mathcal{G}$ is a finite ground set) is non-negative if $f(\emptyset) = 0$ and $f(\mathcal{A}) \geq 0$ for $\forall \mathcal{A} \subseteq \Omega$. $f(\cdot)$ is monotone if $\forall \mathcal{A}_1 \subseteq \mathcal{A}_2 \subseteq \mathcal{G}, f(\mathcal{A}_1) \leq f(\mathcal{A}_2)$. And $f(\cdot)$ is submodular, if and only if $\forall \mathcal{A}_1 \subseteq \mathcal{A}_2 \subseteq \mathcal{G}$ and $\forall e \in \mathcal{G} \backslash \mathcal{A}_2, f(\mathcal{A}_1 \cup \{e\}) - f(\mathcal{A}_1) \geq f(\mathcal{A}_2 \cup \{e\}) - f(\mathcal{A}_2)$.

Any function $f(\cdot)$ is supermodular if $-f(\cdot)$ is submodular. Submodularity has a decreasing returns property while supermodularity captures an increasing returns property, indicating that the added value of an extra element of a bigger set is no less than that to a smaller set [30].

Definition 3.2 (Matroid [31]) Consider a finite ground set G, and a non-empty collection of subsets of G, represented by $\mathcal{I}$. The pair $(G, \mathcal{I})$ is called a matroid, if and only if the following conditions hold: (1) If $\mathcal{A} \subseteq \mathcal{B} \in \mathcal{I}$, then $\mathcal{A} \in \mathcal{I}$; (2) If $\mathcal{A}, \mathcal{B} \in \mathcal{I}$ and $|\mathcal{A}| < |\mathcal{B}|$, then there exists $b \in \mathcal{B}$ such that $\mathcal{A} \cup \{b\} \in \mathcal{I}$.

Definition 3.3 (Partition matroid [31]) A matroid $(G, \mathcal{I})$ is a partition matroid, if there are disjoint sets $G_1, G_2, \ldots, G_m$ and positive integers $i_1, i_2, \ldots, i_m$ for a positive integer m, such that $G := G_1 \cup G_2 \cup \ldots \cup G_m$ and $\mathcal{I} := \left\{ \mathcal{A} : \mathcal{A} \subseteq G, |\mathcal{A} \cap G_j| \leq i_j, j = 1, 2, \ldots, m \right\}$ hold.

Lemma 3.2 The objective function $f(\mathcal{A})$ $(\mathcal{A} \subseteq G)$ in problem **P0$'$** is non-negative and supermodular.

Proof Firstly, the objective function $f(\mathcal{A})$ is non-negative, since if $\mathcal{A} = \varnothing$, the corresponding optimal data allocation $y_{ij}^* = 0$ for $\forall i, j \in \mathcal{N}$ and accordingly $f(\varnothing) = 0$. And $f(\mathcal{A}) \geq 0$ for all $\mathcal{A} \subseteq G$ due to the non-negative expression of the objective function in the problem **P0**. This is reasonable as no placement cost will be caused, and no traffic data transfer will happen if there is no edge node placed.

Second, according to Definition 3.1, to prove the supermodularity, we need to show that, for any feasible $\mathcal{A}_1, \mathcal{A}_2 \subseteq G$ and any $(j_1, s_1) \in G \backslash \mathcal{A}_2$ satisfying that $\mathcal{A}_1 \subseteq \mathcal{A}_2$ and $(\mathcal{A}_2 \cup \{(j_1, s_1)\})$ is feasible, it holds:

$$f(\mathcal{A}_1 \cup \{(j_1, s_1)\}) - f(\mathcal{A}_1) \leq f(\mathcal{A}_2 \cup \{(j_1, s_1)\}) - f(\mathcal{A}_2). \tag{3.14}$$

Suppose that $\mathbf{y}^{(1)} = \left\{ y_{ij}^{(1)} \right\}_{i \in \mathcal{N}, j \in \mathcal{N}}$ and $\widehat{\mathbf{y}}^{(1)} = \left\{ \widehat{y}_{ij}^{(1)} \right\}_{i \in \mathcal{N}, j \in \mathcal{N}}$ is the optimal traffic data allocation solution obtained by solving **P0** under the edge node placement variable $\mathcal{A}_1$ and $\mathcal{A}_1 \cup \{(j_1, s_1)\}$, respectively. Similarly, we can get the optimal traffic data allocation $\mathbf{y}^{(2)} = \left\{ y_{ij}^{(2)} \right\}_{i \in \mathcal{N}, j \in \mathcal{N}}$ and $\widehat{\mathbf{y}}^{(2)} = \left\{ \widehat{y}_{ij}^{(2)} \right\}_{i \in \mathcal{N}, j \in \mathcal{N}}$ under the edge node placement variable $\mathcal{A}_2$ and $\mathcal{A}_2 \cup \{(j_1, s_1)\}$, respectively. Therefore, we can rewrite the objective values of the sub-problem A under $\mathcal{A}_1, \mathcal{A}_1 \cup \{(j_1, s_1)\}, \mathcal{A}_2, \mathcal{A}_2 \cup \{(j_1, s_1)\}$ respectively as follows:

$$f(\mathcal{A}_1) = \sum_{i=1}^{N} \sum_{j=1}^{N} w_i y_{ij}^{(1)} b_{ij} + \sum_{(j, s) \in \mathcal{A}_1} d_{js}, \tag{3.15}$$

$$f(\mathcal{A}_1 \cup \{(j_1, s_1)\}) = \sum_{i=1}^{N} \sum_{j=1}^{N} w_i \widehat{y}_{ij}^{(1)} b_{ij} + \sum_{(j, s) \in \mathcal{A}_1} d_{js} + d_{j_1 s_1}, \tag{3.16}$$

$$f(\mathcal{A}_2) = \sum_{i=1}^{N} \sum_{j=1}^{N} w_i y_{ij}^{(2)} b_{ij} + \sum_{(j, s) \in \mathcal{A}_2} d_{js}, \tag{3.17}$$

$$f(\mathcal{A}_2 \cup \{(j_1, s_1)\}) = \sum_{i=1}^{N} \sum_{j=1}^{N} w_i \widehat{y}_{ij}^{(2)} b_{ij} + \sum_{(j,s) \in \mathcal{A}_2} d_{js} + d_{j_1 s_1}, \qquad (3.18)$$

Then, we obtain:

$$LHS \; of \, (14) = \sum_{i=1}^{N} \sum_{j=1}^{N} w_i \left(\widehat{y}_{ij}^{(1)} b_{ij} - y_{ij}^{(1)} b_{ij} \right) + d_{j_1 s_1}, \qquad (3.19)$$

$$RHS \; of \, (14) = \sum_{i=1}^{N} \sum_{j=1}^{N} w_i \left(\widehat{y}_{ij}^{(2)} b_{ij} - y_{ij}^{(2)} b_{ij} \right) + d_{j_1 s_1}. \qquad (3.20)$$

The first items in Eqs. (3.19) and (3.20) are the negative decremented values in the communication cost before/after deploying the edge node s_1 on traffic station r_{j_1}, respectively. After adding(j_1, s_1) to $\mathcal{A}_1$, the communication cost reduction can be separated into two parts. First, consider some r_{i_2} in the coverage of r_{j_1}. If the data at r_{i_2} is originally transmitted to r_{j_2} in data allocation $\mathbf{y}^{(1)}$ and the communication cost $b_{i_2 j_1}$ to r_{j_1} is lower than $b_{i_2 j_2}$, the communication cost can be reduced by redirecting the data from r_{i_2} to r_{j_1}. Second, the edge nodes in r_{j_2} may be fully-loaded in $\mathcal{A}_1$ and after the redirection, we may redirect the data at other traffic stations to r_{j_2}, which can reduce the communication cost. The operation in the second part might be fulfilled in an iterative manner.

Consider some data transmission from $r_{i'}$ to $r_{j'}$ in $\mathbf{y}^{(1)}$ that is redirected after adding (j_1, s_1) to $\mathcal{A}_1$. As that $\mathcal{A}_2 \backslash \mathcal{A}_1$ may include some (j_3, s_3) and the communication cost $b_{i'j_3}$ may be lower than $b_{i'j'}$, cost reduction caused by (j_1, s_1) can be lower in $\widehat{\mathbf{y}}^{(2)}$ than $\widehat{\mathbf{y}}^{(1)}$. Therefore, the decreasing communication cost caused by (j_1, s_1) under $\mathcal{A}_2$ is lower than the decreasing cost under $\mathcal{A}_1$. So $\sum_{i=1}^{N} \sum_{j=1}^{N} w_i \left(\widehat{y}_{ij}^{(1)} b_{ij} - y_{ij}^{(1)} b_{ij} \right) \le$ $\sum_{i=1}^{N} \sum_{j=1}^{N} w_i \left(\widehat{y}_{ij}^{(2)} b_{ij} - y_{ij}^{(2)} b_{ij} \right)$. The second items in Eqs. (3.19) and (3.20) are the same. Hence, Eq. (3.14) holds, and the lemma is proved.

Note that whether the function $f(\mathcal{A})(\mathcal{A} \subseteq \mathcal{G})$ is monotone or not is unknown with the following reasons. On the one hand, if adding more elements into a feasible set $\mathcal{A} \subseteq \mathcal{G}$, the only affected constraint (3.12) in problem **P0** will be relaxed, and the feasible solution region of the LP problem for $\mathbf{y}$ will be expanded. Given these points, the results in a decreased optimal value. Additionally, adding more elements to $\mathcal{A}$ will inevitably cause a higher cost of placement, which leads to an increase of the second part in the objective function of the sub-problem A. As the increase of a feasible set has an opposite trend in the two parts, the monotonicity of the function $f(\mathcal{A})$ is hard to decide.

Remark 3.1 The monotonicity of function $f(\mathcal{A})$ $(\mathcal{A} \subseteq \mathcal{G})$ is unknown.

Lemma 3.3 Let $G := \{(j,s)| \forall j \in \mathcal{N}, s \in \mathcal{S}\}$ and $\mathcal{I} := \{\mathcal{A}| \mathcal{A} \subseteq G, \forall a_1 := (j_1, s_1), a_2 := (j_2, s_2) \in \mathcal{A}, s_1 \neq s_2\}$. Then, the constraint (3.13) in problem **P0'** is a partition matroid constraint.

Proof We first prove that the constructed pair $(G, \mathcal{I})$ is a matroid. Assume there are at least two traffic stations and two available edge nodes in the problem, *i.e.*, $N \geq 2$ and $S \geq 2$; otherwise, addressing this issue is trivial. In the following, according to Definition 3.2, we prove these three properties of a matroid one by one. First, it is effortless to validate the nonempty property of $\mathcal{I}$ as a consequence of the previous assumption. Secondly, if $\mathcal{A} \subseteq \mathcal{B} \in \mathcal{I}$, we have $\mathcal{A} \in \mathcal{I}$. If not, there exist at least two different elements $a_1, a_2 \in \mathcal{A}$ that share the same second component. Since $\mathcal{A} \subseteq \mathcal{B}$, $a_1, a_2 \in \mathcal{B}$ holds, which clashes with $\mathcal{B} \in \mathcal{I}$ obviously.

Third, suppose that $\mathcal{A}, \mathcal{B} \in \mathcal{I}$ and $|\mathcal{A}| < |\mathcal{B}|$. If there does not exist an element $a' \in \mathcal{B}$ such that $\mathcal{A} \cup \{a'\} \in \mathcal{I}$, we have for any element $a' \in \mathcal{B}$, $\mathcal{A} \cup \{a'\} \notin \mathcal{I}$ holds. Since $\mathcal{A} \in \mathcal{I}$, each element in $\mathcal{B}$ shares the same second component with some element in $\mathcal{A}$. Since $|\mathcal{A}| < |\mathcal{B}|$, there are at least two different elements $a_1, a_2 \in \mathcal{B}$ and an element $a' \in \mathcal{A}$, whose second component is exactly identical. This means that a_1, a_2 share the same second component, which contradicts with $\mathcal{B} \in \mathcal{I}$. Hence, $(G, \mathcal{I})$ is a matroid.

Algorithm 3.1 Local Search-Based Suboptimal Edge Node Deployment Algorithm

Input: Set $G = \{(j,s)| \forall j \in \mathcal{N}, s \in \mathcal{S}\}$, matroid $(G, \mathcal{I})$, value access to function $\tilde{f}(A)$.

    Output: Edge node placement $\mathbf{x} = \{x_{js}\}$, traffic data allocation $\mathbf{y} = \{y_{ij}\}$.

    1: Initialize $\mathbf{x} = \mathbf{0}$, $\mathbf{y} = \mathbf{0}$, $\mathcal{A} = \varnothing$.

    2: Initialize a feasible set $\mathcal{A} \subseteq G$.

    3: while 1 **do**

    4:   **if** there exists $e \in \mathcal{A}$ such that $\tilde{f}(\mathcal{A} \backslash \{e\}) \geq \left(1 + \frac{\epsilon}{N^4 S^4}\right) \tilde{f}(\mathcal{A})\}$ **then**

    5: $\mathcal{A} \leftarrow \mathcal{A} \backslash \{e\}$.

    6:   **else if** there exist $e \in G \backslash \mathcal{A}$, $e' \in \mathcal{A} \cup \{\varnothing\}$ such that $(\mathcal{A} \backslash \{e'\}) \cup \{e\} \in \mathcal{I}$ and $\tilde{f}((\mathcal{A} \backslash \{e'\}) \cup \{e\}) > \left(1 + \frac{\epsilon}{N^4 S^4}\right) \tilde{f}(\mathcal{A})$

    7: $\mathcal{A} \leftarrow (\mathcal{A} \backslash \{e'\}) \cup \{e\}$.

    8:   **else**

    9:   break

    10: Set all $x_{js} = 1$ if $u = (j,s) \in \mathcal{A}$.

    11: Solve problem **P0** with the input of $\mathbf{x}$ to obtain $\mathbf{y}$, and return $\mathbf{x}$ and $\mathbf{y}$.

We further prove that $(G, \mathcal{I})$ under constraint (3.13) is a partition matroid. Since the set G captures all possible pairs of traffic station and edge node, we have

$$G = \bigcup_{s=1}^{S} G_s \quad \text{where } G_s := \{(j,s)| j = 1, 2, \ldots, N\} .$$ Combing with the meaning of

constraint (3.13) and the definition of $\mathcal{I}$, we have $\forall \mathcal{A} \in \mathcal{I}, |\mathcal{A} \cap \mathcal{G}_s| \leq 1$ holds for $s = 1, 2, \ldots, S$. To sum up, $(\mathcal{G}, \mathcal{I})$ is a partition matroid. Lemma 3.3 is thus proved.

Theorem 3.1 Both the sub-problem A and $\mathbf{P0}'$ are NP-hard.

Proof Since the problem $\mathbf{P0}'$ is equivalent to the sub-problem A, we only prove the NP-hardness of the problem $\mathbf{P0}'$. Based on Lemmas 3.2 and 3.3, the problem $\mathbf{P0}'$ is a non-negative supermodular minimization problem with a single matroid constraint, *i.e.*, $\text{Min}_{\forall \mathcal{A} \subseteq \mathcal{G}, \mathcal{A} \in \mathcal{I}} f(\mathcal{A})$. Note that $\text{Min}_{\forall \mathcal{A} \subseteq \mathcal{G}, \mathcal{A} \in \mathcal{I}} f(\mathcal{A})$ is equivalent to$\text{Max}_{\forall \mathcal{A} \subseteq \mathcal{G}, \mathcal{A} \in \mathcal{I}} -f(\mathcal{A})$, which is a submodular maximization problem. It is widely known that the submodular maximization with a matroid constraint is a NP-hard problem [32]. Hence, the problem $\mathbf{P0}'$ is NP-hard, which also establishes the NP-hardness of the sub-problem A.

Local Search-Based Suboptimal Deployment

Considering Lemma 3.2 and Remark 3.1, $-f(\mathcal{A})$ is negative and submodular with unknown monotonicity. There exists a $\left(\frac{1}{4+\epsilon}\right)$ approximation algorithm for maximizing a non-negative submodular subject to a matroid constraint [32]. Thus, we first transform the objective function into a non-negative function, *i.e.*, $\widetilde{f}(\mathcal{A}) := f_{max} - f(\mathcal{A})$, where $f_{max} := \sum_{i=1}^{N} \sum_{j=1}^{N} w_i b_{ij} + \sum_{s=1}^{S} \sum_{j=1}^{N} d_{js}$. Inspired by reference [32], we design a local search-based suboptimal edge node placement algorithm with a performance guarantee as shown in Algorithm 3.1.

We introduce the steps of Algorithm 3.1 in detail as follows. First, in line 1, we initialize both $\mathbf{x}$ and $\mathbf{y}$ as 0, and set $\mathcal{A}$ as an empty set. Second, in line 2, we find a feasible set $\mathcal{A} \subseteq \mathcal{G}$. Third, in lines 3–7, we deploy local search on G (including both deletion operation (lines 4–5) and exchange operation (lines 6–7)) to gain a set $\mathcal{A} \subseteq \mathcal{G}, \mathcal{A} \in \mathcal{I}$, such that the value of $\widetilde{f}(\mathcal{A})$ can be increased by a factor of at least $\left(1 + \frac{\epsilon}{N^4 S^4}\right)$ at each iteration. Last, in lines 10–11, the algorithm outputs the edge node placement decision $\mathbf{x}$, whose value of each element is determined based on the chosen set $\mathcal{A}$ and the traffic data allocation decision $\mathbf{y}$.

The performance guarantee of Algorithm 3.1 and its time complexity is theoretically analyzed as follows.

Theorem 3.2 Let $(\mathbf{x}, \mathbf{y})$ and $(\mathbf{x}^*, \mathbf{y}^*)$ be the output of Algorithm 3.1 and the optimal solution of the sub-problem A, respectively. Then, we have

$$\Omega(\mathbf{x}, \mathbf{y}) \leq \frac{1}{4+\epsilon} \Omega(\mathbf{x}^*, \mathbf{y}^*) + \frac{3+\epsilon}{4+\epsilon} f_{max}, \tag{3.21}$$

where $\Omega(\cdot,\cdot)$ is the objective function of the sub-problem A, $\epsilon > 0$ is the parameter determined by Algorithm 3.1, and $f_{\max} = \sum_{i=1}^{N} \sum_{j=1}^{N} w_i b_{ij} + \sum_{s=1}^{S} \sum_{j=1}^{N} d_{js}$. In addition, the time complexity of Algorithm 3.1 is polynomial.

Proof This theorem is a corollary of Theorem 2.6 in [32], which proves that there is a $\frac{1}{4+\epsilon}$-approximation algorithm to maximize any non-negative submodular set function subject to a matroid constraint. Employing the local search algorithm following that theorem, Algorithm 3.1 actually designs an approximation algorithm for the problem $\text{Max}_{\forall \mathcal{A} \subseteq G, \mathcal{A} \in \mathcal{I}} -f(\mathcal{A})$, where the set $\mathcal{A}$ is obtained by Algorithm 3.1. In light of that theorem, we have $f_{\max} - f(\mathcal{A}) \geq \frac{1}{4+\epsilon}[f_{\max} - f^*]$, where f^* is the optimal objective value of problem **P0**$'$. Remember that the relationship between $f(\cdot)$ and $\Omega(\cdot,\cdot)$; by some operations, we have the inequality as shown in the theorem. For the time complexity, it can be similarly analyzed as Theorem 2.6 in [32], which is omitted here. Thus in the end, the theorem is proven.

3.5.2 Accurate Traffic Data Recovery Based on Low-Rank Theory

Experimental Analysis of Low-Rank

Based on the experimental explorations in Sect. 3.3.2, the traffic data in the ITSs has the temporal correlation at a different time and the spatial correlation on different traffic stations. Therefore, by using SVD as illustrated in Definition 3.4, we further evaluate whether the rank of the traffic data matrix ($\mathbf{V}$) is low in terms of temporal-spatial dimensions.

Definition 3.4 (Singular Vale Decomposition, SVD) For any m n matrix denoted by V, the SVD is a factorization of V as:

$$\mathbf{V} = U_{m \times m} \Sigma_{m \times n} \Xi^*_{n \times n}$$

$$\text{where} \quad \Sigma = \begin{bmatrix} \sigma_1 & & & \\ & \ddots & & \\ & & \sigma_i & \\ & & & \ddots \end{bmatrix}. \tag{3.22}$$

Note that Σ in Eq. (3.4) is a diagonal matrix. Moreover, σ_i ($\forall i \in \{1, \ldots, \min(m, n)\}, \sigma_i \geq 0$) is named as the singular value of $\mathbf{V}$, and $\sigma_i \leq \sigma_j$ if $\forall i, j \in \{1, \ldots, \min(m, n)\}$ and $i < j$.

According to Definition 3.4, we perform experiments to analyze the rank of traffic data matrix at different time and traffic stations. In the first place, we examine its property of low rank in the matter of temporal dimension. Particularly, we make the

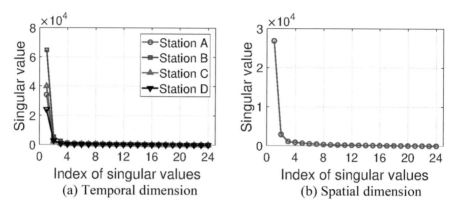

Fig. 3.7 Low-rank analysis of traffic data matrix based on SVD in terms of temporal and spatial dimensions. (**a**) Temporal dimension. (**b**) Spatial dimension

SVD of the traffic data matrix on the stations A–D, where this matrix represents the data of all the weeks on a traffic station. Moreover, each row denotes that of each week. Figure 3.7a demonstrates that the singular values focus mainly on a very limited number of elements. For instance, few singular values (no more than 2) are far larger than others for all of these four stations. More importantly, we investigate the low-rank property of the traffic data matrix in the spatial dimension. This matrix represents the traffic volume of 25 stations, where each row denotes the data of one station at different time. As demonstrated in Fig. 3.7b, similar to Fig. 3.7a, the weights of singular values also concentrate on a few elements regarding spatial dimension.

To sum up, the aforementioned experimental results show that the weights of singular values mainly focus on a very limited number of elements, concerning both the temporal and spatial dimensions. According to the theorem of matrix rank [33, 34], if the weights of singular values for a matrix concentrates on only a few elements, this matrix is roughly low-rank. On the whole, the matrix of traffic volume concerning both temporal and spatial dimensions is approximately low-rank.

Accurate Traffic Recovery Based on Low-Rank Theory

Based on the experimental analysis of low-rank, the traffic data matrix $\mathbf{V}$ is approximately low-rank concerning the temporal-spatial dimensions. As stated by the theorem of the low-rank theory [35], if the matrix $\mathbf{M}$ is roughly low-rank and satisfies that the number of randomly sampled entries is large enough, we can find a low-rank decision matrix Θ to replace $\mathbf{V}$ approximately. Therefore, the sub-problem B in Eqs. (3.7)–(3.11) will be transformed into the low-rank minimization problem as

$$\min \quad \text{rank}(\boldsymbol{\Theta}) \tag{3.23}$$

$$\text{s.t.} \quad \boldsymbol{\Theta}_{ij} = \mathbf{V}_{ij}, (i,j) \in \mathrm{Y}. \tag{3.24}$$

where rank($\cdot$) denotes the function of computing the matrix rank, *i.e.*, the number of non-zero singular values, and Y is the set of index pairs for both $\boldsymbol{\Theta}$ and $\mathbf{V}$. This low-rank minimization problem in Eq. (3.23) is NP-hard, because of the combinational property of the function rank($\cdot$). Hence, it can be equivalently relaxed as Eq. (3.25) by using the nuclear norm $\|\cdot\|_*$ and the ℓ_2-norm $\|\cdot\|_2$ [36].

$$\min \quad \lambda\|\boldsymbol{\Theta}\|_* + \frac{1}{2}\|\mathcal{A}(\boldsymbol{\Theta}) - b\|_2^2, \tag{3.25}$$

$$\|\boldsymbol{\Theta}\|_* = \sum_{i=1}^{\min(m,n)} \sigma_i(\boldsymbol{\Theta}), \tag{3.26}$$

where λ denotes the weight factor for trading off between the nuclear norm and the equality constraint (3.24). The linear map $\mathcal{A} : \mathbb{R}^{m \times n} \to \mathbb{R}^p$ and vector $b \in \mathbb{R}^p$ describe that the observed elements in $\boldsymbol{\Theta}$ are equal to the elements of the same positions in $\mathbf{V}$. $\|\boldsymbol{\Theta}\|_*$ in Eq. (3.25) denotes the sum of all the non-zero singular values of $\boldsymbol{\Theta}$. The minimization of the nuclear norm and square of ℓ_2-norm is a convex optimization problem [37]. Therefore, we equivalently transform the accurate traffic recovery problem—which is an intractable NP-hard one—into a tractable convex optimization problem as Eq. (3.25).

To solve the convex optimization problem, we employ Fixed Point Continuation (FPC) iterative scheme [38] to realize the optimal solution through limited iterations. FPC algorithm is comprised of two key ideas, *i.e.*, the fixed-point-based iterative scheme and the continuation-based accelerated convergence strategy [39].

- **Fixed-Point-Based Iteration**. It iteratively searches the fixed point, which is the optimal solution to the convex optimization problem [37]. Specifically, for any $\varepsilon > 0$, let the matrix shrinkage operator $s_\varepsilon(\mathbf{v}) = \mathbf{x}$, where $x_i = v_i - \varepsilon$ if $v_i - \varepsilon > 0$; otherwise, $x_i = 0$. In each iteration, it updates a new solution based on the previous one, using the matrix shrinkage operator. Let $\boldsymbol{\Theta}^k$ denote the current solution of the k-th iteration. Afterward, the new solution of the $(k + 1)$-th iteration (*i.e.*, $\boldsymbol{\Theta}^{k+1}$) is:

$$\boldsymbol{\Theta}^{k+1} = U_Y \text{Diag}(s_{\tau\lambda}(\sigma))\Xi_Y^T, \tag{3.27}$$

$$\text{where} \quad \mathbf{Y}^k = \boldsymbol{\Theta}^k - \tau\mathbf{g}(\boldsymbol{\Theta}^k). \tag{3.28}$$

Note that τ is a positive constant. U_Y, Ξ_Y, and σ are learned from the SVD of $\mathbf{Y}$, *i.e.*, $\mathbf{Y} = U_Y \text{Diag}(\sigma)\Xi_Y^T$. $\mathbf{g}(\boldsymbol{\Theta}^k)$ represents the gradient of $\frac{1}{2}\|\mathcal{A}(\boldsymbol{\Theta}) - b\|_2^2$ at $\boldsymbol{\Theta}^k$.

- **Continuation-Based Convergence Acceleration**. According to the convergence analysis [38], the speed of convergence is determined by the acceleration factor ζ, *i.e.*, $\lambda_{k+1} = \max\{\zeta_k\lambda_k, \lambda\}$. The smaller ζ is, the faster λ reduce. Hence, the continuation-based convergence strategy is applied to accelerate the convergence. Specifically, in the outer iteration, we iteratively choose the λ in the ascending sequence, which is then utilized to search for the fixed point in the inner iterations.

Algorithm 3.2 FPC-Based Accurate Traffic Data Recovery Algorithm

1: Initialize: Given $\mathbf{v}_i^c$, select $\zeta_1 > 0, \zeta_2 > 0, \ldots, \zeta_n > 0, \overline{\lambda} > 0, \lambda_1 > \lambda_2 > \ldots > \lambda_n = \overline{\lambda}$.

  2: Set $\mathbf{\Theta} = \mathbf{v}_i^c$.

  3: for $\lambda = \lambda_1, \lambda_2, \ldots, \lambda_n$ and $\lambda_{k+1} = max\{\zeta_k \lambda_k, \overline{\lambda}\}\}$ **do**

  4:   **while** Non-convergency **do**

  5:   Select $\tau > 0$;

  6:   Compute $\mathbf{Y} = \mathbf{\Theta} - \tau g(\mathbf{\Theta})$ and SVD of $\mathbf{Y}$, where $g(\mathbf{\Theta}) = \nabla\left(\frac{1}{2}\|\mathcal{A}(\mathbf{\Theta}) - b\|_2^2\right)$;

  7:   Compute $\mathbf{\Theta} = U_Y \mathrm{Diag}(s_{\tau\lambda}(\sigma))\Xi_Y^T$.

  8: return $\widehat{\mathbf{v}}_i^c$

3.6 Traces-Based Evaluations

In this section, we conduct extensive experiments based on an empirical traffic dataset from a large-scale, real-world ITS. In specific, we assess the performance of GTR from two important perspectives, *i.e.*, the cost of edge deployment and the accuracy of traffic data recovery. In the following, we introduce the traffic dataset and the experimental methodologies, including experimental settings, baseline methods, and evaluation metrics. Next, we set forth the experimental results with performance analysis from the perspectives of edge node deployment and traffic data recovery.

3.6.1 Experimental Methodology and Settings

Dataset and Experimental Methodology

This traffic volume dataset is collected from an online Traffic Volume Viewer System (TVVS), which is funded by the Transportation Department of NSW, Australia [4]. The data of traffic volume is generated by roadside collection stations, both permanent and temporary. They monitor the number of vehicles passing on each road with the sampling interval of 1 h [5]. As illustrated in Fig. 3.1, the whole dataset includes data from over 600 traffic stations that are distributed across most areas in the NSW state. For our experimental studies, we collect 12-month traffic data (*i.e.*, Jan. 2018 to Dec. 2018) from 100 major traffic stations.

To assess the performance for edge node deployment, we focus on the workload and navigation distance between different traffic stations of the traffic dataset. For the number of stations N, we consider two kinds of network scenarios, *i.e.*, a large network with $N = 100$ and a small network with $N = 10$. In the large network, we deploy 20 edge nodes with the capacity of each drawn uniformly from the interval $[100k,140k]$. In the range of this small network, 4 edge nodes are deployed, and the capacity of each node is drawn uniformly from the interval $[60k,70k]$. We assume that the communication cost is proportional to the navigation distance among different traffic stations. The deployment cost d_{js} is drawn uniformly from the interval $[17888,35776]$, while the coverage of each traffic station is 2.4 km, suggesting that the traffic data at each traffic station can only be assigned to other traffic stations within this coverage.

To assess the performance of traffic data recovery, we choose N stations in a random manner from the traffic dataset to form a traffic volume matrix for data recovery. Next, a random station is set as the target station for data recovery and generates missing values (with a length of L transformed objective function) in its traffic volume matrix. By leveraging GTR and other baseline methods to fulfill the recovery of the incomplete traffic volume matrix, we make a comparison of their performance in different experimental settings. Note that each experiment is run for 20 times, and average performance is applied as the final results.

Baseline Methods and Evaluation Metrics

To perform a comprehensive study of the edge node deployment' performance, we compare GTR with four baseline methods as follows.

- Brute-Force: This algorithm finds the optimal deployment solutions by constantly searching over all the possible deployment decisions. However, its computational complexity is exceedingly high after solving the NP-hard problem, which in return makes it impossible for large-scale scenarios.
- Random: It randomly chooses a traffic station among all possible stations to deploy an edge node.
- Heuristic: It greedily deploys the edge node at the traffic stations with the largest marginal contribution to the transformed objective function (*i.e.*, $f_{max} - f(\mathcal{A})$).
- LPR: This algorithm uses the LP Relaxation to get the sub-optimal and fractional solution [19]. In order to evaluate the performance in traffic data recovery, we deploy four baseline methods as follows.
- LR (T): Being the simplest baseline, it leverages the linear regression scheme to recover the missing data of a station by applying its remaining data with temporal correlation.
- LR (TS): This method uses temporal and spatial correlations between a target station and its nearby stations. To put it another way, it forms collaboration with

multiple stations to recover missing data of a target station by leveraging linear regression.
- CS: It applies the Compressive Sensing scheme (CS) [34] to recover the missing data of a station by employing the remaining data.
- SVT [40]: Singular Value Thresholding algorithm(SVT) is based on low-rank minimization. It iteratively performs soft-thresholding operations on the singular values of the target matrix until convergence.

For the experimental studies, three metrics are adopted to evaluate the algorithm performance, $i.e.$, Total Cost, Root Mean Squared Error (RMSE), and Mean Absolute Percentage Error (MAPE). Specifically, Total Cost refers to the sum of deployment cost and communication cost as stated in Eq. (3.1). We utilize the Total Cost to assess the cost-efficiency of the edge node deployment. RMSE is the square root of the average squared error between the recovered values and the ground truth of traffic data, as defined in Eq. (3.29). MAPE expresses the accuracy as a percentage ratio by measuring the average ratio of the recovery error to the ground truth, which is defined in Eq. (3.30). Note that RMSE and MAPE are the scale-dependent and scale-independent metrics, both of which are widely exploited to evaluate the recovery accuracy [17, 41].

$$\mathbf{RMSE} = \sqrt{\frac{1}{NT} \sum_{i=1}^{N} \sum_{t=1}^{T} (v_i(t) - \widehat{v}_i(t))^2}, \tag{3.29}$$

$$\mathbf{MAPE} = \frac{1}{NT} \sum_{i=1}^{N} \sum_{t=1}^{T} \left| \frac{v_i(t) - \widehat{v}_i(t)}{v_i(t)} \right|, \tag{3.30}$$

where N denotes the number of stations with incomplete data, and T represents the total length of missing data.

3.6.2 Experimental Results

Evaluations of Edge Node Deployment

We perform the traces-based simulations to validate the deployment performance of GTR with a different number of edge nodes, the workload scale, and the edge capacity.

To begin with, we evaluate the influence of the number of edge nodes on the deployment performance in different network scenarios, both small-scale and large-scale. As illustrated in Fig. 3.8, GTR outperforms other baseline methods in the matter of deployment cost. In contrast to Brute-Force method, which performs computation-intensive search, GTR deploys local search with efficiency. Still, it realizes sub-optimal results by raising the cost just 5.7% above the optimal one. In

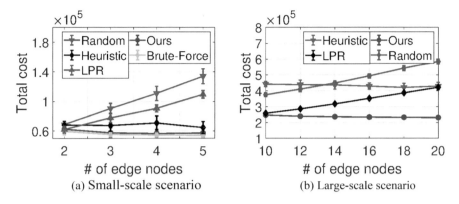

Fig. 3.8 Total cost with different numbers of edge nodes in the small-scale (**a**) and large-scale scenarios (**b**)

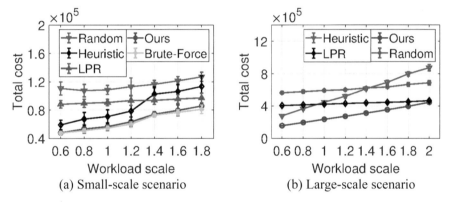

Fig. 3.9 Total cost with different workload scales in the small-scale (**a**) and large-scale scenarios (**b**)

the small network scenario, our algorithm outperforms Random, Heuristic and LPR in average by 37.9%, 13.7%, and 27.6% in Fig. 3.8a, respectively. While in the large network scenario, Fig. 3.8b indicates that our algorithm outperforms Random, Heuristic, and LPR by 48.8%, 45.2%, and 27.4% in average.

Then, as demonstrated in Fig. 3.9, we apply varied workload scales (*i.e.*, the scaling ratio of workload while keeping the workload distribution as the same). In the small network, Fig. 3.9a shows that our algorithm outperforms Random, Heuristic, and LPR in average by 43.2%, 22.4%, and 29.4%, respectively. In the large network, as illustrated in Fig. 3.9b, our algorithm outperforms Random, Heuristic, and LPR by 53.0%, 47.9%, and 32.8% respectively. In addition, as illustrated in Fig. 3.9a in the small scenario, our algorithm realizes sub-optimal performance, *e.g.*, with only 5.4% cost increase in comparison with Brute-Force.

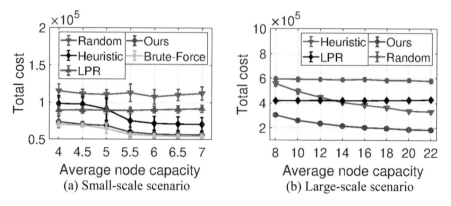

Fig. 3.10 Total cost with different node capacities in the small-scale (**a**) and the large-scale scenarios (**b**)

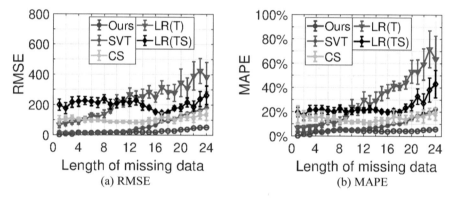

Fig. 3.11 Evaluations of recovery accuracy with a different number of stations in terms of RMSE (**a**) and MAPE (**b**)

Finally, the capacity of edge nodes is changed in both net-work scenarios, as shown in Fig. 3.10. The results in Fig. 3.10a show that our algorithm realizes close-to-optimal performance by comparing it with Brute-Force. Even more, GTR outperforms Random, Heuristic, and LPR in average by 43.3%, 22.6%, and 29.7% in the small network, respectively, while 62.1%, 46.2%, and 47.2% in the large network, respectively, as illustrated in Fig. 3.10a, b.

Evaluations of Traffic Recovery

Based on TVVS dataset, we further perform experiments of traffic data recovery with different numbers of traffic stations and varied lengths of missing traffic data.

To begin with, as illustrated in Fig. 3.11, we assess the impact of missing data (*i.e.*, the length of missing data points in the target station) on the recovery accuracy.

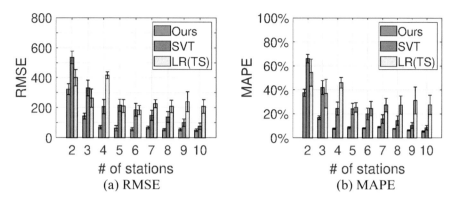

Fig. 3.12 Evaluations of recovery accuracy in a different number of traffic stations, in terms of RMSE (**a**) and MAPE (**b**)

Firstly, we set a random station as a recovery target. Next, we choose 22 adjacent traffic stations to form a traffic volume matrix. We change the length of missing data L from 1 to 24 and employ all stations for recovery of all missing data. As shown in Fig. 3.11a, b, the values of all evaluation metrics in different methods indicate a trend that is generally ascending. This is the evidence to show that the recovery difficulty increases as the length of missing data grows. In spite of that, GTR still preserves a robust performance in the recovery of traffic data, with the averaged RMSE at 22 and MAPE at 4%. Nevertheless, SVT only maintains high-accuracy performance till the length of missing data reaches 12. LR(T) method performs the worst in recovering traffic data under all conditions of missing data, causing an averaged RMSE of 233.9 and MAPE of 30.5%. In conclude, compared with LR(T), LR(TS), CS, and SVT, GTR averagely improves the recovery accuracy by 90.4%, 88.7%, 78.8%, and 63.8% in RMSE respectively, as well as 86.9%, 83.0%, 73.3% and 54.1% in MAPE, respectively.

Then, we evaluate the influence of the number of stations on recovery accuracy. Since LR(T) and CS are only based on the traffic data of an individual station, they are not applied as the baseline methods in evaluation. Empirically, nearby traffic volume data that is with more sufficient would render traffic recovery that is more accurate. As demonstrated in Fig. 3.12a, b, the recovery accuracy in RMSE and MAPE increases as the number of stations rises. Peculiarly, LR(TS) employs temporal-spatial correlations in traffic data, with its performance steady but inaccurate. Similarly, GTR is based on low-rank minimization, and it outperforms other baselines in accuracy and efficiency of the recovery. Specifically, GTR is superior to LR(TS) and SVT on average, decreasing the RMSE by 77.1% and 65.7%, respectively, while the MAPE by 75.5% and 61.6%.

To sum up, the former experimental results further confirm the effectiveness and efficiency of GTR in recovering traffic data. Compared with baseline methods, GTR realizes remarkable improvement in recovery accuracy with three nearby stations applied only, which is capable of reducing the computation overhead essentially.

Furthermore, GTR is stable and robust in performance, which makes it scalable to perform the recovery of traffic data under different conditions.

3.7   Discussion and Future Work

In this section, we discuss the impact of four practical factors on the performance of GTR as well as the future work.

1. **Impacts of Station Group on the Recovery Accuracy**: As illustrated in Fig. 3.4b, the correlations of traffic data among stations are different among stations. Therefore, the difference of station groups might influence the accuracy of traffic data recovery. In addition, experiments are performed to evaluate the impact of station group on the recovery accuracy. As shown in Fig. 3.13a, by randomly choosing seven station groups with the same number of stations, their recovery accuracy (*i.e.*, MAPE) and the Pearson correlations are compared. According to the results, the recovery accuracy varies with the station groups. Particularly, Fig. 3.13a indicates that the recovery accuracy is approximately proportional to the correlation. Therefore, the above analysis is validated. In the future, we will examine how to select the station groups so as to further promote the recovery accuracy.

2. **Impacts of Cost Weight on the Deployment Performance**: By conducting experiments, we evaluate the deployment performance in different cost weights (*i.e.*, α). As illustrated in Fig. 3.13b, the total cost increases with the cost weight for all of these four methods. It shows that the cost of deployment is much higher than that of communication. Additionally, concerning deployment performance, GTR always outperforms Heuristic, LPR, and Random in different settings of cost weight. Therefore, the results further confirm the robustness of GTR.

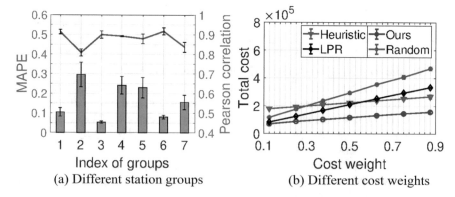

Fig. 3.13 Evaluation of the station group's impact on the traffic recovery and the cost weight's impact on the edge deployment. (**a**) Different station groups. (**b**) Different cost weights

3. **Impacts of Recovery Accuracy on the Node Deployment**: The accuracy of traffic data recovery influences the deployment of edge nodes in the matter of the following aspects. Firstly, if the recovery accuracy is so low that it cannot satisfy the requirement, we can expand the coverage of edge nodes (*i.e.*, l_{ij} in Eq. (3.5)) to improve the accuracy by leveraging traffic data of more stations. Additionally, we can increase the amount of traffic data (*i.e.*, y_{ij} in Eq. (3.2)) to raise the recovery accuracy. In the end, the recovery accuracy is correlated with the coverage of edge nodes and the allocated proportion of traffic data. Therefore, it affects the edge node deployment as Eqs. (3.1), (3.2), and (3.5). In the future, we will further study how to model these impacts, thereby leveraging the feedback of the recovery accuracy so as to realize adaptive deployment.

4. **Applicable Conditions of Accurate Recovery**: GTR employs the low-rank theory to realize accurate traffic recovery based on the incomplete traffic data, which should satisfy the two conditions. First, at least one set of traffic data at any time in any traffic station [35] should be ensured. Second, the total number of missing traffic data should be no more than a maximal threshold. That is highly dependent on the rank and the length of the recovered data matrix [42]. In the future, we will design an adaptive edge node deployment according to the time-varying number of missing traffic data with the use of this recovery condition of low-rank theory.

3.8   Conclusion

In this chapter, we put forward GTR, an edge computing-empowered traffic data recovery system leveraging the low-rank theory. Firstly, we conduct experimental explorations based on a large-scale traffic dataset of ITSs. The results reveal a serious issue of missing traffic data and indicate its spatio-temporal correlations. Due to the inspiration of these observations, we propose a sub-optimal edge node deployment algorithm with a performance guarantee. The extensive theoretical analysis and traces-based evaluations illustrate that GTR outperforms five baseline methods in both the edge node deployment and the traffic recovery.

References

1. C. Meng, X. Yi, L. Su, et al., City-wide traffic volume inference with loop detector data and taxi trajectories. Paper presented at the 25th ACM SIGSPATIAL International Conference on Advances in Geographic Information Systems, 7–10 November 2017
2. S. Guo, C. Chen, J. Wang, et al., Rod-revenue: seeking strategies analysis and revenue prediction in ride-on-demand service using multi-source urban data. IEEE Trans. Mobile Comput. **19**(9), 2202–2220 (2019)

3. Y. Xu, Q.J. Kong, R. Klette, et al., Accurate and interpretable Bayesian mars for traffic flow prediction. IEEE Trans. Intell. Transp. Syst. **15**(6), 2457–2469 (2014)
4. System of traffic volume viewer (2019), https://www.rms.nsw.gov.au/about/corporate-publications/statistics/traffic-vol-umes/aadt-map/index.html
5. Traffic volume viewer (2019), https://www.rms.nsw.gov.au/about/corporate-publications/statistics/traffic-volumes/index.html
6. L. Qu, L. Li, Y. Zhang, et al., PPCA-based missing data imputation for traffic flow volume: a systematical approach. IEEE Trans. Intell. Transp. Syst. **10**(3), 512–522 (2009)
7. A. Mehrabi, M. Siekkinen, A. Ylä-Jääski, Edge computing assisted adaptive mobile video streaming. IEEE Trans. Mobile Comput. **18**(4), 787–800 (2018)
8. P. Mach, Z. Becvar, Mobile edge computing: a survey on architecture and computation offloading. IEEE Commun. Surv. Tutor. **19**(3), 1628–1656 (2017)
9. Y. Mao, C. You, J. Zhang, et al., A survey on mobile edge computing: the communication perspective. IEEE Commun. Surv. Tutor. **19**(4), 2322–2358 (2017)
10. I. Laña, I.I. Olabarrieta, M. Vélez, et al., On the imputation of missing data for road traffic forecasting: new insights and novel techniques. Transp. Res. Part C Emerg. Technol. **90**, 18–33 (2018)
11. C. Xiang, P. Yang, C. Tian, et al., Calibrate without calibrating: an iterative approach in participatory sensing network. IEEE Trans. Parallel Distrib. Syst. **26**(2), 351–361 (2014)
12. S. Tak, S. Woo, H. Yeo, Data-driven imputation method for traffic data in sectional units of road links. IEEE Trans. Intell. Transp. Syst. **17**(6), 1762–1771 (2016)
13. X. Tang, B. Gong, Y. Yu, et al., Joint modeling of dense and incomplete trajectories for citywide traffic volume inference. Paper presented at the World Wide Web Conference 2019, 13–17 May 2019
14. Y. Chen, Y. Lv, F.Y. Wang, Traffic flow imputation using parallel data and generative adversarial networks. IEEE Trans. Intell. Transp. Syst. **21**(4), 1624–1630 (2019)
15. Y. Wang, Y. Zhang, X. Piao, et al., Traffic data reconstruction via adaptive spatial-temporal correlations. IEEE Trans. Intell. Transp. Syst. **20**(4), 1531–1543 (2018)
16. X. Chen, Z. He, J. Wang, Spatial-temporal traffic speed patterns discovery and incomplete data recovery via SVD-combined tensor decomposition. Transp. Res. Part C Emerg. Technol. **86**, 59–77 (2018)
17. X. Fan, C. Xiang, C. Chen, et al., BuildSenSys: reusing building sensing data for traffic prediction with cross-domain learning. IEEE Trans. Mobile Comput. **20**(6), 2154–2171 (2020)
18. L. Li, J. Zhang, Y. Wang, et al., Missing value imputation for traffic-related time series data based on a multi-view learning method. IEEE Trans. Intell. Transp. Syst. **20**(8), 2933–2943 (2018)
19. A. Ceselli, M. Premoli, S. Secci, Mobile edge cloud network design optimization. IEEE/ACM Trans. Netw. **25**(3), 1818–1831 (2017)
20. S. Mondal, G. Das, E. Wong, COMPASSION: a hybrid cloudlet placement framework over passive optical access networks. Paper presented at the IEEE INFOCOM 2018-IEEE Conference on Computer Communications, 16–19 April 2018
21. X. Zhan, Y. Zheng, X. Yi, et al., Citywide traffic volume estimation using trajectory data. IEEE Trans. Knowl. Data Eng. **29**(2), 272–285 (2016)
22. D. Deng, C. Shahabi, U. Demiryurek, et al., Latent space model for road networks to predict time-varying traffic. Paper presented at the 22nd ACM SIGKDD International Conference on Knowledge Discovery and Data Mining, 13–17 August 2016
23. T. Pamuła, Impact of data loss for prediction of traffic flow on an urban road using neural networks. IEEE Trans. Intell. Transp. Syst. **20**(3), 1000–1009 (2018)
24. A. Sarker, H. Shen, J.A. Stankovic, MORP: data-driven multi-objective route planning and optimization for electric vehicles. Proc. ACM Interact. Mobile Wear. Ubiq. Technol. **1**(4), 1–35 (2018)
25. Public Holidays Global, Australia public holidays (2019), https://publicholidays.com.au/zh/anzac-day/

26. T. Idé, T. Katsuki, T. Morimura, et al., City-wide traffic flow estimation from a limited number of low-quality cameras. IEEE Trans. Intell. Transp. Syst. **18**(4), 950–959 (2016)
27. J. Zheng, Y. Cai, Y. Wu, et al., Dynamic computation offloading for mobile cloud computing: a stochastic game-theoretic approach. IEEE Trans. Mobile Comput. **18**(4), 771–786 (2018)
28. C. Xiang, P. Yang, C. Tian, et al., CARM: crowd-sensing accurate outdoor RSS maps with error-prone smartphone measurements. IEEE Trans. Mobile Comput. **15**(11), 2669–2681 (2015)
29. K.G. Murty, *Linear Programming* (Wiley, Hoboken, 1983)
30. G.L. Nemhauser, L.A. Wolsey, M.L. Fisher, An analysis of approximations for maximizing submodular set functions—I. Math. Prog. **14**(1), 265–294 (1978)
31. J.G. Oxley, *Matroid Theory* (Oxford University Press, Oxford, 1992)
32. J. Lee, V.S. Mirrokni, V. Nagarajan, et al., Maximizing nonmonotone submodular functions under matroid or knapsack constraints. SIAM J. Discrete Math. **23**(4), 2053–2078 (2010)
33. D.C. Lay, S.R. Lay, J.J. McDonald, *Linear Algebra and Its Applications* (Pearson, London, 2016)
34. X. Wu, Z. Chu, P. Yang, et al., TW-see: human activity recognition through the wall with commodity Wi-Fi devices. IEEE Trans. Veh. Technol. **68**(1), 306–319 (2018)
35. E. Candes, B. Recht, Exact matrix completion via convex optimization. Commun. ACM **55**(6), 111–119 (2012)
36. V. Chandrasekaran, S. Sanghavi, P.A. Parrilo, et al., Sparse and low-rank matrix decompositions. IFAC Proc. **42**(10), 1493–1498 (2009)
37. S. Boyd, S.P. Boyd, L. Vandenberghe, *Convex Optimization* (Cambridge University Press, Cambridge, 2004)
38. S. Ma, D. Goldfarb, L. Chen, Fixed point and Bregman iterative methods for matrix rank minimization. Math. Prog. **128**(1), 321–353 (2011)
39. S. Foucart, H. Rauhut, *An Invitation to Compressive Sensing* (Birkhäuser, New York, 2013), pp. 1–39
40. J.F. Cai, E.J. Candès, Z. Shen, A singular value thresholding algorithm for matrix completion. SIAM J. Optim. **20**(4), 1956–1982 (2010)
41. L. Gong, Y. Zhao, C. Xiang, et al., Robust light-weight magnetic-based door event detection with smartphones. IEEE Trans. Mobile Comput. **18**(11), 2631–2646 (2018)
42. B. Recht, A simpler approach to matrix completion. J. Mach. Learn. Res. **12**, 3413–3430 (2011)

Part II
How to Use Crowdsensing Data for Smart Cities (Multi-dimensional Applications)

Chapter 4
Environmental Protection Application: Urban Pollution Monitoring

4.1 Introduction

With the urbanization's rapid development and continuous increasing population, more and more people pay attention to the identification of low-level radiation sources for the security of cities [1]. For example, people exploit RFTrax RAD-CZT sensors to detect the gamma radiation from dirty bombs and controlled aerosol injection sources [2, 3]. Even though wireless sensor networks have been put forward to identify the low-level radiation sources [1, 3], the deployment and maintenance of it cost a large amount of money in a large-scale city [4, 5]. With sensor technologies maturing and costs decreasing, smartphones are equipped with abundant sensors, like accelerators, GPS, and microphones [6]. We believe that in the future, the sensors will also be embedded to detect radiation sources [6, 7]. With the widespread use of smartphones, smartphone users inadvertently form a dense, large-scale sensor network, named crowd-sensing networks [4, 8]. Identifying low-level radiation sources based on crowd-sensing networks is promising and low-cost. Nevertheless, building such a system is not an easy task with the following two challenges.

- **Background ghost confusion**. Since the intensity of the low-level radiation sources may be low, the radiations of normal background with the approximate range are always treated as ghost radiation sources. Furthermore, the radiation measurements are Poisson distributed random variables [2], thereby exacerbating this confusion.
- **Unknown measurement errors**. Even worse, users' low-cost sensors have measurement errors, which are characterized by the sensor efficiency [9]. Due to the uncontrollability of users, the users' sensor efficiency are previously unknown.

Existing approaches [1, 2] are on the basis of a ratio of the measurement likelihood, assuming the source is truthful and false, respectively. Their identification accuracy

© The Author(s), under exclusive license to Springer Nature Singapore Pte Ltd. 2023
C. Xiang et al., *Multi-dimensional Urban Sensing Using Crowdsensing Data*, Data Analytics, https://doi.org/10.1007/978-981-19-9006-9_4

is largely dependent on the identification threshold, which is difficult to be set in practice [10, 11]. In addition, these approaches, mainly for wireless sensor networks, are based on the assumption that the sensor efficiency is known in advance, which is difficult to realize in crowd-sensing networks.

To solve the two issues of current approaches, we propose Counter-Strike, [1] which is an accurate and robust approach for the identification of low-level radiation sources in crowd-sensing networks. First, we utilize the true probability of radiation sources for source identification, which is robust with the identification threshold constantly changing. Next, we propose an iterative true-source identification algorithm that iterates alternately between the users' sensor efficiency estimation and the sources' truthful probability estimation, inspired by the expectation maximization (EM) method [13]. This algorithm uses the intermediate estimation results as the feedback of the next iteration's new estimations, hence improving both the sensor efficiency and the true probability's estimation accuracy step by step. Therefore, even when the sensor efficiency of users is unknown, it can realize accurate identification. Finally, we conduct extensive simulations to evaluate our approach's identification performance. To sum up, there are three main contributions of this chapter as follows.

1. To our knowledge, we are the first to identify truthful low-level radiation sources on the basis of crowd-sensing networks, where the sensor efficiency of users is formerly unknown.
2. Illuminated by EM approach, we present an identification algorithm based on an iterative truthful-source. The users' sensor efficiency is estimated based on the estimations of the truthful probability of radiation sources. The feedback of estimation results is for re-estimating the truthful probability.
3. Theoretical analysis and simulation results indicate that our approach is able to achieve a high identification accuracy, converging into the optimal estimations of the truthful probability through limited iterations, where the likelihood of crowd-sensing measurements is maximized. Furthermore, our approach is rather robust in identifying changes of the threshold.

The rest of this chapter is organized as follows. First, we review related work in Sect. 4.2. And then Sect. 4.3 presents the system model, as well as the problem description. Section 4.4 proposes an iterative truthful-source identification approach for addressing this problem. In Sect. 4.5, we conduct extensive simulations to evaluate our approach. Moreover, we discuss the influencing factors and the assumptions of our approach in Sect. 4.6. Finally, we summarize our work and present the future work in Sect. 4.7.

---

[1]Counter-Strike [12] is a video game in which the counters are searching and identifying the terrorists, then killing them. Similar to it, our method aims at accurately identifying the radiation sources which pose threat to the city security.

4.2 Related Work

In recent years, crowd-sensing networks have received extensive attentions from the scientific and industrial community because of the powerful computing and sensing ability of smartphones [6, 8]. Numerous crowdsensing network systems have been proposed in various applications. For example, BikeNet [14], CarTel [15], Nericell [16], and Parknet [17] monitor the urban road's traffic and conditions; ParkSense [18] senses on-street parking in real-time; Ear-phone [19] monitors the ambient noise level in large cities; CARM [20] measures received signal strength of outdoor WiFi APs.

With the development of the cities, detecting the low-level radiation sources has become more and more important, such as the dirty bomb defense strategy [1, 9]. The mean detector is presented in [21] as a simple approach to identify the radiation sources, which uses the mean of the measurements as the detector. If the threshold is below the detector, H1 (*i.e.*, the radiation source is truthful) is assumed; otherwise, the assumption H0 (*i.e.*, it is false) is decided. Although it's easy to leverage this approach in practice, the identification accuracy is poor because the low-level radiation sources' intensity is so low that it cannot distinguish them from the background radiation.

To deal with the shortcomings of mean detector, the likelihood ratio is used for identification. For instance, Sundaresan et al. [22] exploit the likelihood ratio test for identifying truthful radiation sources. To be specific, the maximum likelihood ratio under the assumption H1 to that under the assumption H0 is considered as the detectors. Given the likelihood ratio is above the identification threshold, the radiation source is considered as the truthful one and vice versa. Furthermore, considering the limited bandwidth of wireless sensor networks, they propose a distributed identification approach. Specifically, we exploit the likelihood ratio test for truthful identification on the basis of the local measurements. Then, the local identification results of each user are gathered in the center, which greatly reduces the communication bandwidth. Chin et al. [1, 23] put forward the sequential probability ratio test (SPRT) approach to identify the low-level radiation sources, which is similar to the literature [22]. They sequentially use several times of likelihood ratio tests to identify the truthful sources in order to increase the identification accuracy. Although their identification accuracy is high, the performance of these likelihood ratio test approaches is closely dependent on the identification threshold, however, which is extremely hard to determine [10]. Therefore, it's difficult to apply these approaches in practice. In addition, these approaches mainly consider wireless sensor networks, in which the sensors can be calibrated. However, this chapter is mainly about crowd-sensing networks. Due to the user's uncontrollability, the sensors of users cannot be calibrated and the efficiency of the sensor is not clear [6, 20]. Therefore, these approaches cannot address the issue of identifying truthful radiation sources in crowd-sensing networks. Instead, we put forward an iterative truthful-source identification algorithm that alternately estimates between the truthful provability of sources and the users' sensor efficiency, maximizing the likelihood of

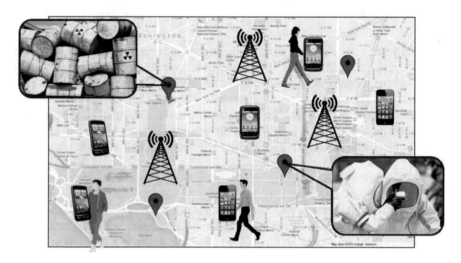

Fig. 4.1 A use-case example for identifying low-level radiation sources based on crowd-sensing networks

measurements. Furthermore, our identification threshold is easy to determine, as its variation has a slight impact on the accuracy of identification.

Furthermore, Yang et al. [24] research on sensor placement, trading off among the sensors numbers, the identification time, and the coverage utility. Liu et al. [25] compare the performance of multiple identification algorithms in wireless sensor networks by leveraging the laboratory experiments and mathematical analysis. Unlike them, we investigate how to accurately identify the truthful radiation sources on the basis of inaccurate crowd-sensing measurements. Meanwhile, multiple approaches [10, 11, 26] have been put forward to identify the diffusive pollution sources, and the measurement model is Gaussian distribution. In contrast, this chapter focuses on the low-level radiation sources, and the measurement model is Poisson distribution.

4.3   System Model and Problem Description

4.3.1   System Model

In this system model, we assume that N users join in the crowd-sensing networks and make measurements about the radiation counts with respect to M candidates of low-level radiation sources, as demonstrated in Fig. 4.1. Make A_j and $\mathbb{X}_j$ respectively represent the intensity and the location of the j-th source, $j = 1, 2, \ldots M$. Based on the radiation intensity decay model [1, 2], the radiation intensity at the location $\mathbb{X}_{ij}$ of the j-th radiation source is:

$$I_{ij} = \frac{A_j}{\left\| \mathbb{X}_j - \mathbb{X}_{ij} \right\|^2}, \qquad (4.1)$$

where $\|\cdot\|$ denotes the Euclidean distance between the two locations.

Ideally, the radiation counts per unit time measured at the location $\mathbb{X}_{ij}$ act in accordance with a Poisson distribution with the parameter I_{ij} [22]. Furthermore, the background radiation is ubiquitous and characterized by a Poisson distribution with the parameter B_j. In addition, each user's low-cost sensor has errors in measurement, which is characterized by sensor efficiency e_i [9]. It expresses the ratio between the mean of measured radiation counts and the mean of ideal radiation counts [9]. c_{ij} denotes the radiation counts measured by the i-th user for the j-th source at the location $\mathbb{X}_{ij}$. Note that unless otherwise stated, the radiation counts represent the radiation counts per unit time. Therefore~∞, the measurement model is given by:

$$\begin{cases} H_0: & c_{ij} \backsim \pi\left(e_i \cdot B_j\right) \\ H_1: & c_{ij} \backsim \pi\left(e_i \cdot (I_{ij} + B_j)\right) \end{cases} \qquad (4.2)$$

where H_1 and H_0 represent the hypothesis that the source is truthful and false, respectively. $\pi(\cdot)$ denotes the Poisson distribution. It should be noted that the above measurement model is widely utilized and validated in references [1, 2].

Based on Eq. (4.2), the conditional probability of the radiation counts c_{ij} with respect to the j-th radiation source measured by the i-th user is denoted as:

$$p\left(c_{ij}|S_j^f\right) = \phi\left(e_i \cdot B_j\right) \qquad (4.3)$$

$$p\left(c_{ij}|S_j^t\right) = \phi\left(e_i \cdot \left(I_{ij} + B_j\right)\right) \qquad (4.4)$$

where S_j^t and S_j^f represent the cases that the j-th radiation source is truthful and false, respectively. $\phi(\cdot)$ represents the probability function for the Poisson distribution, $i.e.$, $\phi(\lambda) = \frac{\lambda^{c_{ij}}}{c_{ij}!} \exp(-\lambda)$ [27].

4.3.2   Problem Description

As demonstrated in Fig. 4.1, each user exploits an available device (such as a smartphone) to measure the radiation sources in the crowd-sensing networks, including both the radiation counts ($i.e.$, c_{ij}) and the measured location ($i.e.$, X_{ij}). Meanwhile, plentiful crowd-sensing measurements are sent to the central server (such as cloud server [28–31]) through available communication networks, like WiFi and cellular networks [4]. Therefore, the server obtains the measurement set of crowdsensing users as:

$$Z = \left\{ z_{ij} | z_{ij} = \left(c_{ij}, \mathbb{X}_{ij} \right), j = 1, 2 \cdots M, i \in \mathbb{U}_j \right\} \tag{4.5}$$

where $\mathbb{U}_j$ denotes the subset of the users who measures the j-th radiation source. It should be noted that each radiation source is sensed only by parts of users because of the roaming behavior of the crowd-sensing users. Therefore, we have $0 \leq \| \mathbb{U}_j \| \leq N$.

The crowd-sensing measurements of the users are susceptible to measurement errors where the sensor efficiency is unknown. In addition, these errors are very hard to be calibrated by the users because of the uncontrollability of users in crowd-sensing networks [6, 20]. Therefore, it is extremely important to identify the truthful radiation sources from these inaccurate crowd-sensing measurements. In this chapter, we investigate how to solve this problem which is described as follows: given M low-level radiation sources, low-level radiation source candidates of known intensity at known locations, how to identify the truthful sources from the measurement set Z of crowd-sensing users when their sensor efficiency is unknown in advance.

4.4 Iterative Truthful-Source Identification Algorithm

4.4.1 Algorithm Design

First of all, We formulate the truthful-source identification problem as a maximum likelihood estimation problem, where the likelihood function is given by:

$$L(Z) = \prod_{j=1}^{M} \prod_{i \in \mathbb{U}_j} \log \left\{ p\left(c_{ij} | S_j^t \right) p\left(S_j^t \right) + p\left(c_{ij} | S_j^f \right) p\left(S_j^f \right) \right\} \tag{4.6}$$

As indicated in Eq. (4.6), this maximum likelihood estimation problem doesn't have complete data, that is, the truthfulness status of the radiation sources, *e.g.*, whether the source is truthful or not. We utilize the EM approach [32] to address this problem in this chapter. To be specific, let V denote the truthfulness of the sources, namely $V = \{v_j, 1, 2 \ldots M\}$, where $v_j = 1(0)$ represents the j-th source is truthful (or false). We select V as the latent variable. Thus, the likelihood function is represented by the following:

$$L(Z|V) = \prod_{j=1}^{M} \prod_{i \in \mathbb{U}_j} \left\{ v_j \cdot \log \left[p\left(c_{ij} | S_j^t \right) \right] + (1 - v_j) \cdot \log \left[p\left(c_{ij} | S_j^f \right) \right] \right\}, \tag{4.7}$$

EM approach is a classical estimation approach in Mathematics Statistics [13], which iterates between E-step and M-step until convergence, gradually maximizing the likelihood value of measurements. Inspired by EM approach, we present an

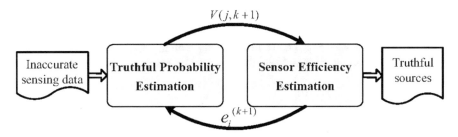

Fig. 4.2 Framework of iterative truthful-source identification algorithm. $V(j, k + 1)$ and $e_i^{(k+1)}$ denote the estimations of truthful probability and sensor efficiency in the $(k + 1)$-th iteration, respectively. They are computed according to Eqs. (4.8) and (4.11), respectively

iterative truthful-source identification algorithm that iterates between the truthful probability and the sensor efficiency estimation, as demonstrated in Fig. 4.2. By iterations, the estimation accuracy of both the truthful probability and the sensor efficiency is gradually improved until the likelihood of measurements converges. Ultimately, according to the identification threshold, the truthful probability estimations of sources are used for truthful-source identification.

Next, we take the $(k + 1)$-th iteration as an example to illustrate the methods of the truthful probability estimation and the sensor efficiency estimation.

Truthful Probability Estimation

We exploit the posterior probability of truthful probability from the newly estimated sensor efficiency as the estimations of truthful probability. To be specific, $\mathcal{E}^{(k)}$ denotes the estimations of sensor efficiency of the k-th iteration, $i.e.$, $\mathcal{E}^{(k)} = \left\{ e_i^{(k)}, i = 1, \cdots N \right\}$, where $e_i^{(k)}$ denotes the estimation of e_i in the k-th iteration. $V(j, k + 1)$ denotes the truthful probability estimation of the j-th source in the $(k + 1)$-th iteration. Thus, deriving from Eqs. (4.1), (4.3), and (4.4), the truthful probability estimation $V(j, k + 1)$ is demonstrated as:

$$
\begin{aligned}
V(j, k + 1) \quad &= p\left(v_j = 1 | Z, \mathcal{E}^{(k)} \right) \\
&= \frac{p\left(Z, \mathcal{E}^{(k)} | v_j = 1 \right) p\left(v_j = 1 \right)}{\sum\limits_{\tau=0}^{\tau=1} p\left(Z, \mathcal{E}^{(k)} | v_j = \tau \right) p\left(v_j = \tau \right)} \\
&= \left\{ 1 + F(j, k) \left(\frac{1}{V(j, k)} - 1 \right) \right\}^{-1}
\end{aligned}
\tag{4.8}
$$

where $F(j, k) = \prod\limits_{i \in \mathbb{U}_j} \left\{ \left[\frac{B_j}{I_{ij} + B_j} \right]^{c_{ij}} \cdot \exp\left(e_i^{(k)} \cdot I_{ij} \right) \right\}$

Sensor Efficiency Estimation

First of all, in line with Eqs. (4.7) and (4.8), based on the new estimations of truthful probability, the expected likelihood function can be computed as:

$$
\begin{aligned}
Q(Z|V) &= E_{V|Z,\mathcal{E}^{(k)}}[L(Z|V)] \\
&= \prod_{j=1}^{M}\prod_{i\in\mathbb{U}_j}\left\{V(j,k+1)\cdot\log\left[p\left(c_{ij}|S_j^t\right)\right]+(1-V(j,k+1))\cdot\log\left[p\left(c_{ij}|S_j^f\right)\right]\right\}
\end{aligned}
$$

$$(4.9)$$

Next, we calculate the new estimations of sensor efficiency (*i.e.*, $e_i^{(k+1)}$), in order to increase the expected likelihood function in Eq. (4.9). Therefore, we have

$$
\frac{\partial Q(Z|V)}{\partial e_i} = 0, i = 1,\dots N
$$

$$(4.10)$$

Finally, we can derive the sensor efficiency estimations $e_i^{(k+1)}$ from Eqs. (4.9) and (4.10) as ($i = 1,\dots N$):

$$
e_i^{(k+1)} = \frac{\sum\limits_{j\in\mathbb{S}_i}c_{ij}}{\sum\limits_{j\in\mathbb{S}_i}\left[B_j + I_{ij}\cdot V(j,k+1)\right]},
$$

$$(4.11)$$

where $\mathbb{S}_i$ denotes the set of sources measured by the i-th user.

Algorithm 4.1 Iterative Truthful-Source Identification Algorithm
Input: Measurement set of crowd-sensing users:
   $Z = \{z_{ij}|z_{ij} = (c_{ij}, \mathbb{X}_{ij}), j = 1, 2\cdots M, i \in \mathbb{U}_j\}$
Output: Truthful identification of sources:
   $\widehat{T} = \{\widehat{t}_j, j = 1, 2\dots, M\}$
   Sensor efficiency estimations of users:
   $\widehat{\mathcal{E}} = \{\widehat{e}_i, i = 1, 2\dots, N\}$
1: Initialize $e_i^{(0)}$ and $V(j, 0)$, $i = 1, 2\dots N, j = 1, 2\dots M$;
2: $k = 0$;
3: **while** $Q(Z|V)$ does not converge **do**
4:   **for** ($j = 1; j \leq M; j$++) **do**
5:      Compute $V(j, k + 1)$ based on $V(j, k)$ and $e_i^{(k)}$, $i = 1, 2\dots, N$, according to Eq. (4.8).
6:   **end for**

(continued)

Algorithm 4.1 (continued)
  7:   **for** $(i = 1; i \leq N; i{+}{+})$ **do**
  8:   Compute $e_i^{(k+1)}$ based on $V(j, k + 1), j = 1, 2 \ldots, M$, according to
Eq. (4.11).
  9:   **end for**
  10: $k = k + 1$
  11: end while
  12: Let e_i^c = the converged value of $e_i^{(k)}$, $i = 1, 2 \ldots, N$;
  13: $\widehat{e}_i = e_i^c$, $i = 1, 2 \ldots, N$;
  14: Let t_j^c = the converged value of $V(j, k), j = 1, 2 \ldots, M$;
  15: for $(j = 1; j \leq M; j{+}{+})$ **do**
  16:   **if** $\{t_j^c \geq \tau\}$ **then**
  17: $\widehat{t}_j = 1$
  18:   **else**
  19: $\widehat{t}_j = 0$
  20:   **end if**
  21: end for
  22: return $\widehat{e}_i$ and $\widehat{t}_j$, $i = 1, 2 \ldots, N, j = 1, 2 \ldots, M$;

4.4.2   Algorithm Description and Analysis

On the basis of the algorithm design of Sect. 4.4.1, we establish the iterative truthful-source identification algorithm as Algorithm 4.1. Its input is the crowd-sensing users' measurement set (*i.e.*, Z). The outputs include both the truthful identification of the radiation sources (*i.e.*, $\widehat{T}$) and the users' sensor efficiency estimations (*i.e.*, $\widehat{\mathcal{E}}$).

From the start of Algorithm 4.1, the truthful probability of sources (*i.e.*, $V(j, 0)$) and the user's sensor efficiency (*i.e.*, $e_i^{(0)}$) are initialized in line 1. It should be noted that the initial values have little effect on the performance of the algorithm due to the convergence of our algorithm.

Next, in lines 3–11, the following two steps are computed iteratively until the expected likelihood function $Q(Z|V)$ converges. In the beginning, the new estimations of the truthful probability (*i.e.*, $V(j, k + 1)$) are calculated from the estimations of the sensor efficiency estimation (*i.e.*, $e_i^{(k)}$) in lines 4–6. Afterward, the new estimations of the sensor efficiency (*i.e.*, $e_i^{(k+1)}$) are calculated from these estimation results (*i.e.*, $V(j, k + 1)$) in lines 7–9.

In lines 12–13, the algorithm calculates the final estimations of sensor efficiency (*i.e.*, $\widehat{e}_i$) after the expected likelihood function $Q(Z|V)$ converges based on the converged values of the sensor efficiency estimations (*i.e.*, e_i^c). Based on the converged values of the truthful probability estimations (*i.e.*, $\widehat{t}_j$) and the identification thresholds τ in lines 14–21, the final results of truthful-source identification (*i.e.*, t_j^c)

are calculated. It should be noted that unless otherwise stated, the identification threshold is generally set to 0.5, and the experiments of section "Algorithm Robustness" indicate that its settings have a slight impact on the performance of identification. Finally, the algorithm returns the results of the truthful-source identification and the users' sensor efficiency estimations in line 22.

Our algorithm is rather simple with the extremely low time complexity O-$(N \cdot M \cdot K)$, where N, M, and K denote the number of users, the radiation sources, and the iterations, respectively. Therefore, our algorithm has polynomial time complexity.

In line with the convergence property [33] of EM approach, as the likelihood function in Eq. (4.6) is a convex function, our algorithm is able to converge into the maximum likelihood of crowd-sensing measurements in limited iterations, hence achieving an optimal estimation of the truthful probability. The proofs of the convergence can be referred to the literature [33], which we will not go into detail.

4.5　Experimental Evaluations

In this section, we perform extensive simulations to evaluate our approach. First of all, we present the methodology and settings of these simulations. Furthermore, we evaluate our approach's identification performance, including our algorithm's convergence and robustness, as well as the impact from different users' number.

4.5.1　Simulation Methodology and Settings

We identify the low-level radiation sources by simulating a medium-scale crowd-sensing networks. To be specific, 100 low-level radiation sources are distributed randomly in a 2000 m × 2000 m square region; the probability of each radiation source is 0.4. The intensity of these sources varies randomly between 2×10^5 and 6×10^5 CPM (counts per minute). The background radiation and the sensor efficiency vary randomly from 10 to 100 CPM and 0.3–0.9, respectively. These settings are in line with the real experiments [1, 2]. N users participate in these crowd-sensing networks. Each user measures a source with the probability of 0.3. Unless otherwise stated, the identification threshold for our approach is set to 0.5. The simulation programs are written in MATLAB, running in a PC with a Win7 Intel Core i5 processor and 4 GB RAM. All the simulations are performed for 100 times, and we get the average results.

We compare our approach with the SPRT approach [1], which performs better than other existing works. Specifically, SPRT approach identifies the truthful source by utilizing the likelihood ratio in accordance with the threshold. In favor of SPRT, we set the ground-truth sensor efficiency in SPRT. Furthermore, we compare our approach with existing approaches according to the following three metrics:

- **False positive rate:** it refers to the proportion of the actual false sources among all identified truthful sources, named false positive in short.
- **False negative rate**: it refers to the proportion of the actual truthful sources among all identified false sources, named false negative concisely.
- **Efficiency estimation error:** it refers to the average estimation error of sensor efficiency for the users of crowdsensing.

4.5.2   Performance Evaluations

Algorithm Convergence

We evaluate the convergence of our algorithm in this section. The number of users N is set to 100. We analyze our approach's performance in terms of different iterations, including the likelihood values and the identification accuracy that includes the false positive rate and the negative rate. It should be noted that the likelihood values represent the values of the expected likelihood function in Eq. (4.9).

As demonstrated in Fig. 4.3, the likelihood values increase rapidly with the number of iterations until convergence. Our approach converges only after ten iterations. In addition, as shown in Fig. 4.4, in terms of both the false positive rate and the false negative rate, the identification errors decrease with the iteration number until convergence. Furthermore, as shown in Fig. 4.4, the false positive rate increases singularly in the first two iterations with the following reasons. During the two iterations, the false negative rate drops rapidly, resulting in more and more identified truthful sources being false. Therefore, the false positive rate increases rapidly in the beginning.

Fig. 4.3 Likelihood values versus the number of iterations in our method. Our method converges only after ten times of iterations

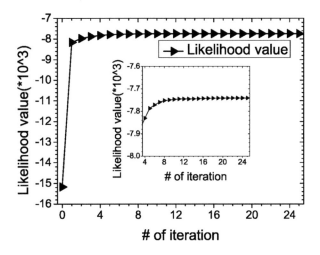

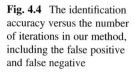

Fig. 4.4 The identification accuracy versus the number of iterations in our method, including the false positive and false negative

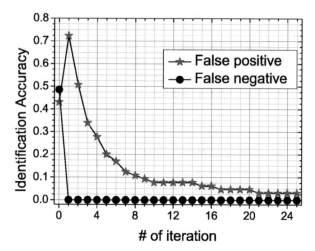

In summary, the experimental results show that our approach is able to achieve the maximum likelihood of measurements by limited iterations. The results are in line with the theoretical analysis in Sect. 4.4.2.

Algorithm Robustness

We compare our approach with SPRT approach in different identification thresholds to evaluate the identification accuracy. The experimental settings are the same as the experiment in section "Algorithm Convergence", except that the identification threshold is uniformly changed from 0.5 to 2 for the following reasons. The SPRT approach utilizes the likelihood ratio, *i.e.*, the ratio between the probability that the sources are truthful and false. In ideal conditions, the identification threshold is 1. If the likelihood ratio is above 1, the source is considered truthful, and vice versa.

First, as illustrated in Fig. 4.5, when the identification threshold is less than 0.9, the false positive rate of SPRT approach is always 100%, and when it is higher than 0.9, the false positive rate decreases with the increased thresholds. In contrast, as shown in Fig. 4.6, when the identification threshold is less than 1, the false negative rate of SPRT approach increases with the identification threshold, and when the identification threshold is above 1, the false negative rate always remains 100%. In the SPRT approach, the false negative rate is the opposite of the false positive rate due to the following reasons. When the identification threshold is less than 1, a lot of false sources are mistakenly identified as truthful ones, resulting in a high false positive rate. Conversely, the false sources are more strictly identified as the false ones. The lower the identification threshold, the stricter the false identification. Therefore, the false negative rate increases with the identification threshold. On the other side, when the identification threshold is higher than 1, the situation is similar. In conclusion, the identification performance of SPRT approach depends

Fig. 4.5 Comparison of false positive between our method and SPRT method in different identification thresholds

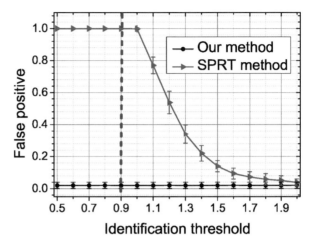

Fig. 4.6 Comparison of false negative between our method and SPRT method in different identification thresholds

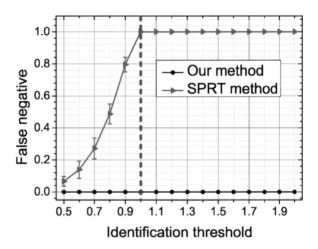

heavily on the identification threshold, which trades between the false positive rate and the false negative rate.

On the contrary, in our approach, the false positive rate varies slightly with the identification threshold, and the false negative rate is always 0. To our surprise, the best results of SPRT approach are worse than our approach when it comes to the false positive and negative rates.

In summary, our approach surpasses the best performance of SPRT approach in both the false positive and negative rate. Furthermore, the identification threshold has a large impact on the identification performance of SPRT approach. However, it has a slight impact on our approach. To make matters worse, how to set the optimal identification threshold based on the requirement of the false positive and negative rate is still an open question [10, 11].

Performance Impact of the Number of Users

We evaluate the effect of the number of the crowd-sensing users on the identification performance of our approach in this section. We set the number of users from 20 to 1000, while other setups are the same as the first experiment.

First, we evaluate the false positive and negative rates for different numbers of users. The false negative rate remains 0, which we do not account for. Furthermore, as demonstrated in Fig. 4.7, the false positive rate varies slightly when the number of users is less than 100. Next, when the false positive rate is above 100, it increases with the number of users rapidly. Until the number of users is more than 400, the false positive rate changes slightly again. In addition, the variation trend for the sensor efficiency estimation error is similar to that for the false positive rate, as shown in Fig. 4.8.

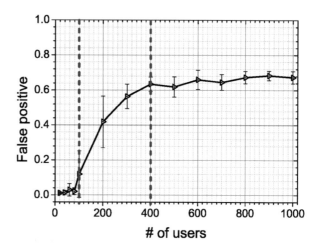

Fig. 4.7 False positive of identification versus the number of users in our method

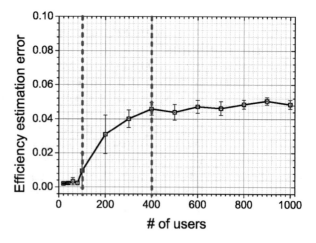

Fig. 4.8 Estimation error of sensor efficiency versus the number of users in our method

To sum up, at the beginning, as the number of users increases, both the identification accuracy and the efficiency estimation accuracy vary slightly, then drop rapidly, and finally reach a steady state. The reasons are as follows. On the one hand, more users can contribute to more measurements, thus improving the identification performance of our approach. On the other hand, the sensor efficiency of crowd-sensing users is unknown beforehand because of the uncontrollability. As a result, more users bring more unknown parameters, the estimation of which is closely tied with source identification, resulting in performance deterioration. Therefore, the identification performance of our approach is a balance between the contribution and the deterioration caused by the increasing number of users.

4.6 Discussion

In the crowd-sensing networks, some sensing data may be lost due to unreliable users [20]. For instance, some users closed the application because of low battery, or they are in places where the smartphones do not have access to the communication networks. The amount of missing data affects the identification performance [26]. Intuitively, the more missing data, the lower identification accuracy. We will exploit the traces-based simulations to further evaluate the impacts of the lost data on the identification performance of our algorithm in the future.

In accordance with the optimal property of EM approach [33], our algorithm is only able to achieve the optimal solution when the likelihood function is convex. Therefore, our approach can be extended to other crowd-sensing scenarios if their likelihood functions are convex, such as locating acoustic sources [34], identifying pollution sources [26], and locating wireless signal sources [20]. Therefore, our approach can be applied to multiple various types of crowd-sensing applications.

4.7 Conclusion

In this chapter, an iterative truthful source identification approach based on EM is proposed to identify the low-level radiation sources accurately and robustly based on inaccurate crowd-sensing measurements, thus successfully solving the problem of poor robustness and unknown sensor efficiency. The users' sensor efficiency and the sources' truthful probability are estimated iteratively and increase the likelihood values of crowd-sensing measurements step by step. The experimental results and theoretical analysis reveal that our approach is able to achieve a maximum likelihood, in which case the sources' truthful probability estimations are optimal. Therefore, we can identify the truthful radiation sources accurately on the basis of the inaccurate crowd-sensing measurements. In addition, the identification accuracy of our approach is slightly influenced by the change of the identification threshold.

References

1. J.C. Chin, N.S.V. Rao, D.K.Y. Yau, M. Shankar, Y. Yang, J.C. Hou, S. Srivathsan, S. Iyengar, Identification of low-level point radioactive sources using a sensor network. ACM Trans. Sens. Netw. **7**(3), 1–35 (2010)
2. J.C. Chin, D.K.Y. Yau, N.S.V. Rao, Y. Yang, C.Y.T. Ma, M. Shankar, Accurate localization of low-level radioactive source under noise and measurement errors, in *Sensys*, (2008)
3. N.S. Rao, M. Shankar, J.C. Chin, D.K. Yau, C.Y. Ma, Y. Yang, J.C. Hou, X. Xu, S. Sahni, Localization under random measurements with application to radiation sources, in *International Conference on Information Fusion*, (IEEE, Washington, DC, 2008), pp. 1–8
4. H. Ma, D. Zhao, P. Yuan, Opportunities in mobile crowd sensing. IEEE Commun. Mag. **52**(8), 29–35 (2014)
5. Y. Zhang, X. Sun, B. Wang, Efficient algorithm for k-barrier coverage based on integer linear programming. China Commun. **13**(7), 16–23 (2016)
6. N.D. Lane, E. Miluzzo, H. Lu, D. Peebles, T. Choudhury, A.T. Campbell, A survey of mobile phone sensing. IEEE Commun. Mag. **48**(9), 140–150 (2010)
7. D. Hasenfratz, O. Saukh, S. Sturzenegger, L. Thiele, Participatory air pollution monitoring using smartphones, in *International Workshop on Mobile Sensing*, Beijing, China, (2012)
8. R.K. Ganti, F. Ye, H. Lei, Mobile crowdsensing: current state and future challenges. IEEE Commun. Mag. **49**(11), 32–39 (2011)
9. J.C. Chin, D.K.Y. Yau, N.S.V. Rao, Efficient and robust localization of multiple radiation sources in complex environments, in *ICDCS*, (IEEE, Washington, DC, 2011), pp. 780–789
10. A. Nehorai, B. Porat, E. Paldi, Detection and localization of vapor-emitting sources. IEEE Trans. Signal Process. **43**(1), 243–253 (1995)
11. T. Zhao, A. Nehorai, Detecting and estimating biochemical dispersion of a moving source in a semi-infinite medium. IEEE Trans. Signal Process. **54**(6), 2213–2225 (2006)
12. Wikipedia, Counter-strike (2016), https://en.wikipedia.org/wiki/Counter-Strike. Accessed 1 Aug
13. A. Dempster, N. Laird, D. Rubin, Maximum likelihood from incomplete data via the EM algorithm. J. R. Stat. Soc. Ser. B **39**(1), 1–38 (1977)
14. S. Eisenman, E. Miluzzo, N. Lane, R. Peterson, G. Ahn, A. Campbell, Bikenet: a mobile sensing system for cyclist experience mapping. ACM Trans. Sens. Netw. **6**(1), 6 (2009)
15. B. Hull, V. Bychkovsky, Y. Zhang, K. Chen, M. Goraczko, A. Miu, E. Shih, H. Balakrishnan, S. Madden, Cartel: a distributed mobile sensor computing system, in *Sensys*, (2006)
16. P. Mohan, V.N. Padmanabhan, R. Ramjee, Nericell: rich monitoring of road and traffic conditions using mobile smart-phones, in *SenSys*, (ACM, New York, NY, 2008), pp. 323–336
17. S. Mathur, T. Jin, N. Kasturirangan, J. Chandrasekaran, W. Xue, M. Gruteser, W. Trappe, Parknet: drive-by sensing of road-side parking statistics, in *Mobisys*, (ACM, New York, NY, 2010), pp. 123–136
18. S. Nawaz, C. Efstratiou, C. Mascolo, Parksense: a smart-phone based sensing system for on-street parking, in *Mobicom*, (2013), pp. 75–86
19. R. Rana, C. Chou, S. Kanhere, N. Bulusu, W. Hu, Ear-phone: an end-to-end participatory urban noise mapping system, in *IPSN*, (2010), pp. 105–116
20. C. Xiang, P. Yang, C. Tian, L. Zhang, H. Lin, F. Xiao, M. Zhang, Y. Liu, CARM: crowd-sensing accurate outdoor RSS maps with error-prone smartphone measurements. IEEE Trans. Mob. Comput. **15**(11), 2669–2681 (2016)
21. A. Jeremic, A. Nehorai, Landmine detection and localization using chemical sensor array processing. IEEE Trans. Signal Process. **48**(5), 1295–1305 (2000)
22. A. Sundaresan, P.K. Varshney, N.S. Rao, Distributed detection of a nuclear radioactive source using fusion of correlated decisions, in *International Conference on Information Fusion*, (IEEE, Washington, DC, 2007), pp. 1–7

23. N.S.V. Rao, M. Shankar, J.C. Chin, D.K.Y. Yau, S. Srivathsan, S.S. Iyengar, Y. Yang, J.C. Hou, Identification of low-level point radiation sources using a sensor network, in *IPSN*, (IEEE, Washington, DC, 2008), pp. 493–504
24. Y. Yang, H. Hou, J.C. Hou, Sensor placement for detecting propagative sources in populated environments, in *INFOCOM*, (IEEE, Washington, DC, 2009), pp. 1206–1214
25. A.H. Liu, J.J. Bunn, K.M. Chandy, Sensor networks for the detection and tracking of radiation and other threats in cities, in *Information Processing in Sensor Networks (IPSN)*, (IEEE, Washington, DC, 2011), pp. 1–12
26. C. Xiang, P. Yang, C. Tian, Y. Yan, X. Wu, Y. Liu, Passfit: participatory sensing and filtering for identifying truthful urban pollution sources. IEEE Sens. J. **13**(10), 3721–3732 (2013)
27. P.J. Bickel, B. Li, *Mathematical Statistics*, Test 15 (1977)
28. Z. Fu, X. Wu, C. Guan, X. Sun, K. Ren, Toward efficient multi-keyword fuzzy search over encrypted outsourced data with accuracy improvement. IEEE Trans. Inf. Forens. Secur. **11**(12), 2706–2716 (2016)
29. Y.J. Ren, J. Shen, J. Wang, J. Han, S.Y. Lee, Mutual verifiable provable data auditing in public cloud storage. J Intern. Technol. **16**(2), 317–323 (2015)
30. Z. Xia, X. Wang, X. Sun, Q. Wang, A secure and dynamic multi-keyword ranked search scheme over encrypted cloud data. IEEE Trans. Parallel. Distrib. Syst. **27**(2), 340–352 (2016)
31. F. Zhangjie, S. Xingming, L. Qi, Z. Lu, S. Jiangang, Achieving efficient cloud search services: multi-keyword ranked search over encrypted cloud data supporting parallel computing. IEICE Trans. Commun. **98**(1), 190–200 (2015)
32. J. Li, X. Li, B. Yang, X. Sun, Segmentation-based image copy-move forgery detection scheme. IEEE Trans. Inf. Forens. Secur. **10**(3), 507–518 (2015)
33. C.F.J. Wu, On the convergence properties of the EM algorithm. Ann. Stat. **11**(1), 95–103 (1983)
34. G. Xing, J. Wang, Z. Yuan, R. Tan, L. Sun, Q. Huang, X. Jia, H.C. So, Mobile scheduling for spatiotemporal detection in wireless sensor networks. IEEE Trans. Parallel. Distrib. Syst. **21**(12), 1851–1866 (2010)

Chapter 5
Urban Traffic Application: Traffic Volume Prediction

5.1 Introduction

As the number of smart buildings equipped with an increasing number of IoT sensors increase rapidly, they produce large amount of building sensing data (also called building data[1] [1–3]). Evidence in reference [4] has shown that the explosive volume of sensing data collected by global smart buildings reached nearly 7.8 ZB (about 7.8×2^{40} G) in 2015, and is predicted to reach nearly 37.2 ZB by 2020. For example, as illustrated in Fig. 5.1a, a CBD building in Sydney which has more than 2000 sensors generates over 100 million sensor readings, including the status of the building, building occupancy, indoor/outdoor environment, etc.

Reusing existing building data is of great importance for smart city sensing, since building data is cost-efficiency and sustainable [5]. We have positive expectations of the use of building sensing data in the long term, which has recently initiated new applications in urban sensing, such as the design of urban 3D mobility models [6] and the abnormal appliance identification [7, 8]. In this chapter, as a fundamental exploration, we reuse building sensing data for nearby traffic sensing with the following reasons. As now most urban buildings are connected by roads, and people pass through these roads to get to their destinations [9]. The report in reference [10] has shown that 93% of Americans' time is spent on enclosed buildings and vehicles (accounting for 87% and 6%, respectively). Considering this, we wonder that there might be some connection between sensing data of buildings and traffic data of its surrounding roads, named as the building-traffic correlations [8]. It is a prospective field of reusing building sensing data, *i.e.*, for the prediction of traffic on nearby roads. Being a proof-of-concept, this chapter chiefly centers around predicting traffic volume, *i.e.*, the number of passing vehicles within 1 h [11]. Accurate prediction of traffic volume is very important for the applications of Intelligent Transportation

---

[1] In the remaining of this chapter, we will use the terms building sensing data and building data interchangeably unless otherwise stated.

© The Author(s), under exclusive license to Springer Nature Singapore Pte Ltd. 2023
C. Xiang et al., *Multi-dimensional Urban Sensing Using Crowdsensing Data*, Data Analytics, https://doi.org/10.1007/978-981-19-9006-9_5

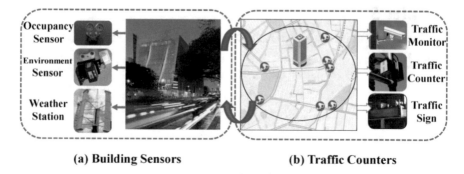

(a) Building Sensors   **(b) Traffic Counters**

Fig. 5.1 Illustrations for reusing building sensing data to predict nearby traffic volume with cross-domain learning. (**a**) Building sensors. (**b**) Traffic counters

Systems (ITSs), such as the control of traffic light, road navigation, and estimation of vehicle emission [8, 12, 13].

Compared with traditional ways of predicting traffic volume [11, 14–18], reusing building data performs exceedingly in many aspects like cost and credibility, both of which are important in traffic sensing [13]. Many traditional ways of traffic prediction depend hugely on the fixed road-based traffic sensing systems, like loop detectors [14] and traffic surveillance cameras [15]. Despite the preciseness of traffic volume information rendered by these ways, installation and maintenance would be a high cost, hence preventing them from being applied in big cities [8]. In contrast, re-using off-the-shelf building sensing data will tremendously lower the cost, for there is no extra installation and maintenance fee [8, 11]. In response to the high cost, concerning opportunistic sensing data of floating vehicles, GPS trajectories [11] and cellular records of passengers [18] have been leveraged to compute traffic volume. Nevertheless, opportunistic sensing is plagued by the uncontrollable property of users and data deficiency of particular roads, resulting in unreliable performance in traffic volume prediction [18]. As the two basic constructions in urban infrastructure, buildings and surrounding roads are unchanged with long-term spatial relations. Hence, compared with the opportunistic sensing [11], buildings can produce sensing data that is more reliable and sustainable, which renders opportunities for predicting nearby traffic volume accurately in the long term [17, 19].

However, it is necessary to solve two principal problems formally as follows.

- Challenge 1: *Investigating unknown building-traffic relationships*. Indeed, some evidence [6, 8] reveals building-traffic correlations. However, they cannot provide further explanation of these relations. It is actually challenging and complex to reveal building-traffic correlations in a precise manner. In addition, it is excessively difficult to reveal the concealed reasons behind the correlations.
- Challenge 2: *Accurate prediction based on cross-domain building traffic correlations*. As the building-traffic relationships are cross-domain and non-linear, the accurate prediction of traffic volume is non-trivial. What is more challenging is that these correlations would vary dynamically as time changes, incuring more difficulties in accurate traffic prediction [20].

To address these challenges, we present BuildSenSys, a system of reusing building sensing data for nearby traffic volume prediction. Firstly, for Challenge 1, based on real-world datasets, we investigate the relationships between building data and nearby traffic volume in Sect. 5.4. The experimental results demonstrate that the building-traffic correlations are non-linear, time-varying, and cross-domain. Next, in response to Challenge 2, we employs cross-domain learning with two attention mechanisms for traffic volume prediction (in Sect. 5.5). At last, we implement a prototype system of BuildSenSys. Moreover, we conduct comprehensive evaluations with 1-year real-world datasets.

To sum up, the three main contributions we made in this chapter are as follows:

1. We conduct a comprehensive building-traffic analysis with real datasets from multiple sources. Based on the multi-source cross-verification, this chapter reveals the reason why building data is related to nearby traffic volume as follows. Residents' commuting activities leads to the changes in building occupancy, which are tremendously related to the dynamics of traffic volume on nearby roads. Moreover, the higher the probability of building occupants pass through a road, the stronger the building-traffic correlation there exists.
2. With the help of cross-domain learning, we put forward a novel network for traffic volume prediction. It uses a cross-domain attention-based encoder and a temporal attention-based decoder to accurately extract the non-linear, time-varying, cross-domain building-traffic correlations. Moreover, it further realizes accurate prediction of traffic volume.
3. Experimental studies indicate that BuildSenSys surpasses all baseline methods with its progress in accuracy up to 65.3%. We believe that this work can pave new path for reusing building sensing data for traffic sensing as well as further building connections between smart buildings and intelligent transportation.

As for the following part of this chapter, they are structured as follows. Section 5.2 is the literature review. Section 5.3 gives a brief and general introduction of the BuildSenSys system. Next, Sect. 5.4 analyzes the connection between building data and nearby traffic data. Section 5.5 formulates the prediction problem. Section 5.5 also covers the cross-domain learning-based recurrent neural network of the traffic prediction. Section 5.6 is the analysis of BuildSenSys through wide experimental studies by using datasets from multiple sources. In the end, Sect. 5.7 examines some critical issues of reusing building data, and Sect. 5.8 marks the conclusion of the chapter.

5.2 Related Work

5.2.1 Reusing Building Data

In the very beginning, building sensing data is used for indoor and control [21]; hence, no extra cost is needed in that process. Apart from building management, it has aroused large research interest in smart city applications, including urban transportation [8], crowd flow patterns [6], and data integration [22]. As demonstrated by reference [23], merely a traffic monitoring system with camera detectors might charge $2500 (USD). However, say in a large-scale city for instance, although such devices might cost 100 million dollars, there's only one fourth of the roads can be covered [8]. In comparison with traditional ways [11, 15–17] that totally depend on sensing data from traffic monitoring systems, reusing building sensing data is totally profitable and trustworthy. For instance, Zheng et al. [6] has studied the effect of buildings on human movements and developed a novel urban mobility model for urban planning. To structure in-building IoT devices with heterogeneous data communication, Hu et al. [24] put forward a communication sharing architecture for smart buildings. In addition, Zheng et al. [8] proposed to leverage indoor CO_2 to forecast building occupancy and created an occupancy-traffic model to predict the speed of traffic. Thanks to the inspiration of the above existing works, it's significant to align traffic monitoring systems with external sensing infrastructures, so as to promote traffic prediction accuracy as well as decreasing marginal cost. Continuing their study, we put forward novel reuse of multi-dimension building sensing data for traffic prediction. Conducting the preliminary steps of the research, we widely delve into the building-traffic correlations. Also, we employ cross-domain learning to ensure the prediction is precise.

5.2.2 Traffic Volume Prediction

Among the present studies of predicting traffic volume, many of them leverage data from fixed road-based traffic sensors, including loop detectors, microwave radars, and video cameras [13]. One major edge of road-based sensors is that their data is valid, for they come from the record of all vehicles passing by [25]. Lately, techniques including opportunistic sensing and crowdsensing have been put into use to gather GPS data [11, 26, 27], and cellular record data [28–30] from floating vehicles and mobile passengers. They render thorough mobility traces for network-wide traffic sensing and prediction. There's a trend in traffic prediction that many existing works have made traffic sensor data and opportunistic sensing data a combination. For instance, to forecast traffic volume, Meng et al. [31] combined loop detector data and taxi trajectories with a spatio-temporal semisupervised learning model. Nevertheless, given the inherent biases and random data deficiency, most trajectory data is incapable of covering the whole traffic dynamics. For example, within a city of large-scale and unique operating time, the GPS data of a 6000-taxi network can only cover 28% of the overall road segments [18]. Because of the data sparsity, using trajectory sensing data is not feasible to ensure sustainability and reliability in traffic prediction, particularly on targeted roads. In this work, the source data for traffic prediction is building sensing data, which is hugely different from many other existing works. Stationary as the buildings and their surrounding roads are, their spatial relations are integrally permanent. Even more, since building-traffic correlations are sustainable, in the long-term traffic prediction, reusing building data is efficient and highly reliable.

5.2.3   Traffic Prediction Models

Traditional ways of traffic prediction in short terms chiefly use parameter-based prediction models, such as Autoregressive Integrated Moving Average (ARIMA) [32], Vector Autoregression (VAR) [33], and Locally Weighted Linear Regression (LWR) [8]. Deep learning has been gaining popularity in recent years, and deep neural networks [34] are employed in traffic prediction, as they are capable of capturing complex temporal-spatial dependencies through feature learning [35]. In addition, Recurrent Neural Networks (RNN) have also been employed by reference [36] to conduct sequence learning on historical traffic data. Admittedly, RNNs fail to preserve long-term dependencies on historical traffic data since the deterioration of their performance with longer input. In the end, Long Short-Term Memory (LSTM) networks are further employed by many research studies [37, 38] to fulfill prediction tasks in the long run. As human can capture a focus on certain visions, attention mechanisms have been made a part of the neural networks for sequence-to-sequence learning [39]. For example, reference [40] puts forward a spatial-temporal dynamic network with a periodically shifted attention mechanism identifying periodic temporal similarity in traffic predictions. In this work, a cross-domain learning-based neural network is created, including a cross-domain attention mechanism and a temporal attention mechanism. This model is capable of identifying cross-domain, non-linear, and time-varying building-traffic correlations with efficiency for accurate traffic prediction.

5.3   System Overview

In this part, a systematic introduction of reusing building data for traffic volume prediction is introduced. As illustrated in Fig. 5.2, the data sources of BuildSenSys consist of a tiny scale building (generating occupancy data and environmental data) and nearby traffic monitors (providing traffic volume data). Moreover, there are two components in BuildSenSys as follows.

- **Building-traffic correlation analysis with multi-source real-world datasets** (in Sect. 5.4). Experimental analysis is performed by employing data from smart buildings, fixed-road sensors, and Google traffic. We examine whether building data is correlated with traffic data. Moreover, we delve into the reasons behind this correlation. The result shows that the answer is affirmative. Also, there are two kinds of cross-domain correlations, including (1) the occupancy correlation between the building occupancy and traffic data (in Sect. 5.4.1); (2) the

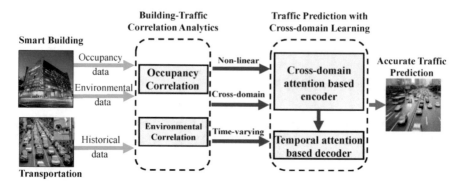

Fig. 5.2 An overview of the BuildSenSys system for reusing building data for nearby traffic prediction

environmental correlation between the building environmental data and traffic data (in Sect. 5.4.2). Apart from that, the building-traffic correlations are dynamic, meaning that they generate the temporal correlations as time changes.

- **Cross-Domain Learning for Accurate Traffic Prediction** (in Sect. 5.5). For cross-domain correlation and time correlation, we propose cross-domain learning to precisely predict traffic volume. In particular, a cross-domain attention mechanism is put forward for the encoder to obtain features from the non-linear, cross-domain correlation between building data and traffic data (in Sect. 5.5.2). After these features are associated with traffic volume data, we identify the most relevant cross-domain association in the training process of the BuildSenSys model. In addition, we propose a time attention mechanism for the decoder to learn the time dependency of the predicted traffic data (in section "Decoder with Temporal Attention"). Then, we employ the output context factors to predict traffic volume.

5.4 Building-Traffic Correlation Analysis with Multi-Source Datasets

In this section, we perform comprehensive experiments to delve into spatial and temporal building-traffic correlations with multi-source real-world datasets as follows. To start with, we introduce building sensing data and traffic volume data as follows.

First, building sensing data is gathered from the Faculty of Engineering and Information Technology's Building (FEIT Building) at the University of Technology Sydney, New South Wales, Australia. As a 16-level building in the campus, the FEIT building has a total usable floor area of 23,500 m^2. Moreover, it allows about 5000 people for accommodation. As shown in Fig. 5.1a, the FEIT building is said to be a 'living laboratory,' for it has 2500 internal environment sensors in the building.

These sensors monitor the environments of the building in a continuous manner. The environment covered by the sensors includes indoor environment (by environmental sensors), outdoor environment (by a roof-top weather station), and building occupancy (by smart cameras). The building sensing data is accessed with the use of an online database server via MySQL workbench. In total, it contains 33 types of building sensing data, and the overall data volume is over 10 GB [41]. To predict traffic, ten kinds of sensor data in the FEIT building are applied.

Next, as illustrated in Fig. 5.1b, the traffic data is the traffic volume collected by the traffic counters of several sections deployed near the FEIT building. These traffic counters are combined into a traffic monitoring system to estimate traffic volume in each hour. We acquire historical traffic volume data from the official website of the Department of Roads and Maritime Services, New South Wales State [42]. Next, we introduce a detailed cross-domain correlation analysis with traffic volume data and different building sensing data.

5.4.1   Correlation Analysis with Building Occupancy Data

In this section, we delve into cross-domain correlations between building occupancy data and traffic volume. With the help of cameras set at entrances, stairways, and walkways in the building, the building occupancy data is gathered to observe the people's daily activity in the building. With the gathered data, the PLCount algorithm [43] is employed to precisely calculate the total building occupancy. Since building occupancy is not the crux of our chapter, some of the details that can be referred from [43] are left out.

Correlation Quantification with Metrics

Having building occupancy calculated before, the connection between building occupancy and nearby traffic volume is further looked into. As a start, we put together building occupancy and the traffic volume of nearby roads in 1 week for contrast. As demonstrated in Fig. 5.3, the normalized building occupancy (dashed blue line) and traffic volume (solid red line) of roads A–D are compared. Particularly, it should be noticed that the aforementioned four roads are of various types. Among the four roads, road A is a minor highway; road B is a major highway; road C is a main street; and road D is a primary street. According to our findings, comparing the building occupancy and traffic volume, the hourly patterns are similar from Monday to Friday, while it differs on Saturday and Sunday. It can be said that the building occupancy is high as it is influenced by the commuting people. Moreover, on Saturday and Sunday, the number of working people is limited in the building. One thing worth noticing is that the building occupancy is tightly related to the peak hour in the morning and evening.

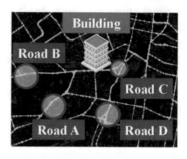

(a)Locations

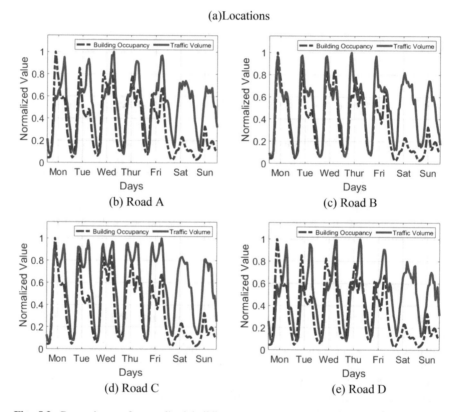

Fig. 5.3 Comparisons of normalized building occupancy and normalized traffic volume on different roads. (**a**) Locations. (**b**) Road A. (**c**) Road B. (**d**) Road C. (**e**) Road D

Nevertheless, we have to admit that what we have learned from comparing the normalized building occupancy and traffic volume is limited. It only tells things about the general dynamics and correlations. Therefore, for further quantification of the connection between building occupancy and traffic volume, two correlation metrics are used, *i.e.*, Cosine Similarity and Pearson Correlation Coefficient. The former one quantifies the similarity between two non-zero vectors on an inner

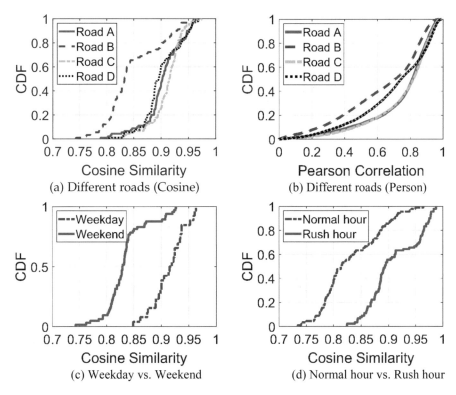

Fig. 5.4 Quantification of correlations between building occupancy data and traffic volume data with two metrics. (**a**) Different roads (Cosine). (**b**) Different roads (Person). (**c**) Weekday vs. weekend. (**d**) Normal hour vs. rush hour

product space. We use s_i to represent the cosine similarity between building occupancy and traffic volume on day i. It is computed as $s_i = \cos(\mathbf{b}_i, \mathbf{t}_i)$, where $\mathbf{b_i} = [b_{i,1}, b_{i,2}, \ldots, b_{i,24}]$ and $\mathbf{t_i} = [t_{i,1}, t_{i,2}, \ldots, t_{i,24}]$ denote the vectors of building occupancy and traffic volume over 24 h on day i, respectively. By doing this, the general cosine similarity between building occupancy and traffic volume for n days is denoted by

$\mathbf{s} = [s_1, \ldots s_i, \ldots s_n]$. Additionally, the Pearson Correlation is computed as $p =$

$$\sum_{j=1}^{k} \left(b_{i,j} - \bar{b}_i\right)\left(t_{i,j} - \bar{t}_i\right) / \sqrt{\sum_{j=1}^{k} \left(b_{i,j} - \bar{b}_i\right)^2 \sum_{j=1}^{k} \left(t_{i,j} - \bar{t}_i\right)^2},$$ where k denotes the time

interval for each Pearson Coefficient, $\bar{b}_i$ and $\bar{t}_i$ are the average building occupancy and traffic volume on day i, respectively. Additionally, the absolute value of Pearson Correlation indicates the strength of the correlation, and the range varies from 0 (weak correlation) to 1 (strong correlation).

The correlations between building occupancy and traffic volume is quantified on four different road segments by using Cosine Similarity and Pearson Correlation. As shown in Fig. 5.4a, the cosine similarities on all four roads are greater than 0.8, indicating that building occupancy is strongly correlated with traffic volume. Additionally, Fig. 5.4b demonstrates that over 70% of traffic volume data has strong and positive ($\geq$0.5) Pearson Correlation with building occupancy data. Moreover, the cosine similarity of building occupancy and traffic volume is calculated by separating the data into different groups, *i.e.*, weekdays/weekends and rush hours/normal hours. According to Fig. 5.4c, d, it is explicit to see that the correlations between building occupancy and traffic volume are higher on weekdays ($\geq$0.85) and rush hours ($\geq$0.82) and lower on weekends ($\geq$0.75) and normal hours ($\geq$0.75).

Correlation Verification with Google Maps

In section "Correlation Quantification with Metrics", we concluded that the building occupancy data is closely related to the traffic volume on nearby roads. A major reason is that most of the building occupants, when getting in or out of a building, have to pass the surrounding roads to get to their destination. That is to say, the correlation between the traffic and the volume lies in the probability of building occupants passing by nearby roads. To put it more specifically, there is a closer correlation between building occupancy and traffic volume when the nearby road is more probable for occupants in the building.

To prove our supposition, we perform cross-verification experiments with Google Maps so as to make progress in the correlation between building occupancy and traffic volume. In the beginning, as shown in Fig. 5.5a, we let this building's location be the starting points or the endpoints. And then, we stochastically choose 500 locations within 10 km distance of this building as the end/starting points. These points, along with the building's location, are packaged as a navigation request and sent to Google Maps for navigation. Next, we receive the best-fit road geometries with a

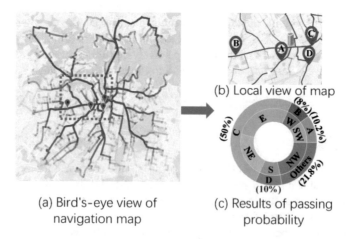

(a) Bird's-eye view of navigation map

(b) Local view of map

(c) Results of passing probability

Fig. 5.5 Cross-verification for building-traffic correlations via Google Maps Navigation. (**a**) Bird's-eye view of navigation map. (**b**) Local view of map. (**c**) Results of passing probability

Table 5.1 Cross-verification: comparison between Roads A, B, C, and D in navigation passing probability, cosine similarity, Pearson correlation and distance to the building

Road name	Passing ratio (%)	Cosine	Pearson	Distance (km)
Road C	50	First	First	0.3
Road A	10.2	Second	Second	1.6
Road D	10	Third	Third	1.9
Road B	8	Fourth	Fourth	3.0

series of GPS locations. Figure 5.5 is the visualization of our results, including 500 navigation outcomes. Note that the routes' colors mean the probability of occupants passing by. Meanwhile, routes of deeper color mean a higher probability of occupants passing by.

As illustrated in Fig. 5.5a, some routes with long-distance would have to get through the main roads, such as major highways and primary streets. Additionally, Fig. 5.5b illustrates a zoom-in view of roads A–D. Figure 5.5c shows different passing probability of roads A–D; the outer circle is the passing probability of four roads; the inner circle represents the major directions of navigation routes. The passing probabilities of roads A, B, C, and D are 10.2%, 8%, 50%, and 10%, respectively; the passing ratio of other roads is about 20%. With the cross-verification being used, these results in Google Maps are compared with building traffic correlations in section "Correlation Quantification with Metrics". As illustrated in Table 5.1, the results which come from datasets of multiple sources are consistent with each other. To put it more specifically, roads of higher passing probability and shorter distance to the building would have stronger building-traffic correlations with this building. As a result, the reason behind building-traffic correlation is verified by the aforementioned results of cross-verification as follows. Since the building occupants going in or out of a building would pass the surrounding roads, the change of building occupancy data (induced by the commuting activity of the building's occupants) is highly correlated to the traffic volume of nearby roads.

5.4.2 Correlation Analysis with Environmental Data

Apart from building occupancy, environmental data have been proved to have impact on traffic on the nearby roads evidently. Also, they contribute to the improvement of traffic prediction accuracy [16, 44]. To conduct cross-domain traffic prediction in this work, we choose five kinds of indoor environmental data (including CO_2 concentration, building humidity, O_2 concentration, building temperature, and building air pollution) and four kinds of outdoor environmental data (including outdoor temperature, rainfall, wind speed, and air quality index) from the FEIT building. Through the studies on correlation between building occupancy and traffic volume, it shows that environmental data differs in the levels of correlations with the data of traffic volume. One special thing is that some of the environmental data have

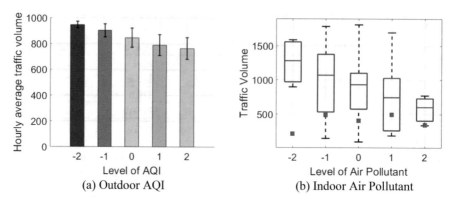

Fig. 5.6 Correlation analysis between the building environmental data and traffic data (-2 stands for the worst level, 0 for the moderate level and 2 for the best level). (**a**) Outdoor AQI. (**b**) Indoor air pollutant

stronger correlations with outdoor traffic volume, while that of the rest is weak. Given this situation, two representative cases are presented for correlations between environmental data and traffic data in the following content.

As shown in Fig. 5.6a, the correlation between the outdoor Air Quality Index (AQI) and traffic volume comes from averaging values of traffic data under air quality conditions after categorization. The air quality values are classified into five levels, which are represented by -2 to 2. We can see that AQI stays lower when the traffic volume is higher. The main reason is that when the daily traffic volume is high, more emissions from vehicles might cause pollution to the air quality directly, thus impacting outdoor AQI.

Also, the correlation between traffic volume and indoor air pollutant levels is estimated. Figure 5.6b shows that the box plot illustrates averaged traffic volume with air pollutant levels after classification. Also, indoor air pollutant increases with the traffic volume. Although we know that indoor environmental factors are not directly correlated with the outdoor traffic volume, we find the indoor environmental data useful in being an indirect sensing data for building occupants [8]. One essential objective of deploying indoor environmental data is to help with traffic prediction when the value of building occupancy shows abnormal signs. For instance, at an emergency evacuation, people inside the building might evacuate rapidly, which will cause higher but false occupancy data produced by smart cameras. If we integrate indoor environmental data into the prediction model, the prediction error in the aforementioned cases can be obliterated with efficiency.

To sum up, there is correlation between the environmental data and the traffic volume; meanwhile, the correlation stays weak. However, both the environmental data and the building data can be applied together in cross-domain traffic prediction.

5.5 Accurate Traffic Prediction with Cross-Domain Learning of Building Data

After analyzing correlation in Sect. 5.4, in this part, we put forward a cross-domain learning approach that forecasts traffic volume with the use of building sensing data. To begin with, we formulate the traffic volume prediction issue of employing cross-domain building sensing data. In response to this challenge, we put forward a cross-domain learning-based recurrent neural network to learn the non-linear, time-varying, and cross-domain building-traffic correlations in pursuit for accurate prediction of traffic volume.

5.5.1 Problem Formulation

In this work, our purpose is to predict traffic volume by applying building sensing data and historical traffic volume data. Suppose there are N types of building sensing data for T time intervals, and we present notations in the following content.

Building data types a building's IoT sensors generate N types of sensing data employed for traffic prediction, including N_o types of occupancy sensing data (*e.g.*, covering different public zones) and N_e types of environmental sensing data (*e.g.*, indoor environmental and outdoor environmental data). Intuitively, $N = N_o + N_e$.

Building sensing data let $x_t(i)$ denote i-th building sensing data at time t and $\mathbf{x}_t = \{x_t(i) | 1 \le i \le N\}$ denote a vector of all building sensing data at time t. Accordingly, $\mathbf{X}_{[1:T]} = [\mathbf{x}_1, \mathbf{x}_2, \ldots, \mathbf{x}_T]_{T \times n}$ denotes a measurement matrix of all building data across T time intervals.

Traffic volume data let y_t represent the traffic volume of a target road segment at time t, $1 \le t \le T - 1$. Correspondingly, $\mathbf{y}_{[1:T-1]}$ denotes a vector of historical traffic volume of the target road segment across $T - 1$ time intervals, where $\mathbf{y} = \{y(j) | 1 \le j \le T - 1\}$.

Future Traffic volume the forecasted traffic volume of a target road is denoted as $\widehat{\mathbf{Y}}_{[T:T+\tau]} = \{y(j) | T \le j \le T + \tau\}$ while using $\mathbf{Y}_{[T:T+\tau]}$ to represent its ground truth, where τ is the time intervals for prediction.

Problem Definition Formally, given n types of building sensing data over T time intervals and historical data of a target road segment over $T - 1$ time intervals, the traffic volume prediction issue for τ future time intervals is defined as

$$\text{Minimize} \left\| \widehat{\mathbf{Y}}_{[T:T+\tau]} - \mathbf{Y}_{[T:T+\tau]} \right\|_F^2, \tag{5.1}$$

$$\text{where} \quad \widehat{\mathbf{Y}}_{[T:T+\tau]} = F\left(\mathbf{y}_{[1:T-1]}, \mathbf{X}_{[1:T]} \right), \tag{5.2}$$

Note that $F(\cdot)$ denotes the non-linear mapping function from building sensing data to traffic data, and a predicting model needs to learn it.

5.5.2   Attention Mechanisms-Based Encoder-Decoder Recurrent Neural Network

To address the cross-domain learning-based traffic volume prediction issue, we put forward BuildSenSys, an LSTM based encoder-decoder architecture with dual-attentions mechanisms. We deploy cross-domain attention on input data to identify the correlations. Also, we pay attention in choosing building sensing data that is the most relevant in the process of forecasting. Then, the temporal attention is used to capture temporal features from historical dependencies. Next, BuildSenSys chooses the most relevant encoder hidden states in all time intervals. Through the integration of the above attention mechanisms with LSTM-based recurrent neural networks, we can jointly promote the train BuildSenSys model with standard back propagation. As a result, BuildSenSys can select the most relevant building sensing data for traffic prediction. Moreover, it is capable of capturing long-term temporal features of traffic volume. The overall framework of BuildSenSys is presented in Fig. 5.7.

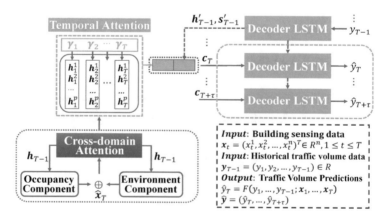

Fig. 5.7 Graphical architecture of cross-domain attention-based recurrent neural networks for cross-domain traffic prediction

Encoder with Cross-Domain Attention

As an LSTM-based recurrent neural network, the encoder in the BuildSenSys framework encodes the input sequence into a feature vector. To forecast cross-domain traffic volume, given N types of building sensing data, the input sequence is denoted as $\mathbf{X} = (\mathbf{x}_1, \ldots, \mathbf{x}_t, \ldots, \mathbf{x}_T)$, where $\mathbf{x}_t \in \mathbb{R}^N$. The hidden state of the encoder at time interval t is computed by

$$\mathbf{h}_t = f_e(\mathbf{h}_{t-1}, \mathbf{x}_t), \tag{5.3}$$

where $\mathbf{h}_{t-1} \in \mathbb{R}^p$ is the previous hidden state of the encoder at time interval $t-1$; p is the size of the hidden state in the encoder, and f_e is an LSTM based recurrent neural network. As LSTMs is capable of learning long-term dependencies, we use the classic LSTM unit with one memory cell as well as three sigmoid gates. At time interval t, the cell state of memory is $\mathbf{s}_t$, the forget gate is $\mathbf{f}_t$, and the input gate is $\mathbf{i}_t$. The encoder LSTM updates its hidden state by

$$\mathbf{f}_t = \sigma\big(\mathbf{W}_f[\mathbf{h}_{t-1}; \mathbf{x}_t] + \mathbf{b}_f\big), \tag{5.4}$$

$$\mathbf{i}_t = \sigma(\mathbf{W}_i[\mathbf{h}_{t-1}; \mathbf{x}_t] + \mathbf{b}_i), \tag{5.5}$$

$$\mathbf{o}_t = \sigma(\mathbf{W}_o[\mathbf{h}_{t-1}; \mathbf{x}_t] + \mathbf{b}_o), \tag{5.6}$$

$$\mathbf{s}_t = \mathbf{f}_t \odot \mathbf{s}_{t-1} + \mathbf{i}_t \odot tanh(\mathbf{W}_s[\mathbf{h}_{t-1}; \mathbf{x}_t] + \mathbf{b}_s), \tag{5.7}$$

$$\mathbf{h}_t = \mathbf{o}_t \odot tanh(\mathbf{s}_t), \tag{5.8}$$

where $[\cdot;\cdot]$ is a concatenation operation; σ is a logistic sigmoid function; $\odot$ is a pointwise multiplication; $\mathbf{W}_f$, $\mathbf{W}_i$, $\mathbf{W}_o$, $\mathbf{W}_s$, $\mathbf{b}_f$, $\mathbf{b}_i$, $\mathbf{b}_o$, and $\mathbf{b}_s$ are the learnable parameters.

Given the fact that visual attention allows human to concentrate on a certain region of images or sentences to create the perception of information, attention mechanism has been made an essential part of the compelling sequence modeling and transduction models [39]. Generally speaking, attention mechanisms are proposed for a soft selection over historical data by calculation and assignment of different weights to them. In this chapter, our purpose is to forecast traffic volume with various data, including building sensing data and historical traffic volume data. In that purpose, cross-domain attention is put forward in order to identify complex building-traffic correlations and promote feature representation of all input data as well. Continuing the study based on the analysis of cross-domain correlation, it is our intent to learn different correlations with the occupancy component as well as environmental component.

Occupancy Component

To forecast traffic volume, we envision a multi-zone scenario, with the j-th zone's occupancy as $\mathbf{x}^j = \left(x_1^j, x_2^j, \ldots, x_t^j\right)^{\top} \in \mathbb{R}^T$ and $1 \leq j \leq N_o$. The cross-domain attention on occupancy components is calculated by referring the previous hidden state $\mathbf{h}_{t-1}$ and previous cell state $\mathbf{s}_{t-1}$ of encoder LSTM as

$$o_t^j = \mathbf{v}_o^{\top} \tanh\left(\mathbf{W}_o[\mathbf{h}_{t-1}; \mathbf{s}_{t-1}] + \mathbf{U}_o \mathbf{x}^j + \mathbf{b}_o\right), \tag{5.9}$$

$$\beta_t^j = \frac{\exp\left(o_t^j\right)}{\sum_{i=1}^{N_o} \exp\left(o_t^i\right)}, \tag{5.10}$$

where $\mathbf{v}_o$, $\mathbf{b}_o \in \mathbb{R}^T$, $\mathbf{W}_o \in \mathbb{R}^{T \times 2p}$ and $\mathbf{U}_o \in \mathbb{R}^{T \times T}$ are learning parameters. By employing another softmax function, we confirm the normalization of all attention weights with occupancy component. Also, we ensure that the total weight for all occupancy input data is 1. With cross-domain attention weights for all public zones, we capture the output vector from the occupancy component at time interval t as

$$\widehat{\mathbf{x}}_t^{occ} = \left(\beta_t^1 x_t^1, \ldots \beta_t^j x_t^j, \ldots \beta_t^{N_o} x_t^{N_o}\right)^{\top}. \tag{5.11}$$

Environmental Component

Let $\mathbf{x}^k$ denote the k-th type of environmental data input, where $\mathbf{x}^k = \left(x_1^k, x_2^k, \ldots, x_t^k\right)^{\top} \in \mathbb{R}^T$ and $1 \leq k \leq N_e$. We deploy the cross-domain attention for the environmental component to adaptively identify the dynamic correlation between traffic volume and k_{th} type of environmental data by

$$e_t^k = \mathbf{v}_e^{\top} \tanh\left(\mathbf{W}_e[\mathbf{h}_{t-1}; \mathbf{s}_{t-1}] + \mathbf{U}_e \mathbf{x}^k + \mathbf{b}_e\right), \tag{5.12}$$

$$\alpha_t^k = \frac{\exp\left(e_t^k\right)}{\sum_{i=1}^{N_e} \exp\left(e_t^i\right)}, \tag{5.13}$$

where $[\cdot; \cdot]$ is a concatenation operation. $\mathbf{v}_e$, $\mathbf{b}_e \in \mathbb{R}^T$, $\mathbf{W}_e \in \mathbb{R}^{T \times 2p}$ and $\mathbf{U}_e \in \mathbb{R}^{T \times T}$ are learnable parameters. By leveraging a softmax function to e_t^k, we obtain the normalized attention weight α_t^k for the k-th environmental data at the time interval t. With cross-domain attention weights for all types of environmental data input, the output vector of the environmental component at time interval t can be adaptively acquired by

$$\widehat{\mathbf{x}}_t^{env} = \left(\alpha_t^1 x_t^1, \ldots \alpha_t^k x_t^k, \ldots \alpha_t^{N_e} x_t^{N_e}\right)^{\boxed{?}}. \tag{5.14}$$

In the end, for encoder LSTM, we adaptively concatenate above output vectors from different components. Also, we extract the final output vector of cross-domain attention mechanism as

$$\widehat{\mathbf{x}}_t = \left[\widehat{\mathbf{x}}_t^{env}; \widehat{\mathbf{x}}_t^{occ}\right], \tag{5.15}$$

where $\widehat{x}_t \in \mathbb{R}^N$. We feed the final output vector $\widehat{\mathbf{x}}_t$ into the encoder LSTM as its new input at time interval t. Consequently, the hidden state of encoder LSTM in Eq. (5.3) is updated by

$$\mathbf{h}_t = f_e(\mathbf{h}_{t-1}, \widehat{\mathbf{x}}_t), \tag{5.16}$$

where f_e is the encoder LSTM network described in Eqs. (5.4)–(5.8).

Decoder with Temporal Attention

For the attention mechanism, the fundamental idea is to distinguish task-related importance of input data in previous time intervals. Also, when calculating attention weights for all the encoder hidden states, the decoder with a temporal attention mechanism can be employed to identify temporal dependency between traffic volume and building data. After the allocation of the temporal attention weights to all the encoder hidden states, decoder LSTM can concentrate on the input data which is the most relevant [39]. To this end, we deploy a temporal attention mechanism which adaptively makes decoder capable of selecting relevant encoder hidden states across each time interval. In the calculation of the attention vector for encoder hidden state at time interval t, the temporal attention mechanism refers to the previous hidden state $\mathbf{h}_{t-1}'$ and previous cell state $\mathbf{s}_{t-1}'$ of decoder LSTM as

$$\mu_t^i = \mathbf{v}_d^{\boxed{?}} \tanh\left(\mathbf{W}_d\left[\mathbf{h}_{t-1}'; \mathbf{s}_{t-1}'\right] + \mathbf{U}_d\mathbf{h}_i + \mathbf{b}_d\right), 1 \le i \le T, \tag{5.17}$$

$$\gamma_t^i = \frac{\exp\left(\mu_t^i\right)}{\sum_{l=1}^{T} \exp\left(\mu_t^l\right)}, \tag{5.18}$$

where $[\cdot]$ represents a concatenation operation; $\mathbf{v}_d, \mathbf{b}_d \in \mathbb{R}^p$; $\mathbf{W}_d \in \mathbb{R}^{p \times 2q}$; $\mathbf{U}_d \in \mathbb{R}^{p \times p}$ are learning parameters. Through a softmax layer, the temporal attention weight γ_t^i is computed for the i-th encoder hidden state at time interval t. As the component of the input sequence is temporally mapped to encoders, the context vector $\mathbf{c}_t$ is calculated as a weighted sum of all encoder hidden states by

$$\mathbf{c}_t = \sum_{i=1}^{T} \gamma_t^i \mathbf{h}_i. \tag{5.19}$$

Aimed at identifying the dynamic temporal correlation in traffic volume data, we integrate the context vector with $\mathbf{y} = (y_1, \ldots, y_t, \ldots, y_{T-1})$ as follows:

$$\widetilde{y}_{t-1} = \widetilde{w}^{\boxtimes}\left[y_{t-1}; \mathbf{c}_{t-1}\right] + \widetilde{b}, \tag{5.20}$$

$$\mathbf{h}_t' = f_d\left(\mathbf{h}_{t-1}', \widetilde{y}_{t-1}\right), \tag{5.21}$$

where f_d is an LSTM-based recurrent neural network as decoder; $\widetilde{w} \in \mathbb{R}^{p+1}$ and $\widetilde{b} \in \mathbb{R}$ are parameters to map the concatenation result to the size of the decoder input. Given the fact that LSTM unit in the decoder shares nearly the same structure with encoder (referred to Eqs. 5.4–5.8), the update process of f_d is left out. Finally, attention mechanisms based on recurrent neural network concatenates the context vector $\mathbf{c}_T$ with decoder hidden state $\mathbf{h}_T'$, predicting the traffic volume at time interval T as

$$\widehat{y}_T = \mathbf{v}_y^{\boxtimes}\left(\mathbf{W}_y\left[\mathbf{c}_T; \mathbf{h}_T'\right] + \mathbf{b}_y\right) + b, \tag{5.22}$$

where $\left[\mathbf{c}_T; \mathbf{h}_T'\right] \in \mathbb{R}^{p+q}$ is a concatenation operation; $\mathbf{W}_y \in \mathbb{R}^{q \times (p+q)}$ and $\mathbf{b}_y \in \mathbb{R}^q$ together map the concatenation to the size of decoder hidden states. The outcome in the end is produced by a mapping function with weights $\mathbf{v}_y \in \mathbb{R}^q$ and $\mathbf{b}_y \in \mathbb{R}$.

5.6 Performance Evaluation

To evaluate the performance of BuildSenSys, we design a prototype system, as illustrated in Fig. 5.8. To begin with, the cross-domain learning-based RNN model is developed by applying a training set of building sensing data and traffic data. BuildSenSys is capable of forecasting traffic volume on nearby roads merely with the input of building sensing data. And then, the experimental settings are introduced, including dataset, baseline methods, evaluation metrics, and model parameters. Next, extensive experimental studies are conducted on BuildSenSys.

5.6.1 Experimental Methodology and Settings

Dataset Description

After observation and research, traffic data from nearby roads and relevant building sensing data are chosen to be the training input data for the BuildSenSys model. As

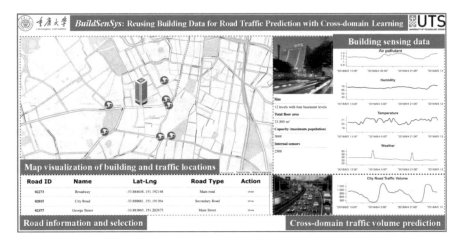

Fig. 5.8 The prototype system of BuildSenSys for data visualization and traffic prediction

for traffic data, we gather traffic volume count data from the official website of the Department of Roads and Maritime Services, New South Wales State [42]. The traffic volume data is generated by roadside collection devices, which records vehicles passing by with the interval of a hour. Among four roads near the building, we collect traffic volume data of 12 months (from 2018/1/1 to 2018/12/31). As for building sensing data, it is gathered from three types of ways, *i.e.*, building occupancy, building environmental data, outdoor environmental data. The generator of building occupancy data is camera sensors distributed at Point-of-Interest Zones inside the building, which are processed by the PLCount algorithm [43] for overall building occupancy. Then, the building environmental data consists of CO_2 concentration, building humidity, O_2 concentration, building temperature, and building air pollution. Meanwhile, the outdoor environmental data is collected from the rooftop weather station of our building, including outdoor temperature, rainfall, and wind speed. Apart from that, as vehicle emission directly impacts outdoor air quality, the hourly AQI data from the Bureau of Meteorology's official website is applied. In addition, we integrate the AQI data with outdoor environmental data to forecast traffic volume. In the end, for training and tests, all building sensing data and traffic volume data are coordinated with the interval of an hour.

Baseline Methods

To assess the performance of BuildSenSys in a comprehensive manner, we compare it with seven baseline methods as follows.

- HA [45]: The historical average (HA) model fulfills the prediction of the traffic volume by averaging the historical value of each corresponding time interval.

- ARIMA [46]: The auto-regressive integrated moving average model is a classic scheme to make a prediction for future time series.
- VAR [47]: The Vector Auto-regressive model serves as an extension of the univariate auto-regressive model, which has been widely applied for multivariate time series forecasting.
- LWR [8]: The Locally Weighted Linear Regression model is non-parametric, performing regressions around points of interest.
- LSTM [37]: The Long Short-Term Memory network is a variation of recurrent neural networks developed to prevent the vanishing gradient issue.
- *Seq2Seq* [48]: It is the Sequence to Sequence model based on an encoder-decoder architecture and recurrent neural networks, which is composed of three parts, *i.e.*, encoder, context vector, and decoder.
- *Seq2Seqw/attn* [48]: It is the Sequence to Sequence model with a temporal attention mechanism.

Note that each baseline method takes a day as a critical feature of input data. Moreover, they apply this feature for traffic prediction from different perspectives. For instance, the HA uses the time of the day with statistical regression, while ARIMA and VAR process it with auto-regression. Additionally, the neural networks of the LSTM and Seq2Seq models learn the time of the day as a feature with their hidden states. In the BuildSenSys model, we further solve the time of the day by deploying a temporal attention mechanism to acquire temporal features of traffic data.

Evaluation Metrics and Parameter Settings

To evaluate the prediction accuracy, we deploy three widely applied evaluation metrics, *i.e.*, Mean Absolute Error (MAE), Root Mean Squared Error (RMSE), and Mean Absolute Percentage Error (MAPE) [49]. Both MAE and RMSE are scale-dependent metrics, while MAPE is a scale-independent metric. Particularly, MAE measures the average magnitude of errors in prediction results as Eq. (5.23). RMSE measures the square root of the average squared differences between prediction results and ground truth as Eq. (5.24). MAPE measures the size of errors in percentage terms for quantifying the prediction accuracy as Eq. (5.25).

$$\mathbf{MAE} = \frac{1}{\tau} \sum_{[T:T+\tau] \in \mathbb{R}^{T}} \left| \mathbf{Y}_{[T:T+\tau]} - \widehat{\mathbf{Y}}_{[T:T+\tau]} \right|, \qquad (5.23)$$

$$\mathbf{RMSE} = \sqrt{\frac{1}{\tau} \sum_{[T:T+\tau] \in \mathbb{R}^{T}} \left(\mathbf{Y}_{[T:T+\tau]} - \widehat{\mathbf{Y}}_{[T:T+\tau]} \right)^{2}}, \qquad (5.24)$$

$$\mathbf{MAPE} = \frac{1}{\tau} \sum\nolimits_{[T:T+\tau] \in \mathbb{R}^T} \left| \frac{\mathbf{Y}_{[T:T+\tau]} - \widehat{\mathbf{Y}}_{[T:T+\tau]}}{\mathbf{Y}_{[T:T+\tau]}} \right|, \qquad (5.25)$$

where $\widehat{\mathbf{Y}}_{[T:T+\tau]}$ and $\mathbf{Y}_{[T:T+\tau]}$ are the prediction results of traffic volume from time interval T to $T + \tau$, respectively.

In this work, we implement the BuildSenSys model with Tensorflow framework and train it together with other baseline models on two NVIDIA Quadro P5000 GPUs with 16 GB memory. In model training, the tunable hyperparameters for BuildSenSys include the time window L (*i.e.*, the length of input data in hours), the length of predicting window τ (the number of days for future traffic prediction), and the size of hidden states in encoder/decoder (denoted by h_a and h_b, respectively). For LSTM, Seq2Seq, Seq2Seqw/attn, and BuildSenSys model, h_a and h_b are tuned from 32, 64, 126, 256 to 512, respectively; L is tuned from 4, 6, 12, 18, 24 to 48 (h), respectively. In the training session, the batch size, the learning rate, and the dropout rate are set to 256, 0.001, and 0.2, respectively. Also, the Adam is the optimizer for the BuildSenSys model. Regarding all the building sensing data and traffic volume data, we chronologically split the dataset into the training set (70%), validation set (10%), and test set (20%).

5.6.2   Experimental Evaluations

Evaluations on Overall Prediction Results

First, we evaluate the overall prediction accuracy of BuildSenSys by comparing prediction results with the ground truth on four different types of roads, *i.e.*, roads A (minor highway), B (major highway), C (main street), and D (primary street). Figure 5.9 indicates the predicted traffic volume and the ground truth over 12 days. As illustrated in Fig. 5.9a–d, the prediction results are hugely close to the ground truth. Therefore, BuildSenSys can effectively capture the cross-domain correlations and temporal dependencies in reusing building data for traffic volume prediction. Additionally, the aforementioned results show that the distance between a road segment and the building can significantly impact the prediction accuracy. For instance, as shown in Fig. 5.9b, prediction errors on road B are much larger than those of roads A, C, and D. As illustrated in Table 5.1, among all four roads, road B is the furthest to the building, *e.g.* 3.0 km.

Comparisons with Baselines

The performance of BuildSenSys is quantified by comparing it with seven baseline methods, using three evaluation metrics. The evaluation experiments are performed on four roads. The basic parameter settings of baseline methods are adopted from

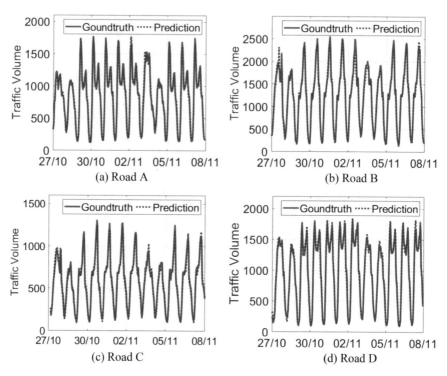

Fig. 5.9 Comparison between predicted traffic volume of BuildSenSys and the ground truth on four different roads. (**a**) Road A. (**b**) Road B. (**c**) Road C. (**d**) Road D

reference [50]. For BuildSenSys, we set the length of input time window $L = 24$ and set the size of hidden states in both encoder LSTM and decoder LSTM as 128 and 512, respectively. Table 5.2 presents the comparison of the performance between BuildSenSys and all baseline methods.

Generally speaking, BuildSenSys has the best performance in prediction accuracy with the lowest RMSE at 30.49%, lowest MAE at 20.29%, and lowest MAPE at 2.05%. It is incredible that it outperforms the best prediction of Seq2Seqw/attn by up to 46.2% in RMSE on road D, 45.6% in MAE on road C, and 65.3% in MAPE on road D. In contrast, the LWR model, which also employs building data for the prediction of traffic volume [8], has the worst performance with RMSE at 239.48%, MAE at 190.79% and MAPE at 22.13% on road D. It is because the LWR model [8] is based on the assumption of linear building-traffic correlation. Also, the actual building-traffic correlations have been proved to be non-linear, time-varying, which is far more complex than the linear model. For other baseline methods applying historical traffic data, we present the detailed comparison results as follows.

First, ARIMA and VAR methods have the worst performance in the prediction because of their incompetency to forecast precisely in the long run, particularly on the 'turning points' (*e.g.*, rush hours). For the Historical Average method, although it is the most naive scheme, it outperforms ARIMA and VAR for the following

Table 5.2 Performance comparison with baseline methods on different roads

Models	Road A			Road B			Road C			Road D		
	RMSE	MAE	MAPE (%)	RMSE	MAE	MAPE (%)	RMSE	MAE	MAPE (%)	RMSE	MAE	MAPE (%)
LWR	244.51	155.69	22.78	257.86	176.94	25.91	206.52	176.35	22.61	239.48	190.79	22.13
ARIMA	152.74	141.22	14.51	192.73	142.66	15.58	149.11	138.09	14.70	173.32	124.31	14.22
VAR	117.35	110.83	12.99	120.37	116.9	13.06	98.65	94.15	11.05	124.61	110.68	12.46
HA	108.01	89.72	11.37	125.88	93.57	12.78	90.71	65.20	10.26	117.03	89.45	11.12
LSTM	74.37	58.30	9.83	91.71	72.47	11.04	70.71	58.9	9.31	90.18	67.37	10.39
Seq2Seq	72.86	51.06	7.40	89.25	64.78	8.29	66.19	53.32	7.12	87.22	63.20	8.14
Seq2Seqw/attn (128)	59.58	45.18	6.89	73.5	59.12	7.75	54.07	46.98	6.73	81.15	56.95	7.49
Seq2Seqw/attn (512)	50.18	39.74	5.71	68.71	50.71	6.97	45.51	37.33	5.49	65.3	46.72	6.4
BuildSenSys (128)	46.89	33.35	4.85	60.18	41.89	4.36	36.42	27.14	5.25	50.45	38.56	5.2
BuildSenSys (512)	33.08	22.78	2.05	58.33	39.71	3.64	30.49	20.29	2.51	35.10	25.75	2.22

reasons. Traffic volumes have daily patterns and weekly patterns which are relatively stable in our dataset. For HA method, there could be some unsatisfied prediction results with many errors, including holidays, extreme weather, and social events. That is because it fails to forecast traffic volume of irregular patterns.

Second, the Recurrent Neural Network-based methods, *i.e.*, LSTM, Seq2Seq, and Seq2Seqw/attn, show superior performance with MAEs lower than 70 and RMSEs lower than 90. Specifically, the performances of LSTM and Seq2Seq are similar, while Seq2Seq surpasses the LSTM by 2.35% and 2.43% in MAPE metric on Road D and Road A, respectively. When it comes to Seq2Seq model based on the encoder-decoder architecture, it encodes the input traffic volume data into a feature vector, from which the decoder produces the fixed-length prediction iteratively. However, the performance of encoder-decoder networks will deteriorate quickly when increasing the lengths of the input sequence data. Both BuildSenSys and Seq2Seqw/attn apply temporal attention mechanisms. Therefore, the decoders of the above models can choose the most relevant encoder hidden states adaptively to improve prediction accuracy. The attention mechanism is validated to be effective, since Seq2Seqw/attn and BuildSenSys have higher accuracy in prediction. With 512 hidden states, both Seq2Seqw/attn and BuildSenSys hugely promote the prediction accuracy in comparison with models which have 128 hidden states. Moreover, as the cross-domain attention makes progress in looking into the correlation between building occupancy and traffic volume, the prediction accuracy of BuildSenSys is further promoted. Compared with Seq2Seqw/attn, BuildSenSys shows 32.3% and 37.8% improvements in MAE and RMSE, respectively. To sum up, in comparison with RNN-based baseline methods, BuildSenSys jointly applies cross-domain attention and temporal attention to learn cross-domain, time-varying, and non-linear building-traffic correlations in an adaptive manner. To conclude, BuildSenSys surpasses all baseline methods with up to 65.3% accuracy improvement (*e.g.*, 2.2% of MAPE) in the prediction of nearby traffic volume.

Evaluation of Parameters

We further evaluate the influence of parameters in RNN networks on BuildSenSys's performance, as BuildSenSys is based on RNN. The parameters include the size of the hidden states in the encoder (h_a) and decoder (h_b), the lengths of the input time window (L) and the prediction window (τ). Additionally, three RNN-based baseline methods, *i.e.*, LSTM, Seq2Seq, and Seq2Seqw/attn, are applied as the benchmarks.

1. *Size of hidden states*: Following reference [51], we set the size of hidden states in both encoder and decoder as the same, *i.e.*, $h_a = h_b$. We let the value of h_a (h_b) range from 32 to 64, 128, 256, and 512 with a grid search. As illustrated in Fig. 5.10a–c, BuildSenSys surpasses LSTM, Seq2Seq, and Seq2Seqw/attn in all settings of hidden states in terms of RMSE, MAE, and MAPE. In addition, the experimental results indicate that the prediction accuracy of BuildSenSys improves with the larger size of hidden states. Generally, BuildSenSys achieves

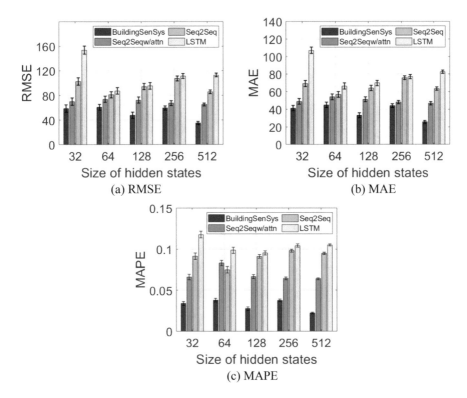

Fig. 5.10 Impact of the hidden states on the performance of BuildSenSys and three RNN-based baseline methods. (**a**) RMSE. (**b**) MAE. (**c**) MAPE

the best prediction results (*i.e.*, RMSE ≤ 33, MAE ≤ 25, and MAPE ≤ 0.22) when $h_a = h_b = 512$.

2. *Length of input time window*: The time window L denotes the number of hours of historical data fed into the traffic prediction models (1 h as the basic unit). To evaluate the impact of L, we let its value range from 4 to 6, 12, 18, 24, and 48 h. Then, the historical data of the last 4, 6, 12, 18, 24, and 48 h will be applied for the prediction of traffic volume in the next hour. As shown in Fig. 5.11a–c, the prediction accuracy of all RNN-based methods rises with the greater length of the time window. In the meantime, the performance of RNN-based methods also declines when the time window is too large, *e.g.*, $L = 48$. Accordingly, BuildSenSys achieves the best performance when $L = 6$, *i.e.*, RMSE $= 31.7$, MAE $= 24$, and MAPE $= 0.019$.

3. *Length of prediction window*: We evaluate the prediction accuracy of BuildSenSys in the matter of the length (τ) of the prediction window. We change τ from 1 day to 12 days. From Fig. 5.12a–c, we notice that the RMSE, MAE, and MAPE boost with the greater length of predicting windows, *i.e.*, the prediction accuracy declines with the longer predicting windows. Nevertheless, except for Road B, the speed of decline of prediction accuracy is quite slow. Hence,

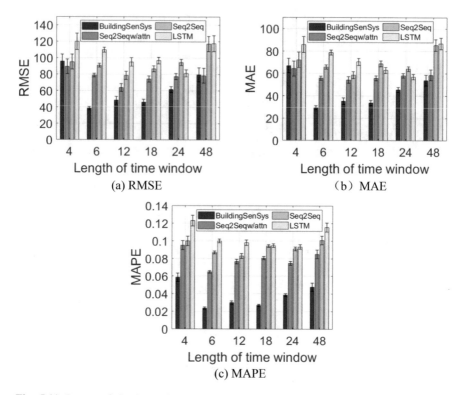

Fig. 5.11 Impact of the input time window on the performance of BuildSenSys and three RNN-based baseline methods. (**a**) RMSE. (**b**) MAE. (**c**) MAPE

BuildSenSys can predict in a stable way with high accuracy by reusing building data, *e.g.*, RMSE and MAE increase from 36 to 52 and 28–30, respectively. In the meantime, as Road B is the furthest road from the building, its building-traffic correlation is not as strong as other roads. Hence, the prediction errors on Road B augment hugely with the increasing value of τ.

Evaluation of Cross-Domain Learning

BuildSenSys includes a cross-domain attention mechanism and a temporal attention mechanism, which jointly extract spatio-temporal features from building-traffic correlations. To evaluate the influence of components on the performance, we perform an ablation study on BuildSenSys with its variants as follows.

- *B*, *i.e.*, BuildSenSys applies cross-domain attention and temporal attention to jointly learn building-traffic correlations and temporal correlations with both occupancy data and environmental data.
- Bwo/o, a variant of B without occupancy component.

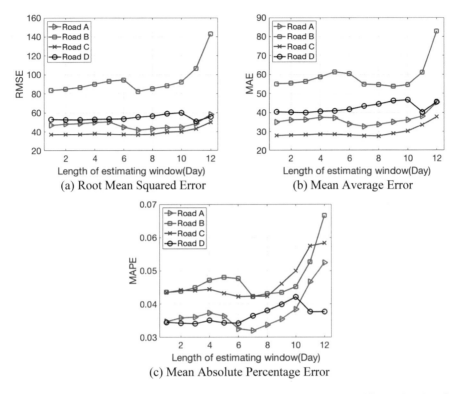

Fig. 5.12 Prediction accuracy of BuildSenSys on four roads by varying different lengths of predicting window. (**a**) Root mean squared error. (**b**) Mean average error. (**c**) Mean absolute percentage error

- Bwo/e, a variant of B without environmental component.
- Bwo/c, a variant of B without cross-domain attention, which only deploys temporal attention to capture temporal dependencies of building sensing data and traffic volume data.
- Bwo/t, a variant of B without temporal attention, which only applies cross-domain attention to learn cross-domain building-traffic correlations.

To begin with, we evaluate the performance of different components of BuildSenSys by changing the size of hidden states. As illustrated in Fig. 5.13, BuildSenSys has the best performance, while Bwo/t shows the worst performance as it lacks temporal correlations for traffic prediction. In the meantime, the prediction accuracy of both Bwo/o and Bwo/e is better than that of Bwo/c. It shows that cross-domain learning with building data can promote the overall performance successfully. Additionally, as shown in Fig. 5.13a–c, the prediction accuracy of Bwo/e is higher than that of Bwo/o. This result indicates that the building occupancy data makes more contribution to cross-domain traffic prediction in comparison with building environmental data.

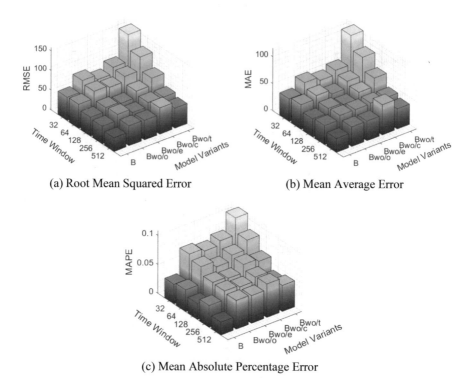

(a) Root Mean Squared Error   (b) Mean Average Error

(c) Mean Absolute Percentage Error

Fig. 5.13 Performance comparison among different variants of BuildSenSys with varying size of hidden states. (**a**) Root mean squared error. (**b**) Mean average error. (**c**) Mean absolute percentage error

Next, we evaluate the performance of different components of BuildSenSys by varying the length of the input time window. As illustrated in Fig. 5.14, the performance of Bwo/t has huge deterioration as it has no temporal attention to learn the temporal correlations in building data and traffic data. As a result, the prediction accuracy of Bwo/t is the worst, *e.g.*, 115% at the RMSE, 80% at the MAE, and 10% at the MAPE, respectively. Simultaneously, BuildSenSys shows the best prediction accuracy when the input time window is 6.

To conclude, the aforementioned results show that each component in cross-domain learning contributes in promoting the prediction accuracy of BuildSenSys. In particular, the occupancy component and the environmental component play a complementary role to each other in reusing building data to predict nearby traffic volume. In addition, it is hugely meaningful to jointly employ cross-domain attention and temporal attention in cross-domain learning of building data. Attention mechanisms have unique contribution to the promotion of prediction accuracy, *e.g.*, up to 45.5% improvement by temporal attention and 30.9% improvement by cross-domain attention.

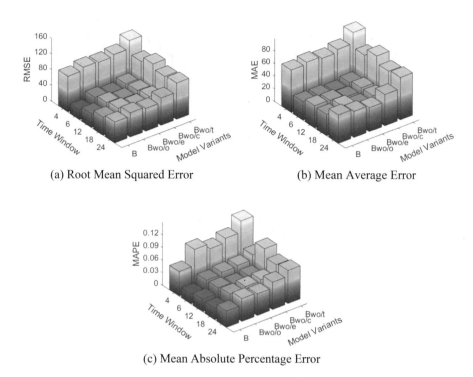

(a) Root Mean Squared Error   (b) Mean Average Error

(c) Mean Absolute Percentage Error

Fig. 5.14 Performance comparison among different variants of BuildSenSys with varying length of the time window (in hours). (**a**) Root mean squared error. (**b**) Mean average error. (**c**) Mean absolute percentage error

Evaluation of Attention Weight

1. *Cross-domain attention*: The attention weights of the proposed traffic prediction model is analyzed in two folds, *i.e.*, cross-domain attention weight and temporal attention weight. Firstly, as the correlations between traffic volume data and different building sensing data are non-linear, BuildSenSys applies a cross-domain attention mechanism to realize the non-linear mapping from building sensing data to traffic data in predicting traffic volume. To show the different attention weights from different types of building sensing data, we perform substantial experiments to analyze their attention weights. As illustrated in Fig. 5.15a, these ten groups of attention weights correspond to ten types of sensing data, including building occupancy (B_occ), CO_2 concentration (B_carb), building humidity (B_hum), O_2 concentration (B_oxy), building temperature (B_temp), building air pollution (B_ap), as well as outdoor temperature (O_temp), rainfall (O_rain) and air quality index (O_aqi). The box-plot in Fig. 5.15a compares the distributions of attention weights by each type of building sensing data.

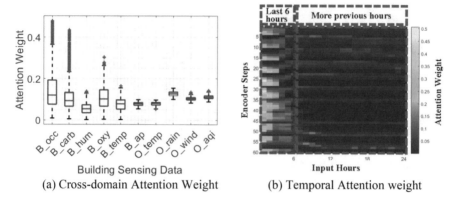

(a) Cross-domain Attention Weight   (b) Temporal Attention weight

Fig. 5.15 Visualization of cross-domain attention and temporal attention. (**a**) Cross-domain attention weight. (**b**) Temporal attention weight

As demonstrated in Fig. 5.15a, different types of building sensing data have their own contribution to traffic prediction while building occupancy data has the highest attention weights across all steps in prediction. Particularly, the whiskers (*i.e.*, lines extending above and below each box) of B_occ have the widest range (from 0.01 to 0.36). B_occ covers the furthest adjacent values of attention weight, revealing the importance of building occupancy data in cross-domain traffic prediction. Additionally, the B_occ and B_carb have the largest group of outliers with the highest values (*i.e.*, up to 0.48 and 0.39, respectively). It shows that they have stronger correlations with traffic data and higher attention weights in traffic prediction. In the end, the median values (*i.e.*, the central marks) of attention weights boxes are approximately close to each other, showing that all types of building data make non-negligible contributions to traffic predictions.

To sum up, the experimental results above demonstrate that, each building data has its own contribution to promoting the prediction accuracy of BuildSenSys. In the meantime, the building occupancy data and the environmental data are complementary to each other in reusing building data for traffic prediction.

2. *Temporal attention*: We further delve into how the temporal attention mechanism captures the correlations between predicted traffic values and historical traffic data. More specifically, we perform the exploring experiment to visualize how BuildSenSys assigns different attention weights to the historical traffic data in the time window '*L*.' As illustrated in the experimental setups, the input time window '*L*' represents the length of input data measured in hours, and we set '*L*' as 24 (hours) in the following experiment.

As a result, the heat map in Fig. 5.15b visualizes the temporal attention weights over 24 h and 60 predicting steps. We split the input time window into two sorts, *i.e.*, the latest 6 h and more previous (last 6–24) hours. The two categories have a huge difference in the allocated attention weights. For the input data of the latest 6 h, BuildSenSys assigns more attention weight to them, as each hour's data has up to 0.5 attention weight. In contrast, most input data in the last 6–24 h have peculiarly small values of attention weights (under 0.05). The above result indicates that the temporal attention mechanism in BuildSenSys would concentrate more on the latest 6 h of the input data. At the same time, since all of the temporal attention weights sum to 1, with the longer input time windows (*e.g.*, 12, 18, 24, and 48 in our ablation studies), the attention weight shared by the latest 6 h would be less. In such cases, BuildSenSys will be unable to concentrate on the most recent data particularly. However, it will be capable of processing the temporal correlations for traffic volume prediction. Therefore, the prediction accuracy of BuildSenSys will be impacted, which is verified by the evaluation results in the previous experimental studies.

Extensive Evaluations of Comparison

Baseline Methods with the Weekday's Data and the Weekend's Data

To delve into the influence of data patterns on the traffic prediction results, extensive experiments are conducted by employing two different models for the prediction of traffic volumes on weekdays and weekends. To start with, a distinct daily average of traffic data is visualized on a target road in Fig. 5.16a. Different colors represent the average values of 1-year traffic data on every single day of the week. Note that the traffic volumes on weekdays and weekends follow two different patterns; the peak hours range from 8 a.m. to 10 a.m. and 4–7 p.m. On weekends, the range for peak hours is longer, *i.e.*, 12 a.m. to 6 p.m. We will study whether employing two different models of BuildSenSys would affect the overall results of traffic volume prediction.

The basic settings in this experiment is the same as that of experiments in 7. The only difference is that the traffic data of a year is divided into two groups (*i.e.*, weekdays and weekends); we train one BuildSenSys model for each group. Meanwhile, a BuildSenSys model applying the whole dataset is developed, and the total epochs for all models are set as 2500. The prediction results of one-model prediction and two-model prediction are shown in Fig. 5.16b, c. Weekday represents a special model of BuildSenSys that is trained only with weekday data for prediction of the data on weekdays. Comparably, Weekend stands for another special model of BuildSenSys which trains only with weekend data to predict the data on weekends. As shown in Fig. 5.16b, c, we compare the prediction accuracy of the Weekday model, the Weekend model, Seq2Seq model, and BuildSenSys model. Compared with the Seq2Seq model, the results indicate that both the Weekday model and the Weekend model can have improvements in prediction accuracy. However, the combined prediction results remain unsatisfactory with even lower accuracy in comparison with the Weekday model. In the meantime, by applying a temporal attention mechanism, BuildSenSys can learn the influence of historical data on the predicting target dynamically, thus surpassing both the Weekday model and the Weekend model. The experimental results also confirm that breaking the continuity

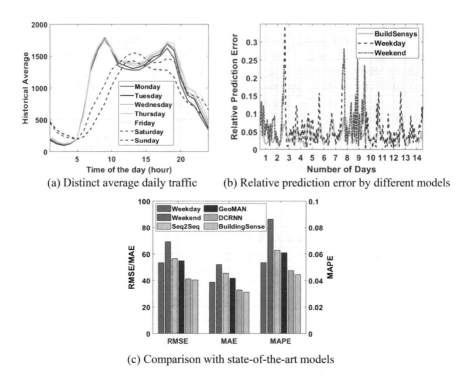

(a) Distinct average daily traffic   (b) Relative prediction error by different models

(c) Comparison with state-of-the-art models

Fig. 5.16 Performance comparison with the Weekday model and Weekend model. (**a**) Distinct average daily traffic. (**b**) Relative prediction error by different models. (**c**) Comparison with state-of-the-art models

of the dataset in the temporal dimension will weaken the performance of temporal attention mechanisms.

Comparison with State-of-the-Art Methods Based on Different Data Sources

To investigate how different data sources affect the traffic prediction results, three baseline methods are used for comparison. Among these baseline methods, the Sequence to Sequence model (Seq2Seq) [48] applies traffic volume data on one road for prediction. The Multi-level Attention Networks for Geospatial Sensors (GeoMAN) [51] exploits the data of one road along with the weather data. Diffusion Convolutional Recurrent Neural Network (DCRNN) [52] leverages the sensing data from multiple roads with the road graph. In this work, BuildSenSys employs building sensing data to predict the traffic volume on nearby roads. The experimental results in Fig. 5.16c show that BuildSenSys has the best performance, even when compared with DCRNN which leverages traffic data from ten road segments for the prediction of traffic volume on the target road. The GeoMAN outperforms Seq2Seq, as it considers both spatial and temporal attention with weather data and historical road data for traffic prediction. At the same time, DCRNN further promotes the prediction accuracy by applying both diffusion convolution and sequence to sequence learning framework on traffic volume data of multiple roads with sensor topology information. The results also verify the practicability and effectiveness of cross-domain traffic prediction in reusing building sensing data.

5.7 Discussion

In this work, in order to forecast the traffic volume on nearby roads, we delve into the possibility of reusing building sensing data. Despite the progress we have made in this new direction, there are still several issues to be further examined as follows.

5.7.1 Applicable Conditions of BuildSenSys

There are a few issues that needs to be discussed: (1) what buildings are appropriate for precise traffic sensing and prediction, and (2) what kind of real-world applications could benefit from cross-domain traffic prediction by reusing building sensing data. With our progress in previous studies, a rough summary of the three critical factors of a building for cross-domain traffic prediction is made, including location, capacity and building types. First, human movement patterns (including traffic) among urban sites are impacted by buildings, which can 'temporarily hold' human mobility [6]. Hence, buildings close to roads are preferred in traffic sensing, for they would have higher probability to affect human mobility on the roads [6]. Second, the capacity of a building, *i.e.*, the volume of occupants it can hold, is critical for accurate cross-domain traffic sensing. For example, Zheng et al. [8] showed that a commercial building with a capacity of 10,000 occupants can affect the traffic on nearby roads with substantial evidence. Third, the types of buildings would affect the applicable conditions of BuildSenSys. Buildings of different types differ in the patterns of occupancy dynamics, which will affect building-traffic correlations in a direct way. Therefore, we believe that commercial building (*e.g.*, office buildings and retail buildings) is the first choice for performing cross-domain traffic sensing with BuildSenSys. Practically, BuildSenSys can be applied in various real-world applications. For instance, BuildSenSys can be employed to provide real-time traffic volume data to help with the control of intelligent traffic lights [53, 54]. Additionally, BuildSenSys can also be leveraged in traffic management systems where accurate traffic predictions are required [55].

5.7.2   Sensing Coverage of BuildSenSys

In this chapter, BuildSenSys is a proof-of-concept in reusing building data for traffic sensing. As illustrated in Sect. 5.6, the prediction accuracy of BuildSenSys is related to the building-traffic correlation of a road. Therefore, we further perform experiments to analyze the coverage of cross-domain traffic prediction by reusing building sensing data. Particularly, as shown in Fig. 5.17, we calculate the correlations between building occupancy and traffic data on nearby roads by employing the Pearson Correlation Coefficient. And then, the building-traffic correlations is further applied as the index of sensing coverage of BuildSenSys. Figure 5.17 demonstrates that BuildSenSys generally has a prediction coverage within 5 km to the building.

5.7.3   Extension to Large-Scale Scenarios

As mentioned above, the BuildSenSys system is capable of predicting traffic volume for road segments within 5 km of the building. To extend this coverage of traffic predictions to a larger scale, it is required to incorporate more sensing data in correlation with traffic volume. Intuitively, traffic data of road segments in the same district would have spatial and temporal correlations [23, 56]. For instance, Liu et al. [27, 57] estimated traffic conditions on different road segments with GPS data from bus riders. In our future work, we will further leverage the aforementioned correlations, multi-road, and multi-region to broaden the coverage of BuildSenSys in traffic sensing and prediction. Additionally, the pervasive street cameras serve as a cost-efficient data source to aggregate urban crowd flow, which may be correlated with traffic volume on nearby roads directly or indirectly. Existing works in computer vision have put forward highly effective approaches to generate density maps

Fig. 5.17 Illustrations of prediction coverage by BuildSenSys

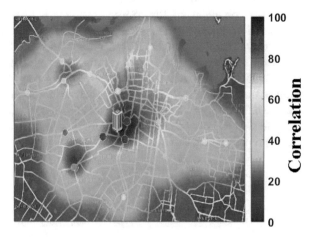

[58] and realized accurate crowd counting [59], which is promising to make contribution in cross-domain traffic sensing and prediction.

5.7.4 Privacy and Security of Building Data

As smart buildings produce large amount of IoT data, protecting privacy become an important task when reusing building data. In our work, data provider ensures the anonymity of the building datasets, including occupancy data and environmental data. Therefore, these data will be harmful in jeopardizing people's privacy, as no personal information can be traced. Also, since facial recognition is not feasible at people counters (cameras), so personal privacy leakage from the building occupancy data would be less likely to come true. Additionally, we can use existing privacy protection methods [60, 61] to avoid privacy leakage during the utilization of building sensing data.

5.8 Conclusion

In this work, we have put forward BuildSenSys, a building sensing data-based traffic volume prediction system with cross-domain learning. We have performed a comprehensive experimental analysis on building-traffic correlations by applying real-world datasets from multiple sources. They have shown that building data is hugely related to traffic data. Then, we have put forward a cross-domain learning-based RNN with cross-domain and temporal attention mechanisms to cooperatively identify building-traffic correlations for accurate traffic prediction. Additionally, we have implemented a prototype system of BuildSenSys and conducted a large number of experiments. The experimental results prove that BuildSenSys outperforms seven baseline methods with up to 65.3% accuracy improvement in the prediction of nearby traffic volume. This work can pave new path for the reuse of building sensing data for traffic sensing, thus revealing an interconnection between smart buildings and intelligent transportation.

References

1. A.P. Plageras, K.E. Psannis, C. Stergiou, et al., Efficient IoT-based sensor BIG Data collection–processing and analysis in smart buildings. Futur. Gener. Comput. Syst. **82**, 349–357 (2018)
2. O. Bates, A. Friday, Beyond data in the smart city: repurposing existing campus IoT. IEEE Pervas. Comput. **16**(2), 54–60 (2017)
3. N. Nesa, I. Banerjee, IoT-based sensor data fusion for occupancy sensing using Dempster–Shafer evidence theory for smart buildings. IEEE Intern. Things J. **4**(5), 1563–1570 (2017)

4. T. C. Team, A to Z of smart buildings (2019), https://www.comfyapp.com/blog/d-data/. Accessed Aug 2019
5. D. Snoonian, Smart buildings. IEEE Spectr. **40**(8), 18–23 (2003)
6. Z. Zheng, F. Wang, D. Wang, et al., Buildings affect mobile patterns: developing a new urban mobility model. Paper presented at Proceedings of the 5th Conference on Systems for Built Environments, 7–8 November 2018
7. H. Rashid, N. Batra, P. Singh, Rimor: towards identifying anomalous appliances in buildings. Paper presented at Proceedings of the 5th Conference on Systems for Built Environments, 7–8 November 2018
8. Z. Zheng, D. Wang, J. Pei, et al., Urban traffic prediction through the second use of inexpensive big data from buildings. Paper presented at Proceedings of the 25th ACM International on Conference on Information and Knowledge Management, 24–28 October 2016
9. D. Jo, B. Yu, H. Jeon, et al., Image-to-image learning to predict traffic speeds by considering area-wide spatio-temporal dependencies. IEEE Trans. Veh. Technol. **68**(2), 1188–1197 (2018)
10. N.E. Klepeis, W.C. Nelson, W.R. Ott, et al., The National Human Activity Pattern Survey (NHAPS): a resource for assessing exposure to environmental pollutants. J. Expos. Sci. Environ. Epidemiol. **11**(3), 231–252 (2001)
11. X. Zhan, Y. Zheng, X. Yi, et al., Citywide traffic volume estimation using trajectory data. IEEE Trans. Knowl. Data Eng. **29**(2), 272–285 (2016)
12. D. Deng, C. Shahabi, U. Demiryurek, et al., Latent space model for road networks to predict time-varying traffic. Paper presented at Proceedings of the 22nd ACM SIGKDD international conference on knowledge discovery and data mining, 13–17 August 2016
13. A.M. Nagy, V. Simon, Survey on traffic prediction in smart cities. Pervas. Mob. Comput. **50**, 148–163 (2018)
14. J. Tang, G. Zhang, Y. Wang, et al., A hybrid approach to integrate fuzzy C-means based imputation method with genetic algorithm for missing traffic volume data estimation. Transport. Res. C. Emerg. Technol. **51**, 29–40 (2015)
15. T. Idé, T. Katsuki, T. Morimura, et al., City-wide traffic flow estimation from a limited number of low-quality cameras. IEEE Trans. Intell. Transp. Syst. **18**(4), 950–959 (2016)
16. L. Lin, J. Li, F. Chen, et al., Road traffic speed prediction: a probabilistic model fusing multi-source data. IEEE Trans. Knowl. Data Eng. **30**(7), 1310–1323 (2017)
17. J. Wan, J. Liu, Z. Shao, et al., Mobile crowd sensing for traffic prediction in internet of vehicles. Sensors **16**(1), 88 (2016)
18. Z. Qin, Z. Fang, Y. Liu, et al., EXIMIUS: a measurement framework for explicit and implicit urban traffic sensing. Paper presented at Proceedings of the 16th ACM Conference on Embedded Networked Sensor Systems, 4–7 November 2018
19. B. Balaji, A. Bhattacharya, G. Fierro, et al., Brick: towards a unified metadata schema for buildings. Paper presented at Proceedings of the 3rd ACM International Conference on Systems for Energy-Efficient Built Environments, 16–17 November 2016
20. Z. Pan, Y. Liang, W. Wang, et al., Urban traffic prediction from spatio-temporal data using deep meta learning. Paper presented at Proceedings of the 25th ACM SIGKDD international conference on knowledge discovery & data mining, 4–8 August 2019
21. S.P. Mohanty, U. Choppali, E. Kougianos, Everything you wanted to know about smart cities: the Internet of things is the backbone. IEEE Consum. Electron. Mag. **5**(3), 60–70 (2016)
22. D. Minoli, K. Sohraby, B. Occhiogrosso, IoT considerations, requirements, and architectures for smart buildings—energy optimization and next-generation building management systems. IEEE Intern. Things J. **4**(1), 269–283 (2017)
23. Z. Liu, Z. Li, M. Li, et al., Mining road network correlation for traffic estimation via compressive sensing. IEEE Trans. Intell. Transp. Syst. **17**(7), 1880–1893 (2016)
24. C. Hu, W. Bao, D. Wang, et al., sTube+ an IoT communication sharing architecture for smart after-sales maintenance in buildings. ACM Trans. Sens. Netw. **14**(3–4), 1–29 (2018)
25. K. Nellore, G.P. Hancke, A survey on urban traffic management system using wireless sensor networks. Sensors **16**(2), 157 (2016)

26. X. Kong, X. Song, F. Xia, et al., LoTAD: long-term traffic anomaly detection based on crowdsourced bus trajectory data. World Wide Web **21**(3), 825–847 (2018)
27. Z. Liu, P. Zhou, Z. Li, et al., Think like a graph: real-time traffic estimation at city-scale. IEEE Trans. Mob. Comput. **18**(10), 2446–2459 (2018)
28. Y. Cui, B. Jin, F. Zhang, et al., Mining spatial-temporal correlation of sensory data for estimating traffic volumes on highways. Paper presented at Proceedings of the 14th EAI International Conference on Mobile and Ubiquitous Systems: Computing, Networking and Services, 7–10 November 2017
29. A. Janecek, D. Valerio, K.A. Hummel, et al., The cellular network as a sensor: from mobile phone data to real-time road traffic monitoring. IEEE Trans. Intell. Transp. Syst. **16**(5), 2551–2572 (2015)
30. C. Costa, G. Chatzimilioudis, D. Zeinalipour-Yazti, et al., Towards real-time road traffic analytics using telco big data. Paper presented at Proceedings of the international workshop on real-time business intelligence and analytics, 28 August 2017
31. C. Meng, X. Yi, L. Su, et al., City-wide traffic volume inference with loop detector data and taxi trajectories. Paper presented at Proceedings of the 25th ACM SIGSPATIAL International Conference on Advances in Geographic Information Systems, 7–10 November 2017
32. A. Sarker, H. Shen, J.A. Stankovic, MORP: data-driven multi-objective route planning and optimization for electric vehicles. Proc. ACM Int. Mob. Wear. Ubiq. Technol. **1**(4), 1–35 (2018)
33. D. Pavlyuk, Short-term traffic forecasting using multivariate autoregressive models. Proc. Eng. **178**, 57–66 (2017)
34. Y. Lv, Y. Duan, W. Kang, et al., Traffic flow prediction with big data: a deep learning approach. IEEE Trans. Intell. Transp. Syst. **16**(2), 865–873 (2014)
35. Z. Liu, Z. Li, K. Wu, et al., Urban traffic prediction from mobility data using deep learning. IEEE Netw. **32**(4), 40–46 (2018)
36. J. Xu, R. Rahmatizadeh, L. Bölöni, et al., Real-time prediction of taxi demand using recurrent neural networks. IEEE Trans. Intell. Transp. Syst. **19**(8), 2572–2581 (2017)
37. Z. Zhao, W. Chen, X. Wu, et al., LSTM network: a deep learning approach for short-term traffic forecast. IET Intell. Transp. Syst. **11**(2), 68–75 (2017)
38. Y. Tian, K. Zhang, J. Li, et al., LSTM-based traffic flow prediction with missing data. Neurocomputing **318**, 297–305 (2018)
39. A. Vaswani, N. Shazeer, N. Parmar, et al., Attention is all you need. Adv. Neural Inf. Proces. Syst. **30** (2017)
40. H. Yao, X. Tang, H. Wei, et al., Revisiting spatial-temporal similarity: a deep learning framework for traffic prediction. Paper presented at Proceedings of the AAAI conference on artificial intelligence, 22 February– 1 March 2019
41. EIF, Research data interface (2019), https://eif-research.feit.uts.edu.au/. Accessed Aug 2019
42. Roads and N. Maritime Services, Roads and maritime services collects traffic volume information from roadside traffic collection devices across the NSW road network (2019), https://www.rms.nsw.gov.au/about/corporate-publications/statistics/traffic-volumes/index.html. Accessed Aug 2019
43. F.C. Sangoboye, M.B. Kjærgaard, Plcount: a probabilistic fusion algorithm for accurately estimating occupancy from 3d camera counts. Paper presented at Proceedings of the 3rd ACM International Conference on Systems for Energy-Efficient Built Environments, 16–17 November 2016
44. A. Koesdwiady, R. Soua, F. Karray, Improving traffic flow prediction with weather information in connected cars: a deep learning approach. IEEE Trans. Veh. Technol. **65**(12), 9508–9517 (2016)
45. J. Zhang, Y. Zheng, D. Qi, Deep spatio-temporal residual networks for citywide crowd flows prediction. Paper presented at Thirty-first AAAI conference on artificial intelligence 2017
46. W. Min, L. Wynter, Real-time road traffic prediction with spatio-temporal correlations. Transport. Res. C. Emerg. Technol. **19**(4), 606–616 (2011)

47. S.R. Chandra, H. Al-Deek, Predictions of freeway traffic speeds and volumes using vector autoregressive models. J. Intell. Transp. Syst. **13**(2), 53–72 (2009)
48. I. Sutskever, O. Vinyals, Q.V. Le, Sequence to sequence learning with neural networks. Adv. Neural Inf. Proces. Syst. **27** (2014)
49. Y. Qin, D. Song, H. Chen, et al., A dual-stage attention-based recurrent neural network for time series prediction. arXiv, 1704.02971 (2017)
50. G. Lai, W.C. Chang, Y. Yang, et al., Modeling long-and short-term temporal patterns with deep neural networks. Paper presented at The 41st international ACM SIGIR conference on research & development in information retrieval, 8–12 July 2018
51. Y. Liang, S. Ke, J. Zhang, et al., GeoMAN: multi-level attention networks for geo-sensory time series prediction. Paper presented at IJCAI 2018
52. Y. Li, R. Yu, C. Shahabi, et al., Diffusion convolutional recurrent neural network: data-driven traffic forecasting. arXiv, 1707.01926 (2017)
53. H. Zhang, S. Feng, C. Liu, et al., Cityflow: a multi-agent reinforcement learning environment for large scale city traffic scenario. Paper presented at The world wide web conference, 13–17 May 2019
54. H. Wei, G. Zheng, H. Yao, et al., Intellilight: a reinforcement learning approach for intelligent traffic light control. Paper presented at Proceedings of the 24th ACM SIGKDD International Conference on Knowledge Discovery & Data Mining, 19–23 August 2018
55. L. Zhu, F.R. Yu, Y. Wang, et al., Big data analytics in intelligent transportation systems: a survey. IEEE Trans. Intell. Transp. Syst. **20**(1), 383–398 (2018)
56. H. Zhu, Y. Zhu, M. Li, et al., SEER: metropolitan-scale traffic perception based on lossy sensory data. Paper presented at IEEE INFOCOM 2009, 19–25 April 2009
57. Z. Liu, S. Jiang, P. Zhou, et al., A participatory urban traffic monitoring system: the power of bus riders. IEEE Trans. Intell. Transp. Syst. **18**(10), 2851–2864 (2017)
58. C. Xu, K. Qiu, J. Fu, et al., Learn to scale: generating multipolar normalized density maps for crowd counting. Paper presented at Proceedings of the IEEE/CVF international conference on computer vision, 27 October 2019–02 November 2019
59. X. Cao, Z. Wang, Y. Zhao, et al., Scale aggregation network for accurate and efficient crowd counting. Paper presented at Proceedings of the European conference on computer vision (ECCV), 8–14 September 2018
60. R. Jia, F.C. Sangogboye, T. Hong, et al., Privacy-preserving building-related data publication using pad. Paper presented at Proceedings of the 4th ACM International Conference on Systems for Energy-Efficient Built Environments, 8–9 November 2017
61. K. Zhang, J. Ni, K. Yang, et al., Security and privacy in smart city applications: challenges and solutions. IEEE Commun. Mag. **55**(1), 122–129 (2017)

Chapter 6
Airborne Sensing Application: Reusing Delivery Drones

6.1 Introduction

The drones (also called Unmanned Aerial Vehicles, UAVs) are extensively applied by a large number of tech giants (*e.g.,* Amazon and JD) in delivering packages for cities' last-mile deliveries and emergency responses [1, 2]. For instance, drone delivery is exploited by JD in China in substitution of the traditional delivery ways which have been impacted by the COVID-19 pandemic in 2020 [3]. Additionally, in recent years, an increasing number of companies (*e.g.*, Amazon, Alphabet, UPS, and JD) have gained government-approved licenses for drone delivery [4]. A recent report demonstrates that [1] it is estimated that the global market size of drone delivery, including retail, medical goods, etc., will reach US$ 2.1 billion by 2023. As the market grows, urban package delivery leverages more and more delivery drones.

Delivery drones with many kinds of on-board sensors (*e.g.*, GPS and camera) are promising in multiple urban sensing applications in terms of delivering packages, like crowd surveillance [5], disaster response [6], and Air Quality Index (AQI) monitoring [7], as shown in Fig. 6.1a. This fact demonstrates the practicability of urban crowdsensing based on the re-utilization of delivery drones. In order to confirm its feasibility, as illustrated in Fig. 6.1b, we analyze service stations/warehouses' distribution (top) and their heatmap (bottom) for seven major express companies in Beijing City, on the basis of a real-world dataset [8]. The downtown area (about 6084 km^2) of Beijing has over 625 delivery service stations and 15 warehouses distributed in a dense manner. These results indicate that reusing delivery drones could become a trending business, as it is possible to realize large-scale urban crowdsensing, which is far beyond the coverage of conventional vehicles [9]. Additionally, it can hugely decrease the cost of deployment and maintenance due to drone resource sharing [10]. Therefore, *re-utilizing the delivery drones can offer a novel and promising way for urban sensing by enabling large-scale crowdsensing at an considerable low cost.*

© The Author(s), under exclusive license to Springer Nature Singapore Pte Ltd. 2023
C. Xiang et al., *Multi-dimensional Urban Sensing Using Crowdsensing Data*, Data Analytics, https://doi.org/10.1007/978-981-19-9006-9_6

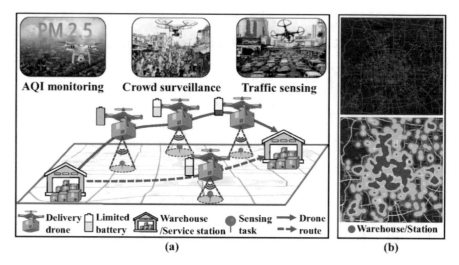

Fig. 6.1 (**a**) Illustration of urban crowdsensing by delivery drones reutilization. (**b**) The distribution (top) and coverage heatmap (bottom) of express delivery stations in Beijing, China

However, most of current works [6, 9, 11, 12] overlook the re-utilization of *available delivery drone resources* and only take into consideration crowdsensing on the basis of *dedicated drones*. In this work, we research the re-utilization of delivery drones in urban crowdsensing to fill this void. Hence, as illustrated in Fig. 6.1a, drones execute each sensing task within different duration (named *sensing time*) on their *selected flying routes* under the energy capacities, while delivering packages with different weights (called *delivery weight*) from the warehouses to the service stations. For instance, to collect the sensor data in Internet of Things (IoT) [12], the sensing time is the required data collection time [13] when applying drones for this task. In order to further strengthen our proposal, we perform real-world experiments to explore the relationship between delivery drones' energy consumption and delivery weights. According to the result, the delivery weight of drones mostly affects the energy costs of flying and sensing. Therefore, aiming at maximizing the delivery and sensing utility, we concentrate on jointly optimizing route selection, sensing time, and delivery weight allocation with the restriction of the drones' energy. This problem is challenging because of the following two difficulties:

1. *Performance guarantee for the NP-hard problem*: When taking into consideration the Route-Time (RT) joint optimization problem with fixed delivery weight, it is a Mixed Integer Non-Linear Programming (MINLP) problem, combinatorially optimizing integer route selection variables as well as continuous sensing/ hovering time variables. As a result, achieving a theoretical performance guarantee for such an MINLP problem is difficult and proved to be NP-hard.
2. *Tight coupling of multiple optimization variables*: Considering adjustable delivery weight further impose great challenges in addressing this MINLP problem, as delivery weight allocation is tightly coupled with route selection and sensing time

assignment because of the energy capacities of drones. Even worse, such coupling renders both the corresponding objective function and constraints non-convex.

We solve these difficulties as follows: (1) we create a new objective function merely with the route selection variables to solve the first problem, thus decomposing the coupling route-time optimization. Then, we transform the RT problem in an equivalent manner into a *problem of* maximizing *a non-monotone, submodular objective function* under two *partition matroid constraints*. This problem can be successfully addressed by a *constant approximation algorithm*. (2) For the second problem, based on the solution to the RT problem, we concern the *Route-Time-Weight* (RTW) joint optimization problem with adjustable delivery weights. Then, we put forward an iterative joint optimization algorithm. Particularly, given the current results of route selection and sensing time allocation, the delivery weight of routes is optimized, which is fed back to update route selection and sensing time allocation.

In all, we make the following three major contributions:

1. *Novel crowdsensing by reusing available drones*: we are the *first* to re-utilize existing delivery drones for large-scale urban crowdsensing. It enables large-scale urban crowdsensing at a low cost by leveraging the shared drone resources between the package delivery and the urban crowdsensing.
2. *Guaranteed near-optimal algorithms*: We put forward the near-optimal algorithms by employing the equivalent objective function transformation, the local search method, and the alternating iteration scheme. According to a series of theoretical analyses, the $\frac{1}{4+\varepsilon}$-approximation ratio and the convergence guarantee can be realized by the proposed algorithms for the scenarios of fixed and adjustable delivery weights, respectively.
3. *Trace-based simulations and field experiments*: We deploy a prototype system to perform large-scale trace-based simulations, field experiments, and real-world application. The results indicate that the proposed algorithms can averagely promote the sensing and delivery utility and the energy utilization rate by 124.7% and 72.2% respectively, in comparison with the original drone delivery without re-utilization.

The indicated results are expected as an inspiring demonstration that the drone sharing, like ride sharing (*e.g.*, Uber and DiDi), will develop into an up-and-coming drive in the sharing economy [10]. Hence, novel multifunctional UAV applications will be possible, like LTE communication [14, 15], disaster response [6], and airdropping sensor networks [16].

The rest of this chapter is structured as follows. To start with, in Sect. 6.3, based on real-world experiments, we build the system model and formulate the problem. Section 6.2 reviews the related works. Next, we put forward the solution design and the theoretical analysis in Sect. 6.4. We perform the trace-based simulations and implement the prototype system to make field experiments and the real-world application in Sect. 6.5. In the end, we take over our work in Sect. 6.6 and conclude in Sect. 6.7.

6.2   Related Work

First, we survey the current crowdsensing works which use other kinds of mobile equipments, like human subjects and vehicles. And then, we summarize the drone-based crowdsensing works and route planning approaches.

6.2.1   Crowdsensing Based on Other Mobile Devices

Many outstanding works have been committed to crowdsensing on the basis of other mobile devices, like human subjects [17–21] and vehicles [22–29]. For instance, Karaliopoulos et al. [17] investigated how to optimally assign the sensing tasks to each user while considering the bounded rationality of human agents. He et al. [26] presented a user recruitment strategy for vehicular crowdsensing, maximizing the time and space coverage under a limited budget. In addition, Zhu et al. [27] proposed a scheme of deep learning-based vehicular crowdsensing. It utilizes RNN network to predict vehicle mobility, which is used to select vehicles to maximize their coverage under a limited budget. Considering the situation where participants strategically misreport their costs, Xiao et al. [28] put forward a truthful incentive mechanism design for vehicular crowdsensing that is non-deterministic. The works in [23, 29] explored how to simultaneously schedule vehicles trajectory and design incentive mechanisms for vehicular crowdsensing.

In conclusion, the previous works based on human subjects and vehicles rarely consider energy consumption, because their energy limitations are almost negligible [17, 29]. On the contrary, most drones have extremely limited energy [2, 12, 30], making route selection, sensing time, and delivery weight distribution limited [9, 11, 31]. Therefore, the aforementioned works cannot deal with this problem related to the optimization of drone energy consumption.

6.2.2   Crowdsensing Based on Drones

For the past few years, due to the inherent advantages of swift deployment and flexible mobility, drones have been extensively utilized in the applications of urban crowdsensing [5–7, 32, 33]. For instance, Rashid et al. [6] presented SocialDrone, a comprehensive social-physical sensing system that utilizes social media to initially sense disasters. The results are then utilized to manipulate the drones for field verification. For the application of indoor localization, Piao et al. [34] exploited drone sensing to build the CSI fingerprint map automatically. Yang et al. [7] proposed a drone-based AQI monitoring system called ImgSensingNet, which utilizes the haze images collected by the drones to infer the coarse-grained AQI scale. The results are fed back to drive on-ground sensors to sense the fine-grained sensing. Motlagh et al. [5] used drones' cameras to monitor the crowds based on edge computing and face recognition. These works which focus on particular applications do not consider the optimization of drone energy consumption.

Some works have investigated optimizing the energy consumption in drone routing. For instance, references [9, 35, 36] proposed new public bus-based delivery drone systems. They utilized buses to deliver and recharge these delivery drones, and thus not only reduce the energy cost of battery-constrained drones but also increase their load capacity. Moreover, Huang et al. [36] presented an optimal solution to the round trip routing problem under the delivery deadline and the energy budget limitations. Liu et al. [31] proposed crowdsensing schemes, using deep reinforcement learning. It is energy-efficient for drones based on charging stations which are randomly deployed. Zhou et al. [12] proposed a joint optimization algorithm for route planning and task allocation in the drone-assisted mobile crowdsensing. To sum up, the above works mainly optimize the route selection and the sensing time allocation, while neglecting the delivery weight allocation. Though Dorling et al. [2] investigated the problem of routing planning of delivery drones through optimizing the distribution of delivery weight, they did not consider the sensing time allocation. Therefore, unlike the above works, this chapter optimizes route selection, sensing time allocation, and delivery weight allocation. Since it is a new non-convex MINLP problem, current approaches cannot address this complicated problem.

Furthermore, some existing works [2, 9, 11, 12, 30, 31, 37] study the optimization of UAV energy efficiency in crowdsensing. More specifically, Wang et al. [37] took into account the interchangeable energy capacities for hovering and servicing, thus trading off the hovering time against service capacity and maximizing energy efficiency. Zeng et al. [30] proposed a joint optimization scheme of UAV trajectory and communication time to minimize the energy cost of flying and communication. Shan et al. [11] only considered speed dispatching with the time and space limitation in wireless communication.

Summary

For one thing, current works about human agents and vehicles do not consider the limited energy consumption and cannot address the problem of drone-based crowdsensing because the energy is very limited. For another, current drone-based works focus on either urban crowdsensing based on dedicated drones or drone delivery only. In contrast, we are the *first* to reuse *non-dedicated* delivery drones to explore new mobile crowdsensing. It *jointly* optimizes the routing, sensing time, and delivery weight distribution to maximize energy consumption efficiency, thereby reusing available delivery drones for large-scale urban crowdsensing at a considerably low cost.

6.3 Models and Problem Formulation

6.3.1 Delivering and Sensing Models for Delivery Drones

Drones are employed by huge amounts of drone delivery companies (like Amazon, UPS, and JD) to deliver packages from package warehouses to the corresponding service stations. The delivery drones of a company with the same pair of warehouse and service station are defined as a Delivery Group (DG), as illustrated in Fig. 6.1a. Suppose that there are totally I DGs; the set of DGs is represented by $\mathcal{I} = \{1, \ldots, I\}$. Each DG i has the delivery drone constraints $\{l_i^0, l_i^1, a_i, E_i\}$ as follows:

1. *Delivery location constraint* (l_i^0, l_i^1), *i.e.*, each drone in DG i should deliver its packages from the location of warehouse l_i^0 to that of service station l_i^1;
2. *Drone number limitation* (a_i), *i.e.*, the number of available delivery drones in DG i for crowdsensing doesn't exceed a_i;
3. *Drone energy constraint* (E_i), *i.e.*, the energy capacity of each drone in DG i is E_i.

The drones of DGs in package delivery can be concurrently re-utilized for urban crowdsensing. Suppose that totally K sensing tasks are assigned at different locations, and $\mathcal{K} = \{1, \ldots, K\}$ denotes the set of all the tasks. Once the task is performed by one drone, the task $k \in \mathcal{K}$ will return the sensing utility that can be formally calculated through a non-decreasing function $G_k(\cdot)$ with sensing time of drone t_k, *i.e.*, $g_k = G_k(t_k)$. Like current works [38–40], we apply $G_k(t_k) = \min(u_k t_k, \overline{U}_k)$, where u_k indicates the utility weight of task k per unit time, and $\overline{U}_k$ represents its utility threshold beyond which the utility will not improve with more sensing time.

The number of feasible drone routes for each DG is limited. These routes mainly depend on its warehouse and service station locations. Also, the position distribution of all the tasks [12] impacts them. Additionally, the schedule of feasible routes should be responsible for the privacy and security of citizens; its detailed schemes are referred to [9, 12]. We assume that there exists J feasible routes for all drones in total, and $\mathcal{J} = \{1, \ldots, J\}$ denotes the set of feasible routes. Each route $j \in \mathcal{J}$ covers a few sensing tasks, and $\mathcal{K}_j$ denotes the set of tasks covered by route j. Additionally, d_{ij} denotes the length of route j for DG i and is easily computed according to l_i^0, l_i^1, and all the tasks' locations in route j. Moreover, all the DGs performs sensing tasks by being assigned with several routes when delivering their packages with drones. We let $x_{ij} \in \{0, 1\}$ denote the route selection variable, *i.e.*, $x_{ij} = 1$ if route j is selected for DG i, and $x_{ij} = 0$ otherwise. Besides, w_{ij} denotes the delivery weight assignment variable for route j of DG i. w_{ij} is discrete, since packages are the combination of several indivisible goods. In addition, s_{ij}^k denotes task k on route j of DG i. t_{ij}^k denotes the allocated sensing time for s_{ij}^k.

To sum up, $\mathbf{x} := \{x_{ij}\}$, $\mathbf{w} := \{w_{ij}\}$, and $\mathbf{t} := \{t_{ij}^k\}$ are the decision variables, which involve both discrete and continuous variables. Frequently used notations are illustrated in Table 6.1.

Table 6.1 Frequently used notations

Symbols	Definitions
$i, I, \mathcal{I}$	DG i, its total number, set of DGs
$k, \mathcal{K}, \mathcal{K}_j$	Task k, set of all the tasks, set of route j's tasks
$j, J, \mathcal{J}$	Route j, its total number, set of routes
s_{ij}^k, t_{ij}^k	Task k of route j of DG i, its sensing time
d_{ij}	Length of route j for DG i w/ crowdsensing
d_i^0	Flying length of DGi' drones wo/ crowdsensing
e_{ij}, E_i	Drone energy cost for route j of DG i, its capacity
$G_k(\cdot), U$	Sensing utility function of task k, total utility
u_k	Utility weight per unit time
$\overline{U}_k$	Task k's utility bound
x_{ij}	Indicator of whether route j is selected for DG i
w_{ij}	Delivery weight of route j of DG i
x, t, w	$\mathbf{x} := \{x_{ij}\}, \mathbf{t} := \left\{t_{ij}^k\right\}, \mathbf{w} := \{w_{ij}\}$
$P^{\mathrm{f}}(\cdot), P^{\mathrm{h}}(\cdot)$	Drone energy power for flying and hovering

6.3.2 Energy Consumption Model for Delivery Drones

Drones execute the sensing tasks and deliver the package, incurring energy consumption, which is one of the main works for UAVs [9, 37]. Next, on-site experiments are performed to investigate the delivery drones' energy consumption, which are exploited to construct the practical energy cost model.

On-Site Experimental Explorations

A sensing prototype system based on delivery drones is leveraged and specified in Sect. 6.5.2. Applying this system, real experiments are conducted to investigate the drone energy consumption with varied flying time and delivery weight settings.

1. *Impact of flying time on drone energy consumption*: A drone is set to fly at 5 m/s for 2 min. Then, we let it hover at a spot for 2 min when the delivery weight is fixed, *i.e.*, 0 kg. Our settings are in accordance with real-world drone delivery [1, 2]. As illustrated in Fig. 6.2a, the results show that the drone power approximately remains the same in the matter of both flying and hovering, when the drone speed and the delivery weight are fixed.
2. *Impact of delivery weight on drone energy consumption*: We vary the delivery weight from 0 to 600 g with the interval of 50 g; the drone's net weight is 2 kg. Let the drone fly and hover for 2 min in each delivery weight. Next, we measure the average consumed powers. As illustrated in Fig. 6.2b, for both hovering and flying, the consumed power has a roughly linear increment with the delivery weight. However, the flying and hovering power's model parameters differ from

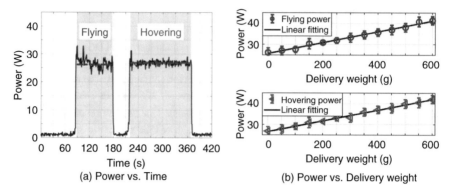

Fig. 6.2 Experimental results for consumed powers of delivery drone when flying and hovering. (**a**) Power vs. time. (**b**) Power vs. delivery weight

each other, *e.g.*, the hovering's parameters are 26.62 and 0.026, and those for flying are 25.75 and 0.026.

To sum up, the above results demonstrate that: irrespective of flying at a constant speed or hovering at a position, the delivery drone's consumed power remains almost the same with the time change but grows linearly in terms of the delivery weight.

Energy Consumption Model

As illustrated in Fig. 6.3, the experimental results have shown that the drones fulfill the delivery of packages by flying from warehouses to service stations, generating the *flying energy cost*. In the meantime, they perform sensing tasks by hovering for a period of sensing time. As a result, they cause the *hovering energy cost*, also called *sensing energy cost*. Therefore, the delivery drone's energy cost is primarily composed of the flying energy cost and the sensing energy cost. Note that the energy consumption for each drone's sensors and communication are much lower than those of flying and hovering, hence ignored like references [9, 11, 12].

In particular, let $P^{\mathrm{h}}(w_{ij})$ and $P^{\mathrm{f}}(w_{ij})$ denote the drone's power of hovering and flying with the delivery weight w_{ij}, respectively. The above experimental results in Fig. 6.2a, b indicate that hovering and flying's power remains invariant as time changes, but grows linearly in terms of the delivery weight. Hence, we have

$$P^{\mathrm{h}}\left(w_{ij}\right) = \rho_0^{\mathrm{h}} + \rho_1^{\mathrm{h}} w_{ij}, \quad 0 \le w_{ij} \le \overline{w}, \tag{6.1}$$

$$P^{\mathrm{f}}\left(w_{ij}\right) = \rho_0^{\mathrm{f}} + \rho_1^{\mathrm{f}} w_{ij}, \quad 0 \le w_{ij} \le \overline{w}, \tag{6.2}$$

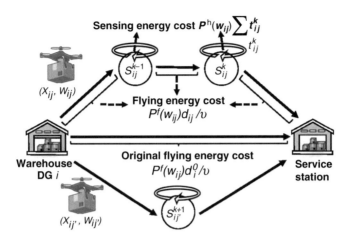

Fig. 6.3 Illustration for the energy consumptions of delivery drone-based crowdsensing, consisting of the flying energy cost and the sensing energy cost

where $\overline{w}$ indicates the maximal delivery weight of the drone, *e.g.*, 600 g in our experiments. ρ_0^f, ρ_1^f, ρ_0^h, and ρ_1^h represent the power model parameters, and they depend on the surrounding environments (*e.g.*, the air density and the weather), the UAV mechanical structure (*e.g.*, the blade area), and the fly speed v [11, 30, 41].

Let e_{ij} represent the drone's energy consumption with w_{ij} on route j of DG i, which primarily include the flying energy cost $P^f(w_{ij})d_{ij}/v$ and the hovering energy cost $P^h\left(w_{ij}\right)\sum_{k\in\mathcal{K}_j}t_{ij}^k$. Therefore, as shown in Fig. 6.3, according to Eqs. (6.1) and (6.2), the *energy consumption model of delivery drone* is

$$e_{ij}=P^f\left(w_{ij}\right)\frac{d_{ij}}{v}+P^h\left(w_{ij}\right)\sum_{k\in\mathcal{K}_j}t_{ij}^k, 0\le w_{ij}\le\overline{w}. \tag{6.3}$$

It should be noticed that we leverage the steady straight-and-level flight assumption [30], which overlooks the minor influence of acceleration/deceleration and flying altitude on energy consumption, like most existing works [11, 12, 30, 41]. Additionally, like references [9, 31, 34], we set v constant; while the energy-efficient speed scheduling was investigated well in references [11, 41].

Model Analysis

We make the following comparison of our energy consumption model and current ones:

- Some of the current works [34, 42, 43] suppose that the energy cost is proportional to the flight distance and time, which is similar to our model. However, these models do not take into consideration the influence of delivery weight, which is vital to delivery drones.

- Researches in references [11, 12, 30] put forward complex theoretical models, which are dependent on the speed, the drone weight, the blade profile, etc. On the contrary, we build a model that is uncomplicated but practical on the basis of real-world experiments for the following reasons: Firstly, we only model the energy cost of the drone within the capacity of its delivery weight $\overline{w}$. Additionally, the speed of the drone is assumed to be fixed. Hence, the energy cost model can be presumably streamlined into a linear one. Moreover, our approach is also practical to these complicated non-linear models [12, 30] with slight extensions.

6.3.3   Problem Formulation

Exploiting the previous system models, we put forward the following two popular scenarios. The first is the routes' fixed delivery weight. For instance, some companies arrange beforehand the packages carried from a warehouse to a station. The other is the different routes' adjustable delivery weight. We name the problems with fixed delivery weight and adjustable deliver weight as the Route-Time (RT) joint optimization problem and the Route-Time-Weight (RTW) joint optimization problem, respectively. We formulate the RT problem and the RTW problem as follows:

RT Problem

Given the delivery drone constraints of I DGs $\left\{ \left(l_i^0, l_i^1, a_i, E_i \right) \right\}$, the set of sensing tasks $\mathcal{K}$ with J feasible routes, and each DG i's drone's delivery weight assignment $\{ w_{ij} \}$ on route j, choosing routes $\{ x_{ij} \}$ for each DG i and allocating the sensing time $\left\{ t_{ij}^k \right\}$ for each task s_{ij}^k so as to maximize the total utility of sensing tasks and package deliveries, concurrently fulfilling both the delivery drone constraints $\left\{ \left(l_i^0, l_i^1, a_i, E_i \right) \right\}$ and the total extra energy cost's budget δ. Formally,

$$\max_{\mathbf{x}, \mathbf{t}} \sum_{i \in \mathcal{I}} \sum_{j \in \mathcal{J}} x_{ij} \left(\lambda \sum_{k \in \mathcal{K}_j} G_k \left(t_{ij}^k \right) + (1 - \lambda) \tau w_{ij} \right), \tag{6.4}$$

$$\text{s.t.} P^{\text{h}} \left(w_{ij} \right) \sum_{k \in \mathcal{K}_j} t_{ij}^k + P^{\text{f}} \left(w_{ij} \right) \frac{d_{ij}}{v} \leq E_i, \forall i \in \mathcal{I}, \tag{6.5}$$

$$\sum_{j \in \mathcal{J}} x_{ij} \leq a_i, \forall i \in \mathcal{I}, \tag{6.6}$$

$$\sum_{i \in \mathcal{I}} x_{ij} \leq 1, \forall j \in \mathcal{J}, \tag{6.7}$$

$$\sum_{i \in \mathcal{I}} \sum_{j \in \mathcal{J}} x_{ij} \left(P^{\mathrm{h}}\left(w_{ij}\right) \sum_{k \in \mathcal{K}_j} t_{ij}^k + e_{ij}^{\Delta} \right) \leq \delta, \tag{6.8}$$

$$e_{ij}^{\Delta} = P^{\mathrm{f}}\left(w_{ij}\right)\left(d_{ij} - d_i^0\right)/v, \forall i \in \mathcal{I}, \forall j \in \mathcal{J}, \tag{6.9}$$

$$x_{ij} \in \{0, 1\}, t_{ij}^k \geq 0, \forall i \in \mathcal{I}, \forall j \in \mathcal{J}, \forall k \in \mathcal{K}. \tag{6.10}$$

RTW Problem

Given the delivery drone constraints of I DGs $\left\{\left(l_i^0, l_i^1, a_i, E_i\right)\right\}$ and the set of sensing tasks $\mathcal{K}$ with J feasible routes, choose routes $\{x_{ij}\}$ for each DG i and assign the delivery weight $\{w_{ij}\}$ for each route j together with the sensing time $\left\{t_{ij}^k\right\}$ for each task s_{ij}^k, to maximize the total utility of the sensing tasks and the package deliveries, concurrently fulfilling both the delivery drone constraints $\left\{\left(l_i^0, l_i^1, a_i, E_i\right)\right\}$ and the budget of the total extra energy cost δ. Formally,

$$\max_{\mathbf{x}, \mathbf{w}, \mathbf{t}} \sum_{i \in \mathcal{I}} \sum_{j \in \mathcal{J}} x_{ij} \left(\lambda \sum_{k \in \mathcal{K}_j} G_k\left(t_{ij}^k\right) + (1 - \lambda)\tau w_{ij} \right), \tag{6.11}$$

s.t. Eqs. (6.5)–(6.10),

$$w_{ij} \in \{\overline{w}_1, \overline{w}_2, \dots, \overline{w}_m\}, \forall i \in \mathcal{I}, \forall j \in \mathcal{J}. \tag{6.12}$$

Next, we specify the objective and the constraints of the RT problem and the RTW problem, and then analyze their challenges.

Objective and Constraints

The objectives in Eqs. (6.4) and (6.11) are to maximize the delivery drones' overall utility for crowdsensing, containing the sensing utility and the delivery utility. It should be noticed that, τ represents the delivery utility per kilogram, and λ indicates the trade-off coefficient between the utility of sensing and delivery, *i.e.*, $0 < \lambda < 1$. Equation (6.5) denotes the constraint of drones' energy cost, and Eq. (6.6) indicates the number limit of available delivery drones of each DG for crowdsensing. Equation (6.7) demonstrates the reasonable assumption that each route is assigned to at most one DG, which is similar to current works [2, 12].

Additionally, $\sum_{i \in \mathcal{I}}\sum_{j \in \mathcal{J}} x_{ij} P^f (w_{ij}) d_i^0 / v$ in Eqs. (6.8) and (6.9) denotes the general energy cost without sensing, *i.e.*, all the drones' energy consumption when each DG i's drone with its package directly flies from l_i^0 to l_i^1, as shown in Fig. 6.3. It should be noticed that, d_i^0 represents the distance of flying from l_i^0 to l_i^1 directly.

$$\sum_{i \in \mathcal{I}}\sum_{j \in \mathcal{J}} x_{ij} \left(P^h (w_{ij}) \sum_{k \in \mathcal{K}_j} t_{ij}^k + P^f (w_{ij}) \frac{d_{ij}}{v} \right)$$ denotes the total energy cost with sensing,

i.e., the energy consumption of all the drones after reusing delivery drones for sensing. Therefore, the left hand side of Eq. (6.8) indicates the *total extra energy cost*, *i.e.*, the difference between the total energy cost with sensing and the one without it, which is caused by the sensing tasks. On the basis of constraint (6.5), all the drones' general battery capacity restricts the total energy cost with sensing. Moreover, we set δ to limit the total extra energy cost for sensing, guaranteeing a lower bound of the energy cost for sorely the package delivery, which is important and essential for the delivery of drones. Furthermore, the crowdsensing company and the delivery drone company decide δ. For instance, it depends on the monetary budget that is provided by the crowdsensing company in order to recruit the delivery drones for crowdsensing [44, 45]. In the meantime, there may be precise requirements for energy cost under some practical scenarios from the delivery drone company [2, 35]. Lastly, Eq. (6.12) represents the delivery weight assignment's range, where $0 < \overline{w}_1 < \overline{w}_2 < \cdots < \overline{w}_m \le \overline{w}$.

Challenges

(1) Based on the results of Theorem 6.1, both the RT and RTW problems are MINLP problems and NP-hard. For instance, two different kinds of decision variables are coupled in the RT problem, *i.e.*, 0–1 integral route selection variables $\{x_{ij}\}$ and the continuous sensing time variables $\left\{ t_{ij}^k \right\}$. (2) As shown in Fig. 6.4, the above variables and the delivery weight variables are closely related to each other, therefore making both the objective functions (6.4), (6.11) and constraint (6.8) of the RT and RTW problems non-convex.

Theorem 6.1 *Both the RT and RTW problems are NP-hard.*

Proof Consider an instance of the RT and RTW problems, where the energy capacity E_i ($\forall i \in \mathcal{I}$) and the energy budget δ are large enough to satisfy all the drones. Therefore, constraints (6.5) and (6.8) can be relaxed. In the meantime, the available drones' total number for DGs (*i.e.*, $\sum_{i \in \mathcal{I}} a_i$) is bigger than that of the routes. Therefore, constraint (6.7) can be re-written as $\forall j \in \mathcal{J}, \sum_{i \in \mathcal{I}} x_{ij} = 1$. Therefore, this problem can be reduced from the classical NP-hard Generalized assignment problem [46]: *i.e.*, given I knapsacks (*i.e.*, DGs), each with capacity a_i ($\forall i \in \mathcal{I}$), assign each item j (*i.e.*, route $j \in \mathcal{J}$) to exactly one knapsack i ($i \in \mathcal{I}$) with profit

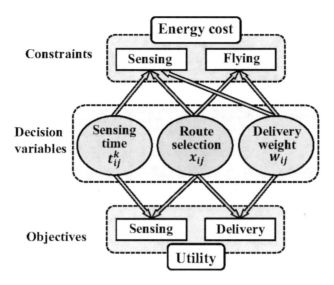

Fig. 6.4 Coupling among route selection, sensing time, and delivery weight with constraints of the sensing and flying energy cost and objectives of the sensing and delivery utility

$(\lambda \sum_{k \in \mathcal{K}_j} G_k \left(t_{ij}^k \right) + (1-\lambda)\tau w_{ij})$, in order to realize maximize the total profit under the capacity of knapsacks. Thus, Theorem 6.1 is proved.

6.4 Solution Design

6.4.1 Overview

As illustrated in Fig. 6.5, we put forward two near-optimal algorithms with performance guarantees in this section to solve the RT problem and the RTW problem respectively. And then, we perform the analysis of these algorithms.

1. *Route-Time joint allocation algorithm* (*RT-alg*, Sect. 6.4.2): To address the RT problem, we put forward a constant-factor approximation route-time joint allocation algorithm named *RT-alg* in Sect. 6.4.2. Particularly, we construct a novel objective function in section "Equivalent Objective Function Construction" as a start, and it is applied to equivalently transform the RT problem with two kinds of highly coupled variables (*i.e.*, **x** and **t**) into a simple problem only with **x**. Next, to solve this new problem, an approximation route selection algorithm is proposed in section "Approximation Algorithm for Route-Time Joint Allocation", utilizing the *p*-exchange local search strategy to achieve the constant-factor near-optimal solution iteratively.

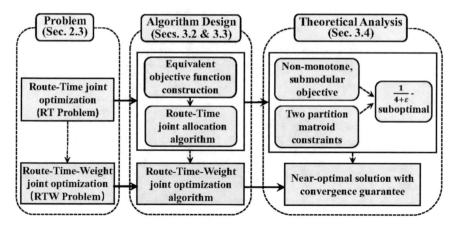

Fig. 6.5 Overview of solution design and analysis

2. *Route-Time-Weight joint optimization algorithm* (*RTW-alg*, Sect. 6.4.3): An iterative route-time-weight joint optimization algorithm called *RTW-alg* is proposed to solve the RTW problem, on the basis of the solution of the RT problem in Sect. 6.4.3. Particularly, in each iteration, given the delivery weight allocation, it utilizes the *RT-alg* algorithm to improve route selection and sensing time allocation, which are fed back for the update of the delivery weight allocation on the basis of the greedy scheme.

3. *Theoretical analysis of algorithms* (Sect. 6.4.4): The performance of *RT-alg* and *RTW-alg* algorithms is analyzed in theory. Particularly, we put forward a set of theoretical analyses, which concern the constructed novel objective functions as well as the constraints in section "Analysis of Objective Function and Constraints". Employing the aforementioned results, in section "Analysis of Algorithm Performance", we can prove the $\frac{1}{4+\varepsilon}$ -approximation ratio and the convergence guarantee for the *RT-alg* algorithm and the *RTW-alg* algorithm, respectively.

6.4.2　Route-Time Joint Allocation Algorithm

Equivalent Objective Function Construction

Let $U(\mathbf{x}, \mathbf{t})$ represent the objective function of the RT problem in Eq. (6.4). Next, we put forward the greedy sensing time allocation scheme with the intention to build a novel objective function $H(\mathbf{x})$ merely with the variables $\mathbf{x}$. Such a novel function can equally replace $U(\mathbf{x}, \mathbf{t})$, hence decoupling the complex interdependence between $\mathbf{x}$ and $\mathbf{t}$.

Given the route selections $\mathbf{x}$, as shown in Algorithm 6.1, we greedily assign sensing time for each task s_{ij}^k in the following: To start with, all the tasks are categorized based on their utility weights $\{u_k\}$ in lines 2–3. We sort $\Gamma\left(s_{ij}^k\right)$ as the index function that s_{ij}^k pertains to, $i.e.$, $\Gamma\left(s_{ij}^k\right) : \mathbf{U} \rightarrow \{1, \ldots, N^s\}$, where the number of all the sensing tasks are denoted as N^s. Therefore, in lines 4–8, it greedily allocates the sensing time for tasks according to this order of tasks, until each task, each route, and all the routes' sensing time does not meet the utility bound $\overline{U}_k$, constraints (6.5), and (6.8), respectively. Hence, the assigned sensing time for s_{ij}^k is denoted as

$$
\begin{aligned}
&\widehat{t}_{ij}^k(\mathbf{x}) \\
&= \min\left(\frac{\overline{U}_k}{u_k}, \frac{E_i v - p_{ij}^f d_{ij}}{p_{ij}^h v} - \sum_{k' \in \mathcal{K}_j/\{k\}} \widehat{t}_{ij}^{k'}(\mathbf{x}), \frac{E^s}{p_{ij}^h} - \frac{1}{p_{ij}^h}\sum_{i \in \mathcal{I}}\sum_{j \in \mathcal{J}}\sum_{k' \in \mathcal{K}_j/\{k\}} x_{ij} p_{ij}^h \widehat{t}_{ij}^{k'}(\mathbf{x})\right),
\end{aligned}
$$

(6.13)

where the first term in the min($\cdot$) function indicates the constraint of the sensing time allocation because of the utility bound $\overline{U}_k$. The second term represents the constraint by the restricted capacity of drone energy, $i.e.$, constraint (6.5). The third term demonstrates the constraint impacted by the budget of total extra energy cost ($i.e.$, constraint 6.8); $E^s := \delta - \sum_{i \in \mathcal{I}}\sum_{j \in \mathcal{J}}\left(x_{ij}e_{ij}^\Delta\right)$, which indicates the sensing energy cost restriction for all drones. p_{ij}^f and p_{ij}^h denote $P^f(w_{ij})$ and $P^h(w_{ij})$, respectively. Meanwhile, the delivery weight of each route ($i.e.$, $w_{ij}, \forall i \in \mathcal{I}, j \in \mathcal{J}$) is fixed beforehand.

Therefore, substituting $\widehat{\mathbf{t}}(\mathbf{x}) := \left\{\widehat{t}_{ij}^k(\mathbf{x})\right\}$ ($i.e.$, Eq. 6.13) into the original objective function $U(\mathbf{x}, \mathbf{t})$ ($i.e.$, Eq. 6.4), the new objective function $H(\mathbf{x})$ can be denoted as

$$
H(\mathbf{x}) = U\left(\mathbf{x}, \widehat{\mathbf{t}}(\mathbf{x})\right) = \sum_{i \in \mathcal{I}}\sum_{j \in \mathcal{J}} x_{ij}\left(\lambda \sum_{k \in \mathcal{K}_j} u_k \widehat{t}_{ij}^k(\mathbf{x}) + (1-\lambda)\tau w_{ij}\right).
$$

(6.14)

On the basis of the new objective function $H(\mathbf{x})$ in Eq. (6.14), we get Lemma 6.1. Hence, the RT problem can be equally transformed into the new optimization problem merely with the route selection variables $\mathbf{x}$, $i.e.$, $\max_{\mathbf{x}} H(\mathbf{x})$.

Lemma 6.1 *The optimization problem with the new objective function $H(\mathbf{x})$ is equal to the RT problem, i.e., $\max_{\mathbf{x}} H(\mathbf{x}) = \max_{\mathbf{x},\mathbf{t}} U(\mathbf{x},\mathbf{t})$.*

Proof To begin with, we demonstrate that $\widehat{t}_{ij}^k(\mathbf{x})$ in Eq. (6.13) is the optimal solution to the RT problem given $\mathbf{x}$ as follows. Since constraints (6.6) and (6.7) only involve the variables $\mathbf{x}$, they can be neglected. In addition, we can add constraint (6.18) to equally transform the non-linear objective function (*i.e.*, Eq. 6.4) into a linear one (*i.e.*, Eq. 6.15). Therefore, given $\mathbf{x}$, we can equivalently transform the RT problem into

$$\max_{\mathbf{t}} \sum_{i \in \mathcal{I}} \sum_{j \in \mathcal{J}} \sum_{k \in \mathcal{K}_j} x_{ij} u_k t_{ij}^k, \tag{6.15}$$

$$\text{s.t.} \sum_{i \in \mathcal{I}} \sum_{j \in \mathcal{J}} \sum_{k \in \mathcal{K}_j} x_{ij} p_{ij}^{\text{h}} t_{ij}^k \leq E^{\text{s}}, \tag{6.16}$$

$$\sum_{k \in \mathcal{K}_j} t_{ij}^k \leq \frac{E_i v - p_{ij}^{\text{f}} d_{ij}}{p_{ij}^{\text{h}} v}, \forall i \in \mathcal{I}, \forall j \in \mathcal{J}, \tag{6.17}$$

$$t_{ij}^k \leq \frac{\overline{U}_k}{u_k}, \forall i \in \mathcal{I}, \forall j \in \mathcal{J}, \forall k \in \mathcal{K}_j. \tag{6.18}$$

Based on Eqs. (6.15)–(6.18), this problem is recognized as a bounded knapsack problem [46] with continuous variables $\left\{ t_{ij}^k \right\}$, *i.e.*, assigning continuous sensing time t_{ij}^k for each sensing task s_{ij}^k with weight w_{ij} and utility u_k to maximize the overall utility with weight capacity E^{s}. At the same time, $\overline{U}_k/u_k$ should restrict the time allocation t_{ij}^k for each sensing task s_{ij}^k, while the time allocation for all the drones of DG i on route j is restricted by $\frac{E_i v - p_{ij}^{\text{f}} d_{ij}}{p_{ij}^{\text{h}} v}$. The optimal solution in polynomial time can be realized by the greedy sensing time allocation algorithm (*i.e.*, Algorithm 6.1), since the allocation variables $\left\{ t_{ij}^k \right\}$ are continuous [46]. It is worth noting that it is still challenging to get a clear expression of the optimal solution, even though this problem is a Linear Programming (LP) problem which can be addressed by many classical LP methods [47]. Therefore, we get the explicit solution $\widehat{t}_{ij}^k(\mathbf{x})$ as Eq. (6.13) by using Algorithm 6.1, in order to analyze the properties of the objective function. Therefore, $\widehat{t}(\mathbf{x})$ in Eq. (6.13) is the optimal solution to the RT problem given $\mathbf{x}$, and we have $\max_{\mathbf{x}, \mathbf{t}} U(\mathbf{x}, \mathbf{t}) = \max_{\mathbf{x}} U\left(\mathbf{x}, \widehat{t}(\mathbf{x})\right)$. As $H(\mathbf{x})$ is equivalent to $U(\mathbf{x}, \mathbf{t})$ by substituting t_{ij}^k with $\widehat{t}_{ij}^k(\mathbf{x})$, $H(\mathbf{x}) = U\left(\mathbf{x}, \widehat{t}(\mathbf{x})\right)$. Hence, $\max_{\mathbf{x}, \mathbf{t}} U(\mathbf{x}, \mathbf{t}) = \max_{\mathbf{x}} H(\mathbf{x})$, and Lemma 6.1 is proved.

Algorithm 6.1 Sensing Time Allocation Algorithm for Equivalent Objective Function Construction

Input: 1) Set of feasible routes: $\mathcal{J}$;

      2) Set of sensing tasks: $\left\{ \left(u_k, \overline{U}_k \right) \right\}$

      3) Delivery constraints of DGs: $\left\{ \left(l_i^0, l_i^1, a_i, E_i \right) \right\}$;

(continued)

Algorithm 6.1 (continued)
    4) Budget: δ
    5) Delivery weight: $\mathbf{w} = \{w_{ij}\}$;
    6) Route selection: $\mathbf{x} = \{x_{ij}\}$;
  Output: 1) Sensing time of tasks: $\widehat{\mathbf{t}} = \left\{\widehat{t}_{ij}^{k}\right\}$;
    2) Total utility: U;
  1: Initialize $\widehat{t}_{ij}^{k} \leftarrow 0, \forall i \in \mathcal{I}, \forall j \in \mathcal{J}, \forall k \in \mathcal{K}$;
  2: Sort all the tasks $\left\{s_{ij}^{k}\right\}$ based on their utility weights $\{u_k\}$ in descending order.
  3: Let $n \leftarrow \Gamma\left(s_{ij}^{k}\right)$ denote its order of s_{ij}^{k}, $n \in \{1, \ldots, N^s\}$;
  4: for $n = 1:N^s$ **do**
  5: $(i,j,k) \leftarrow \Gamma^{-1}(n)$;
  6:   **if** $((x_{ij} \neq 0)$ && (constraints (6.5) and (6.8) are true)) **then** Compute $\widehat{t}_{ij}^{k}$ according to Eq. (6.13)
  7: Set $\widehat{\mathbf{t}} \leftarrow \left\{\widehat{t}_{ij}^{k}\right\}$;
  8: Compute U based on $\widehat{\mathbf{t}}$, $\mathbf{x}$, and $\mathbf{w}$ according to Eq. (6.14);
  9: return $\widehat{\mathbf{t}}$ and U

Algorithm 6.2 *RT-alg* **Algorithm**
Input: 1) Set of feasible routes: $\mathcal{J}$;
    2) Set of sensing tasks: $\left\{\left(u_k, \overline{U}_k\right)\right\}$
    3) Delivery constraints of DGs: $\left\{\left(l_i^0, l_i^1, a_i, E_i\right)\right\}$;
    4) Budget: δ
    5) Delivery weight: $\mathbf{w} = \{w_{ij}\}$;
  Output: 1) Sensing time of tasks: $\widehat{\mathbf{t}} = \left\{\widehat{t}_{ij}^{k}\right\}$;
    2) Route selection: $\widehat{\mathbf{x}} = \left\{\widehat{x}_{ij}\right\}$;
    3) Total utility: U;
  1: $\mathcal{R}_1 \leftarrow \mathcal{R}$;
  2: for $n = 1:N^s$ **do**
  3:   Initialize $\mathcal{A}_n \leftarrow \{r_0\}$, where $r_0 = \arg\max_{r \in \mathcal{R}_n} \{H(\{r\})\}$ and r_0 satisfies constraints (6.6) and (6.7);
  4:   **while 1 do**

(continued)

Algorithm 6.2 (continued)

   5:   **If** there exists a route $r \in \mathcal{A}_n$, such that $H(\mathcal{A}_n \backslash \{r\}) > \left(1 + \frac{\varepsilon}{I^4 J^4}\right) H(\mathcal{A}_n)$

then

   6:      Delete the route r, *i.e.*, $\mathcal{A}_n \leftarrow \mathcal{A}_n \backslash \{r\}$;

   7:   **else If** there exist $\lfloor p \rfloor$ routes $r_j^e \in \mathcal{R}_n \backslash \mathcal{A}_n \cup \{\varnothing\} \sim (j \in \{1, \ldots, \lfloor p \rfloor\})$

and $\lfloor p \rfloor$ routes $r_i^d \in \mathcal{A}_n \cup \{\varnothing\} \sim (i \in \{1, \ldots, \lfloor p \rfloor\})$, such that $\mathcal{A}_n' = $

$\mathcal{A}_n \backslash \left\{r_j^e\right\}_{\lfloor p \rfloor} \cup \left\{r_i^d\right\}_{\lfloor p \rfloor}$ satisfies constraints (6.6) and (6.7), and $H(\mathcal{A}_n') > $

$\left(1 + \frac{\varepsilon}{I^4 J^4}\right) H(\mathcal{A}_n)$

     then

   8:      Exchange the routes $\left\{r_j^e\right\}_{\lfloor 2p \rfloor}$ for $\left\{r_i^d\right\}_{\lfloor p \rfloor}$, *i.e.*, $\mathcal{A}_n \leftarrow \mathcal{A}_n'$;

   9:   **else**

 10:     **Break;**

 11: $\mathcal{R}_{n+1} = \mathcal{R}_n \backslash \mathcal{A}_n$

 12: $\mathcal{A} \leftarrow \arg \max_{\mathcal{A}_n} \{H(\mathcal{A}_n) | \forall n \in \{1, \ldots, N^c\}\}$

 13: Set $\widehat{\mathbf{x}} \leftarrow \left\{\widehat{x}_{ij} = 1 | \forall i, j, (i, j) \in \mathcal{A}\right\}$;

 14: Set $\widehat{\mathbf{t}} = H(\widehat{\mathbf{x}})$;

 15: Compute U based on $\widehat{\mathbf{t}}, \widehat{\mathbf{x}}$, and $\mathbf{w}$ according to Eq. (6.4);

 16: return $\widehat{\mathbf{t}}, \widehat{\mathbf{x}}$, and U.

Approximation Algorithm for Route-Time Joint Allocation

The new problem comes to a combinatorial optimization problem only with the 0–1 variables $\mathbf{x}$, after the equivalent problem transformation with the new objective function $H(\mathbf{x})$. Also, it has been proved that this problem was maximizing a *non-monotone, submodular* function subject to *two partition matroid* constraints in section "Analysis of Objective Function and Constraints". Therefore, we put forward the *p*-exchange local-search-based route-time joint allocation algorithm named *RT-alg* based on the inspiration of the local search scheme [48]. As illustrated in Algorithm 6.2, *RT-alg* algorithm is composed of two-level iterations, including the outer loop (*i.e.*, lines 2–12) and the inner loop (*i.e.*, lines 4–10). In the following, we present two core ideas behind the design of this algorithm:

1. In the inner loop, we leverage two operations of *p*-exchange local search, *i.e.*, deletion of one route and exchange of *p* routes. The algorithm based on two operations can get a feasible solution that satisfies the partition matroid constraints (6.6) and (6.7) in each iteration, as the matroid constraints have the basis exchange property [48]. Moreover, it iteratively finds new solutions of higher

utility in the neighborhood of the old one until it fails to promote the utility, which results in a locally optimal solution.

2. Due to the non-monotone objective function, it often achieves a solution that is locally optimal in the inner loop. Therefore, we look for multiple different locally optimal solutions and select the best one, in order to get a globally optimal solution in the outer loop, which ensures an approximation ratio of $\frac{1}{4+\epsilon}$ (demonstrated in the proof of Theorem 6.2).

Particularly, we define the set of all the DG-route candidate selections as $\mathcal{R}:=\{r=(i,j)|\forall i \in \mathcal{I}, \forall j \in \mathcal{J}\}$. $\mathcal{A}$ denotes the set of the selected DG-route pairs, i.e., $\mathcal{A}=\{(i,j)|x_{ij}=1, \forall i \in \mathcal{I}, \forall j \in \mathcal{J}\}$, and $\mathcal{A} \subseteq \mathcal{R}$. $\forall \mathcal{A} \subseteq \mathcal{R}$, $H(\mathcal{A}):=\{H(\mathbf{x})|\forall (i,j) \in \mathcal{A}, x_{ij}=1; \forall(i,j) \notin \mathcal{A}, x_{ij}=0\}$. It should noticed that though $H(\mathcal{A})$ and $H(\mathbf{x})$ serve as different functions, we utilize the same symbol $H(\cdot)$ to denote their functions to simplify the process. As illustrated in Algorithm 6.2, we initialize $\mathcal{R}_1$ with $\mathcal{R}$ in line 1. Next, it searches multiple locally optimal route sets in lines 2–12 in the outer loop. As illustrated in lines 4–10, it iteratively substitutes the current route set with its best neighbor to find one locally optimal route set in the inner loop; a neighbor represents a route set in the neighborhood of the current route set. The neighborhood is a collection of route sets resulting from two operations: (1) deletion of one route in lines 5–6; (2) exchange of p routes in lines 7–8. It should be noticed that, as the matroid constraints have the exchange property [48], the deletion operation on a feasible solution in lines 5–6 still results in a feasible solution that satisfies the matroid constraints (6.6) and (6.7). In addition, in lines 5 and 7, the utility increment ratio in each iteration should be more than $\frac{\epsilon}{l^4 J^4}$ so as to get the near-optimal solution in polynomial time, where ϵ is an arbitrarily small positive parameter. p is a parameter related to ϵ, which is set according to [48], i.e., $p=\left\lceil\frac{4}{\epsilon}\right\rceil$, $H(\cdot)$ in Algorithm 6.2 is computed by Algorithm 6.1. N^c represents the number of matroid constraints, e.g., $N^c=2$ in the RT problem.

6.4.3   Route-Time-Weight Joint Optimization Algorithm

Based on the *RT-alg* algorithm in Sect. 6.4.2, we put forward *RTW-alg*, an iterative joint route-time-weight optimization algorithm to address the RTW problem. As shown in Algorithm 6.3, given the delivery weight, it alternately optimizes the route selection and the sensing time, which are fed back to update the allocation of delivery weight for higher utility. Particularly, let N represent the maximal number of iterations, which is a limited constant due to the algorithm convergency proved in section "Analysis of Algorithm Performance". We use $\mathbf{x}^{(n)}$, $\mathbf{t}^{(n)}$, and $\mathbf{w}^{(n)}$ to denote the results of route selection, sensing time, and delivery weight in the n-th iteration, respectively. In each iteration $n+1$, it includes two steps as follows:

1. *Optimizing route selection and sensing time allocation*: As shown in line 3 of Algorithm 6.3, given the delivery weight allocation $\mathbf{w}^{(n)}$ of the n-th iteration, we

optimize the route selection $\mathbf{x}^{(n+1)}$ and the sensing time assignment $\mathbf{t}^{(n+1)}$ by using Algorithm 6.2 with the initial solution $\mathbf{x}^{(n)}$.

2. *Optimizing delivery weight allocation*: In line 4, based on the new route selection $\mathbf{x}^{(n+1)}$ and the new sensing time allocation $\mathbf{t}^{(n+1)}$, according to Eqs. (6.4), (6.5), (6.8), and (6.12), the RTW problem is a bounded knapsack problem with integral variables $\{w_{ij}\}$, which is NP-hard [46]. Therefore, we leverage the greedy algorithm [46] to achieve a constant-factor near-optimal solution. This algorithm is not specified due to the page limit.

Algorithm 6.3 *RTW-alg* Algorithm
Input: 1) Set of feasible routes: $\mathcal{J}$;
     2) Set of sensing tasks: $\{(u_k, \overline{U}_k)\}$
     3) Delivery constraints of DGs: $\{(l_i^0, l_i^1, a_i, E_i)\}$;
     4) Budget: δ

Output: 1) Sensing time of tasks: $\widehat{\mathbf{t}} = \{\widehat{t}_{ij}^k\}$;
     2) Route selection: $\widehat{\mathbf{x}} = \{\widehat{x}_{ij}\}$;
     3) Delivery weight: $\widehat{\mathbf{w}} = \{\widehat{w}_{ij}\}$;
     4) Total utility: U;
1: Initialize $\mathbf{x}^{(0)}$, $\mathbf{t}^{(0)}$, and $\mathbf{w}^{(0)}$; $n \leftarrow 1$;
2: while $(U^{(n)} > (1 + \varepsilon)U^{(n+1)})$ && $(n \leq N)$ **do**
3:   Given $\mathbf{w}^{(n)}$, optimize $\mathbf{x}^{(n+1)}$ and $\mathbf{t}^{(n+1)}$ by using Algorithm 6.2 with initial solution $\mathbf{x}^{(n)}$;
4:   Given $\mathbf{x}^{(n+1)}$ and $\mathbf{t}^{(n+1)}$, optimize $\mathbf{w}^{(n+1)}$ by exploiting Greedy algorithm;
5:   Compute $U^{(n+1)}$ based on $\mathbf{x}^{(n+1)}$, $\mathbf{t}^{(n+1)}$, and $\mathbf{w}^{(n+1)}$, according to Eq. (6.4);
6: $n \leftarrow n + 1$;
7: return $\mathbf{t}^{(n)}$, $\mathbf{x}^{(n)}$, $\mathbf{w}^{(n)}$, and $U^{(n)}$;

6.4.4   Theoretical Analysis of Algorithms

Analysis of Objective Function and Constraints

To start with, we reformulate the RT problem with $H(\mathbf{x})$ into a set function optimization problem as Eqs. (6.19)–(6.21), followed by the analysis of the properties of its objective function and constraints.

$$\max_{\mathcal{A} \subseteq \mathcal{R}} \; H(\mathcal{A}), \tag{6.19}$$

$$\text{s.t.} \sum_{j:(i,j)\in\mathcal{A}} \mathbf{1}_{(i,j)\in\mathcal{A}} \leq a_i, \forall i \in \mathcal{I}, \tag{6.20}$$

$$\sum_{i:(i,j)\in\mathcal{A}} \mathbf{1}_{(i,j)\in\mathcal{A}} \leq 1, \forall j \in \mathcal{J}. \tag{6.21}$$

where $\mathbf{1}$ represents the indicator function to demonstrate whether an element (i, j) is in the set $\mathcal{A}$ or not.

Definition 6.1 (*Non-negativity, Monotonicity, Submodularity* [48]) A set function $f : 2^{\mathcal{R}} \to \mathbb{R}$ ($\mathcal{R}$ is a finite ground set) is (1) *non-negative* if $f(\varnothing) = 0$ and $f(\mathcal{A}) \geq 0$ ($\forall \mathcal{A} \subseteq \mathcal{R}$); (2) *monotone* if for $\forall \mathcal{A} \subseteq \mathcal{B} \subseteq \mathcal{R}, f(\mathcal{A}) \leq f(\mathcal{B})$; (3) *submodular*, if and only if $\forall \mathcal{A} \subseteq \mathcal{B} \subseteq \mathcal{R}$ and $\forall r \in \mathcal{R}\backslash\mathcal{B}, f(\mathcal{A} \cup \{r\}) - f(\mathcal{A}) \geq f(\mathcal{B} \cup \{r\}) - f(\mathcal{B})$.

Lemma 6.2 *The objective function* $H(\mathcal{A})(\mathcal{A} \subseteq \mathcal{R})$ *is nonnegative, non-monotone, and submodular.*

Proof (1) Non-negativity. When $\mathcal{A} = \varnothing, \forall i, j, k, \overset{\curvearrowright k}{t_{ij}} = 0$, and $H(\mathcal{A}) = 0$. Furthermore, $\forall \mathcal{A} \subseteq \mathcal{R}, \mathcal{A} \neq \varnothing, H(\mathcal{A}) \geq 0$ due to the non-negative utility in Eq. (6.14). Thus Therefore, $H(\mathcal{A})$ is non-negative. (2) Submodularity. According to Based on Definition 6.1, we should can prove that $\forall \mathcal{A} \subseteq \mathcal{B} \subseteq \mathcal{R}, \forall r_1 = (i_1, j_1) \in \mathcal{R}\backslash\mathcal{B}$, the following relationship holds

$$H(\mathcal{A} \cup \{r_1\}) - H(\mathcal{A}) \geq H(\mathcal{B} \cup \{r_1\}) - H(\mathcal{B}). \tag{6.22}$$

Let $\mathbf{t}^{(0)}$, $\mathbf{t}^{(1)}$, $\mathbf{t}^{(2)}$, and $\mathbf{t}^{(3)}$ denote to represent the optimal sensing time allocations according to based on Eq. (6.13) under the route selections $\mathcal{A}$, $\mathcal{A} \cup \{r_1\}$, $\mathcal{B}$, and $\mathcal{B} \cup \{r_1\}$, respectively. Hence Therefore, according to Eq. (6.14), we have

$$H(\mathcal{A}) = \sum_{(i,j)\in\mathcal{A}} \left(\lambda \sum_{k\in\mathcal{K}_j} u_k t_{ij}^{k(0)} + (1-\lambda)\tau w_{ij} \right), \tag{6.23}$$

$$H(\mathcal{B}) = \sum_{(i,j)\in\mathcal{B}} \left(\lambda \sum_{k\in\mathcal{K}_j} u_k t_{ij}^{k(2)} + (1-\lambda)\tau w_{ij} \right), \tag{6.24}$$

$$
\begin{aligned}
H(\mathcal{A} \cup \{r_1\}) \quad &= \lambda \sum_{k\in\mathcal{K}_{j_1}} u_k t_{i_1 j_1}^{k(1)} + (1-\lambda)\tau w_{i_1 j_1} \\
&+ \sum_{(i,j)\in\mathcal{A}} \left(\lambda \sum_{k\in\mathcal{K}_j} u_k t_{ij}^{k(1)} + (1-\lambda)\tau w_{ij} \right),
\end{aligned} \tag{6.25}
$$

$$H(\mathcal{B} \cup \{r_1\}) \quad = \lambda \sum_{k \in \mathcal{K}_{j_1}} u_k t_{i_1 j_1}^{k(3)} + (1-\lambda)\tau w_{i_1 j_1}$$
$$+ \sum_{(i,j) \in \mathcal{B}} \left(\lambda \sum_{k \in \mathcal{K}_j} u_k t_{ij}^{k(3)} + (1-\lambda)\tau w_{ij} \right). \tag{6.26}$$

$$\text{LHS of}(22) \quad = \sum_{k \in \mathcal{K}_{j_1}} \lambda u_k t_{i_1 j_1}^{k(1)} + (1-\lambda)\tau w_{i_1 j_1}$$
$$- \lambda \sum_{(i,j) \in \mathcal{A}} \sum_{k \in \mathcal{K}_j} u_k \left(t_{ij}^{k(0)} - t_{ij}^{k(1)} \right), \tag{6.27}$$

$$\text{RHS of } (22) \quad = \sum_{k \in \mathcal{K}_{j_1}} \lambda u_k t_{i_1 j_1}^{k(3)} + (1-\lambda)\tau w_{i_1 j_1}$$
$$- \lambda \sum_{(i,j) \in \mathcal{B}} \sum_{k \in \mathcal{K}_j} u_k \left(t_{ij}^{k(2)} - t_{ij}^{k(3)} \right). \tag{6.28}$$

The first and second terms in Eq. (6.27) show the increased sensing utility and the delivery utility in r_1's tasks, illustrated as $\Delta U_1^+(\mathcal{A} \cup \{r_1\})$ and $\Delta U_2^+(r_1)$, respectively. The third term in Eq. (6.27) denotes the decreased sensing utility in $\mathcal{A}$'s tasks, including two parts. (1) $\Delta U_1^-(\mathcal{A} \cup \{r_1\})$:

Based on Eqs. (6.8) and (6.13), the extra flying energy $e_{i_1 j_1}^\Delta$ induced by r_1 reduces the total sensing energy budget, thereby reducing the sensing utility of $\mathcal{A}$'s tasks. (2) $\Delta U_2^-(\mathcal{A} \cup \{r_1\})$: The new distribution of sensing energy for r_1's tasks decreases this sensing utility. Therefore, we get

$$\text{LHS of } (22) \quad = \left(\Delta U_1^+(\mathcal{A} \cup \{r_1\}) - \Delta U_2^-(\mathcal{A} \cup \{r_1\}) \right)$$
$$+ \Delta U_2^+(r_1) - \Delta U_1^-(\mathcal{A} \cup \{r_1\}), \tag{6.29}$$

$$\text{RHS of } (22) \quad = \left(\Delta U_1^+(\mathcal{B} \cup \{r_1\}) - \Delta U_2^-(\mathcal{B} \cup \{r_1\}) \right)$$
$$+ \Delta U_2^+(r_1) - \Delta U_1^-(\mathcal{B} \cup \{r_1\}). \tag{6.30}$$

Since we utilize the greedy sensing time allocation strategy and $\mathcal{A} \subseteq \mathcal{B}$, based on Eqs. (6.8), (6.13), and (6.14), we get

$$\Delta U_1^+(\mathcal{A} \cup \{r_1\}) - \Delta U_2^-(\mathcal{A} \cup \{r_1\}) \geq \Delta U_1^+(\mathcal{B} \cup \{r_1\})$$
$$- \Delta U_2^-(\mathcal{B} \cup \{r_1\}), \tag{6.31}$$

$$\Delta U_1^-(\mathcal{A} \cup \{r_1\}) \leq \Delta U_1^-(\mathcal{B} \cup \{r_1\}). \tag{6.32}$$

Therefore, based on Eqs. (6.29)–(6.32), Eq. (6.22) holds and $H(\mathcal{A})$ is submodular. Furthermore, since proving $H(\cdot)$ is non-monotone by constructing a counter-example is easy, we do not illustrate its proof due to the space limit. Therefore, Lemma 6.2 is proved.

Definition 6.2 (Partition Matroid [49]) Consider a finite ground set $\mathcal{R}$, and a non-empty collection of subsets of $\mathcal{R}$ denoted as $\mathcal{M}$. The pair $(\mathcal{R}, \mathcal{M})$ is a partition matroid, if and only if it holds the four conditions: (1) $\varnothing \in \mathcal{M}$; (2) If $\mathcal{A} \subseteq \mathcal{B} \in \mathcal{M}$, then $\mathcal{A} \in \mathcal{M}$; (3) If $\mathcal{A} \in \mathcal{M}$, $\mathcal{B} \in \mathcal{M}$ and $|\mathcal{A}| < |\mathcal{B}|$, then $\exists r \in \mathcal{B} \backslash \mathcal{A}$ such that $\mathcal{A} \cup \{r\} \in \mathcal{M}$. (4) there exist l disjoint sets (*i.e.*, $\mathcal{R}_1, \cdots, \mathcal{R}_l$) and l positive integers (*i.e.*, $o_1, \ldots, o_l$), such that $\mathcal{R} := \bigcup_{i=1}^{l} \mathcal{R}_i$ and $\mathcal{M} := \{\mathcal{A} : \mathcal{A} \subseteq \mathcal{R}, |\mathcal{A} \cap \mathcal{R}_i| \le o_i, \forall i \in \{1, \ldots, l\}\}$ hold.

Lemma 6.3 Constraints (6.20) and (6.21) are partition matroid constraints.

Proof Based on Definition 6.2, we prove that the pair $(\mathcal{R}, \mathcal{M})$ constructed by constraint (6.20) meets the four conditions of partition matroid in the following.

1. According to Eq. (6.20), It is easy to prove that $\varnothing \in \mathcal{M}$
2. We utilize the proof by contradiction, assuming that the second condition does not hold. Therefore, $\exists \mathcal{A} \subseteq \mathcal{B} \in \mathcal{M}$, $\mathcal{A} \notin \mathcal{M}$. Based on Eq. (6.20), $\exists i_1, \sum_{j:(i_1,j)\in\mathcal{A}} 1_{(i_1,j)\in\mathcal{A}} > a_{i_1}$. Since $\mathcal{A} \subseteq \mathcal{B}$, $\sum_{j:(i_1,j)\in\mathcal{B}} 1_{(i_1,j)\in\mathcal{B}} > a_{i_1}$. Therefore, $\mathcal{B} \notin \mathcal{M}$, which is not true, and the second condition holds.
3. When both $\mathcal{A}$ and $\mathcal{B}$ have the same set of DG i, as $\mathcal{A} \in \mathcal{M}$, $\mathcal{B} \in \mathcal{M}$, and $|\mathcal{A}| < |\mathcal{B}|$, $\exists i_1$ which meets the following condition:

$$\sum_{j:(i_1,j)\in\mathcal{A}} 1_{(i_1,j)\in\mathcal{A}} < \sum_{j:(i_1,j)\in\mathcal{B}} 1_{(i_1,j)\in\mathcal{B}} \le a_{i_1}. \tag{6.33}$$

Therefore, according to Eq. (6.33), $\exists r_1 = (i_1, j_1) \in \mathcal{B} \backslash \mathcal{A}$ which meets the following inequation:

$$\sum_{j:(i_1,j)\in\mathcal{A}\cup\{r_1\}} 1_{(i_1,j)\in\mathcal{A}\cup\{r_1\}} \le \sum_{j:(i_1,j)\in\mathcal{B}} 1_{(i_1,j)\in\mathcal{B}}. \tag{6.34}$$

On the basis of Eqs. (6.33) and (6.34), we get

$$\sum_{j:(i_1,j)\in\mathcal{A}\cup\{r_1\}} 1_{(i_1,j)\in\mathcal{A}\cup\{r_1\}} \le a_{i_1}. \tag{6.35}$$

Hence, $\mathcal{A} \cup \{r_1\} \in \mathcal{M}$, and the third condition holds. In addition, we can prove that the third condition holds when $\mathcal{A}$ and $\mathcal{B}$ differ in sets of DG i.
4. To divide $\mathcal{R}$ based on the index of DGs, we get $\mathcal{R} = \cup_{i=1}^{I} \mathcal{R}_i$, where $\mathcal{R}_i := \{(i,j) | \forall j \in \mathcal{J}\}$. Therefore, according to Definition 6.2, $\forall \mathcal{A} \in \mathcal{M}$, we get

$$\sum_{j:(i,j)\in\mathcal{A}\cap\mathcal{R}_i} 1_{(i,j)\in\mathcal{A}\cap\mathcal{R}_i} \le a_i, \forall i \in \{1, \ldots, I\}. \tag{6.36}$$

Hence, there are I disjoint sets and positive integers $\{(\mathcal{R}_i, a_i)\}$ that meet the fourth condition. In summary, as constraint (6.20) meets all the four conditions, it is a partition matroid constraint. Likewise, by setting a_i to 1, constraint (6.21) is also a partition matroid. Therefore, Lemma 6.3 is proved.

Analysis of Algorithm Performance

Based on Lemmas 6.2 and 6.3, we analyze the performance of the proposed algorithms as follows.

Theorem 6.2 *RT-alg* algorithm can achieve a near-optimal solution with the $\frac{1}{4+\varepsilon}$-approximation ratio ($\varepsilon > 0$) in the polynomial time complexity $O((IJ)^6 K \lg(IJ) \lg K)$, where I, J, and K denote the number of DGs, feasible routes, and tasks, respectively.

Proof According to Lemmas 6.1–6.3, the RT problem with the new objective function $H(\mathbf{x})$ is equivalently transformed into maximizing a non-negative, non-monotone, and submodular function under the constraints of two partition matroid. Reference [48] addresses the pure mathematical problem of maximizing non-monotone submodular functions under the constraints of matroid and knapsack, and gives an approximation ratio by utilizing the p-exchange local search. Therefore, referring to [48], the rout-time joint allocation algorithm base on the p-exchange local search can achieve $\frac{1}{4+\varepsilon}$-approximation ratio. For the rest content, we only summarize three basic ideas behind the proof, while the details can be found in [48].

1. *Partition matroid constraints make it possible to acquire feasible solutions with p-exchange local search.* The reason is as follows: the constraints of partition matroid have the partition basis exchange property [48]. Thus, for a set of feasible routes, there is always another set of feasible routes; the exchange of at most p routes between them still gets two feasible solutions. It should be pointed out that adding or deleting routes can be considered as an exchange between the routes and the trivial entity $\emptyset$.
2. *One locally optimal solution in the inner loop has a lower bound for utility, but the approximation ratio is not guaranteed.* The locally optimal solution of the local search in the inner loop is denoted as S, and the globally optimal solution is denoted as C. Due to local optimality of the S, it is the best solution in its neighborhood, *i.e.*,

$$f(S) \geq f\left(S \backslash \left\{r_j^e\right\}_{\lfloor p \rfloor} \cup \left\{r_i^d\right\}_{\lfloor p \rfloor}\right). \tag{6.37}$$

From the first basic idea, given a locally optimal solution S, it is feasible to acquire the globally optimal solution C after many steps of route exchange. Thus, we can measure the difference in utility between S and C by evaluating the change in utility at each step. Owing to the submodularity of the objective function, after union and division of exchanged routes at each step, we can get an inequality based on Eq. (6.37):

$$2f(S) \geq (1 - 1/p)f(S \cup C) + f(S \cap C). \tag{6.38}$$

When the objective function is monotone, the inequality in Eq. (6.38) can provide an approximation ratio of $\frac{1-1/p}{2}$, when the objective function is monotone. Nevertheless, our objective function is non-monotone, so the approximation ratio does not hold, and the solution requires to be expanded further as in the third basic idea.

3. In the outer loop, Searching multiple locally optimal solutions improves utility, thus obtaining the near-optimal solution with an approximation ratio. Specifically, after obtaining the best solution among N^c locally optimal solutions in the outer loop, from Eqs. (6.37) and (6.38), we get the following inequality:

$$4\left(1 + \frac{1}{p-1}\right)f(S) \geq f(C). \tag{6.39}$$

Since $p = \frac{4}{\varepsilon}$, according to Eq. (6.39), we have

$$f(S) \geq \frac{1}{4+\varepsilon}f(C). \tag{6.40}$$

Therefore, the solution is near-optimal with an approximation ratio of $\frac{1}{4+\varepsilon}$.

Finally, we analyze the time complexity of the *RT-alg* algorithm, which has at most $O((IJ)^4 \lg(IJ))$ iterations, and each iteration's time complexity is $O((IJ)^2 K \lg (K))$.

Therefore, the time complexity of *RT-alg* algorithm is polynomial, *i.e.*, $O((IJ)^6 K \lg(IJ) \lg K)$.

Theorem 6.3 *RTW-alg* algorithm with non-decreasing utilities in each iteration can realize the convergency in polynomial time complexity $O((IJ)^6 K \lg(IJ) \lg K)$, where I, J, and K denote the number of DGs, feasible routes, and tasks, respectively.

Proof Make $U(\mathbf{x}^{(n+1)}, \mathbf{t}^{(n+1)}, \mathbf{w}^{(n)})$ and $U(\mathbf{x}^{(n+1)}, \mathbf{t}^{(n+1)}, \mathbf{w}^{(n+1)})$ represent the n-th iteration's utilities implemented by steps 3 and 4 of Algorithm 6.3 respectively. $\mathbf{x}^{(n+1)}$ and $\mathbf{t}^{(n+1)}$ are updated by exploiting Algorithm 6.2 with the initial solution $\mathbf{x}^{(n)}$. As shown in lines 5–8 of Algorithm 6.2, the new solution replaces the old one in each iteration, only if it has at least $\frac{\varepsilon}{I^4 J^4}$ utility improvement. Therefore, we get

$$U\left(\mathbf{x}^{(n+1)}, \mathbf{t}^{(n+1)}, \mathbf{w}^{(n)}\right) \geq U\left(\mathbf{x}^{(n)}, \mathbf{t}^{(n)}, \mathbf{w}^{(n)}\right). \tag{6.41}$$

Furthermore, $\mathbf{w}^{(n+1)}$ is calculated from $\mathbf{x}^{(n+1)}$, $\mathbf{t}^{(n+1)}$, and $\mathbf{w}^{(n)}$ by leveraging Greedy algorithm. Because the RTW problem given $\mathbf{x}$ and $\mathbf{t}$ is a bounded knapsack problem with integral variables $\mathbf{w}$, we get

$$U\left(\mathbf{x}^{(n+1)}, \mathbf{t}^{(n+1)}, \mathbf{w}^{(n+1)}\right) \geq U\left(\mathbf{x}^{(n+1)}, \mathbf{t}^{(n+1)}, \mathbf{w}^{(n)}\right). \tag{6.42}$$

Therefore, from Eqs. (6.41) and (6.42), Algorithm 6.3 achieves non-decreasing solutions in each iteration. In addition, as there must be an upper bound on the values of RTW problem, the convergency of Algorithm 6.3 is ensured. Furthermore, according to the time complexity of Algorithm 6.2 in Theorem 6.2, that of Algorithm 6.3 is also $O(N(IJ)^6 K \lg(IJ) \lg K)$.

6.5 Experimental Evaluations

We make comprehensive simulations for the evaluation of the performance of our algorithms leveraging real-world traces, including the dataset of delivery stations in Beijing City illustrated in Fig. 6.1 and the drone energy consumption traces shown in Fig. 6.2a, b. In addition, we perform field experiments for the algorithms' performance evaluation by implementing a prototype system, followed by deploying a real-world application to demonstrate its feasibility in practice.

6.5.1 Traces-Based Simulations

Evaluation Methodology and Settings

Employing the delivery dataset, we perform extensive simulations in a large-scale area (about 6084 km^2) of Beijing City with 239 DGs. The number of drones available in each DG randomly varies from 3 to 7. In addition, the drone battery capacity, the delivery weight, and the energy cost with various weights are set according to the real energy consumption traces. There are 10,000 sensing tasks in total that are randomly distributed in this area. As is shown in the delivery and sensing model in Sect. 6.3.1, the utility function is set as $G_k(t_k) = \min\left(u_k t_k, \overline{U}_k\right)$. Additionally, the utility weight (u_k) and the utility bound ($\overline{U}_k$) of tasks follow the randomly uniform distributions in [25, 50] and [1000, 2000], respectively. Moreover, we regard 235,872 J from the battery of field experiments in Sect. 6.5.2 as the reference battery capacity. To mimic drones from different DGs, we let E_i vary in [100, 200] KJ. The total utility is computed according to Eqs. (6.4) and (6.11). The budget of the overall extra energy cost changes from 150 to 200 kJ [2, 11]. $\varepsilon = 0.01$, $\lambda = 0.5$, $p = 1$, $N^c = 2$, $N = 100$. All the experiments are conducted on the Asus computer (3 GHz, 192 GB RAM), and the average results of 20 runs is computed.

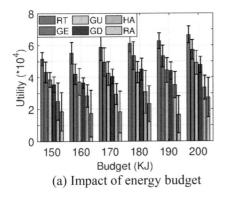
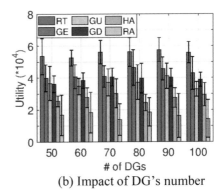

(a) Impact of energy budget   (b) Impact of DG's number

Fig. 6.6   Performance evaluations of *RT-alg* in terms of different energy budget and DGs' number, respectively. (**a**) Impact of energy budget. (**b**) Impact of DG's number

To evaluate the performance of our algorithms in a comprehensive manner, we exploit six baseline methods as follows.

1. *Greedy utility algorithm* (GU) [50]: It greedily chooses the route with maximal utility.
2. *Greedy cost-efficiency algorithm* (GE) [39]: It greedily selects the route of the maximal cost efficiency, *i.e.*, the ratio of the utility to its extra energy cost.
3. *Greedy distance algorithm* (GD): It greedily selects the route with minimal incremental distance.
4. *Heuristic algorithm* (HA) [37]: We borrow the idea of reference [37] and leverage the heuristic algorithm (*e.g.*, the simulated annealing [2]) to search near-optimal routes.
5. *Random route algorithm* (RA): It randomly selects the routes under constraints (6.5)–(6.7).
6. *Optimal method* (OPT): It utilizes the brutal-force search approach to get the optimal solution. Owing to the exponential time complexity, we only employ the OPT method in the small-scale scenarios.

It is worth noting that, GU, GE, GD, HA, and RA methods use the greedy sensing time allocation scheme and the iterative joint optimization scheme with the greedy delivery weight allocation, similar to *RTW-alg*. Also, due to the space limit, in Figs. 6.6, 6.7, 6.8, 6.9, 6.10, 6.11, 6.12, and 6.13, we use RT and RTW to represent *RT-alg* and *RTW-alg*, respectively.

Performances of RT-alg Algorithm

In the beginning, we evaluate the performances of *RT-alg* algorithm with varied budgets and DGs' numbers. Specifically, as shown in Fig. 6.6a, *RT-alg* always has higher utility than other methods in different budgets, while averagely surpassing

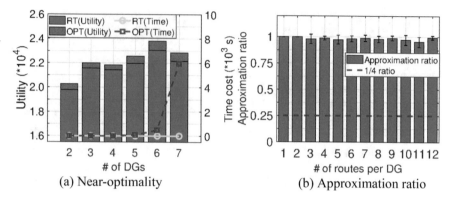

Fig. 6.7 Evaluations of the near-optimality and the approximation ratio by comparing *RT-alg* with OPT method. (**a**) Near-optimality. (**b**) Approximation ratio

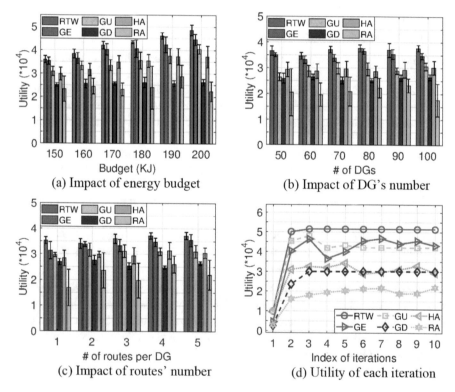

Fig. 6.8 Performance evaluations of *RTW-alg* in terms of different energy budgets (**a**), DGs' numbers (**b**), and routes' numbers per DG (**c**). Evaluation of its convergency in terms of different iteration numbers (**d**)

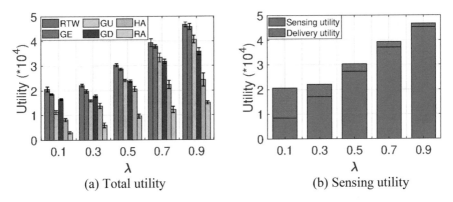

(a) Total utility (b) Sensing utility

Fig. 6.9 Influence of the model parameter λ on the performance of *RTW-alg*. (**a**) Total utility. (**b**) Sensing utility

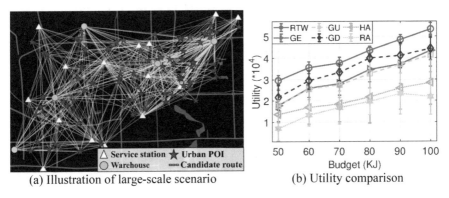

(a) Illustration of large-scale scenario (b) Utility comparison

Fig. 6.10 Trace-based case study, *i.e.*, reusing 120 delivery drones to monitor AQI of 83 POIs in Beijing City. (**a**) Illustration of large-scale scenario. (**b**) Utility comparison

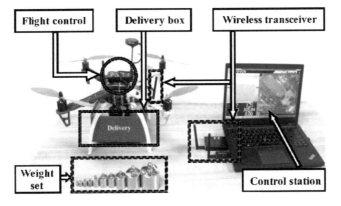

Fig. 6.11 The prototype system of urban crowdsensing based on a delivery drone

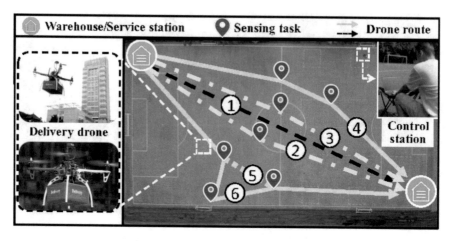

Fig. 6.12 Small-scale field experiments based on two delivery drones with the prototype system on a football pitch

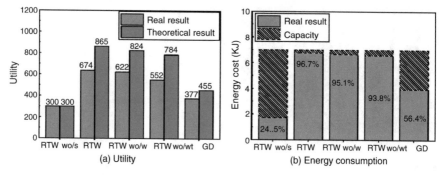

Fig. 6.13 The experimental results evaluate the utility (**a**) and the energy cost (**b**) of *RTW-alg* and four baselines

GE, GU, GD, HA, and RA by 19.6%, 39.8%, 43.0%, 95.7%, and 199.4%, respectively. Meanwhile, the utilities of *RT-alg*, GE, GU, GD, and HA roughly increase with the budget except for RA, since RA has fluctuating performances because of the random route selection. In addition, Fig. 6.6b indicates that *RT-alg* averagely outperforms GE, GU, GD, HA, and RA by 29.6%, 51.4%, 41.9%, 101.8%, and 242.0% respectively in different numbers of DGs. Moreover, Fig. 6.6b demonstrates that the variation of DG's number has a mild effect on the utility.

At last, we compare *RT-alg* with OPT in the matter of both utility and time cost in a small-scale scenario (*i.e.*, 7 DGs). As shown in Fig. 6.7a, the time cost of OPT has an exponential rising with the number of DGs, while the cost of *RT-alg* is negligible. For instance, when there are 7 DGs with 28 candidate routes, OPT has a time cost that is up to about 1.7 h, while *RT-alg* spends only 2.3 s. In comparison with OPT, *RT-alg* can averagely get 97.5% of the optimal utility with the time cost of merely

Table 6.2 Runtime comparison between *RT-alg* and five baselines in different numbers of routes per DG

Algorithm	Runtime (s)			
	$J = 12$	$J = 18$	$J = 24$	$J = 32$
RT	1.0606	1.2261	1.2965	1.4044
GE	0.1394	0.1424	0.1531	0.1814
GU	0.0744	0.0755	0.0761	0.0914
GD	0.0102	0.0119	0.0125	0.0139
RA	0.0127	0.0148	0.0148	0.0145
OPT	1.1700e+03	3.6335e+04	[a]	[a]

[a] The algorithm cannot output results in several days

0.04%. In the meantime, we also evaluate the approximation ratio of *RT-alg* in varied numbers of routes per DG. As shown in Table 6.2, the OPT method requires time cost that is tremendously high, *e.g.*, when the amount of routes per DG is over 18, the runtime is over 10 h. Therefore, we only evaluate the approximation ratio of *RT-alg* under the condition that the number of routes per DG is below 18. As indicated in Fig. 6.7b, the average approximation ratio of *RT-alg* is 98.3% (much higher than 1/4). Therefore, the 1/4-approximation ratio is merely the lower bound of *RT-alg*, and its real approximation ratio is generally much higher than this bound.

Performances of RTW-Algorithm

We evaluate the performance of *RTW-alg* algorithm in various budgets, DGs' number, and routes' number per DG. As illustrated in Fig. 6.8a–c, RTW-alg averagely surpasses GE, GU, GD, HA, and RA by 6.0%, 20.2%, 64.2%, 23.2%, and 75.0% in different budgets, respectively; 5.8%, 27.1%, 42.3%, 25.7%, and 79.4% in different number of DGs, respectively; 6.6%, 16.3%, 37.3%, 20.2%, and 69.4% in different number of routes per DG, respectively. It is worth noticing that, Fig. 6.8b indicates that the rise of the number of DGs fails to promote the utilities of these six methods. That is because the 50 DGs randomly distributed in the area have sufficient feasible routes to cover most of the tasks. Therefore, the key factor to boost utility is not the DGs' number. Instead, the key factor is the energy budget when the tasks of given routes cover the total task utility weight distribution. In addition, we evaluate the convergence of *RTW-alg* algorithm. As illustrated in Fig. 6.8d, the utility of *RTW-alg* is promoted in every iteration, and the algorithm rapidly converges after six iterations. These experiments are in line with the theoretical proof in section "Analysis of Algorithm Performance".

At last, we evaluate the performance of *RTW-alg* algorithm in different settings of the model parameter λ, compared with five baselines. As illustrated in Fig. 6.9a, if we change λ from 0.1 to 0.9, *RTW-alg* always outperforms the five baselines in the general utility. Particularly, the general utility of *RTW-alg* averagely improves by 49.2%, 110.0%, 14.0%, 34.8%, and 348.1% in comparison with GU, HA, GE, GD, and RA, respectively. Moreover, we present the impacts of λ on the utility of sensing and delivery. As shown in Fig. 6.9b, the parameter λ trades off the sensing utility against the delivery utility. The sensing utility of *RTW-alg* rises with λ. In contrast, the delivery utility declines with it. We can set this parameter according to the significance of the sensing utility in comparison with the delivery utility in particular applications.

Case Study of Drone-Based AQI Monitoring

We emulate a large-scale trace-based case study that stems from the inspiration of the exceptional drone-based urban AQI sensing applications [7, 51]. In particular, the dataset of 83 important Points of Interest (POIs) [8] is collected within the 4-th Ring road of Beijing City, including factories, shopping malls, etc. Leveraging the datasets of the POIs and the delivery stations in Beijing City, as shown in Fig. 6.10a, the application of reusing delivery drones is emulated to monitor the AQI of urban POIs [7, 51]. As illustrated in Fig. 6.10b, the utility of all these approaches improves with the increase of budget. Additionally, ours can achieve the best utility in various budgets and averagely outperform GE, GU, GD, HA, and RA by 36.2%, 39.4%, 19.6%, 100.5%, and 163.3%, respectively.

In summary, the trace-based simulations demonstrate that *our method can averagely improve the sensing and delivery utility by 36.2% than five baselines despite the restricted budget. Additionally, we can averagely have 97.5% of the optimal utility with the time cost of the OPT method at only 0.04%.*

6.5.2   Field Experiments

System Implementation

We build a delivery quadcopter (about 2 kg) fixed with a flight controller (*i.e.*, Pixhawk 2.4.8) and a battery (12.6 V, 5200 mAh, 235,872 J), as illustrated in Fig. 6.11. Next, we leverage a computer with Mission Planner [52] as the control station. This station communicates with the drone by using the wireless transceiver. This station is capable of controlling the drone's flight (*e.g.*, its route and sensing time). Also, it can receive its real-time flight state, energy consumption, and sensing data [6]. In addition, we employ an onboard power module to supervise the drone's current and voltage in real-time, which are leveraged to precisely measure the drone's flying/hovering energy consumption. Also, we accurately alter the delivery weight by employing a delivery box with a weight set.

Experimental Settings and Baselines

As illustrated in Fig. 6.12, we take into consideration a small-scale experimental scenario that two drones of a DG are delivering 600 g packages in total at the speed of 5 m/s from the warehouse to the service station on a football pitch. In addition, seven sensing tasks are assigned on this pitch with different utility weights and bounds. Since the number of candidate routes of these small-scale experiments is only six, GE, GU, HA, and RA cannot be utilized as the baselines. Therefore, we only leverage GD as the baseline. Moreover, to evaluate the influence of each component of the route-time-weight joint optimization in total performance, we construct ablation studies on *RTW-alg* (called RTW for short) with three variants as follows.

1. RTWwo/w exploits *RTW-alg* without using the delivery weight.
2. RTWwo/wt exploits *RTW-alg* without optimizing the delivery weight and the sensing time.
3. RTWwo/s only delivers packages without crowd sensing.

Experimental Results

As shown in Fig. 6.13a, considering the utilities, *RTW-alg* averagely outperforms GD, RTWwo/wt, RTWwo/w, and RTWwo/s by 78.8%, 22.1%, 8.4%, and 124.7%, respectively. Therefore, it shows that the components of the route-time-weight joint optimization is capable of promoting the utility. For instance, instead of choosing the routes of the minimal distance for GD, RTWwo/wt optimizes the route selection for maximal utility, hence choosing routes 4 and 6. As a result, the utility is promoted by 46.4%. In comparison with RTWwo/w which selects routes 4 and 5 that are in the same delivery weight (300 g), *RTW-alg* considers the optimal allocation of delivery weight. For example, it lets one drone with the lowest weight (*i.e.*, 50 g) fly on route 6 instead of route 5, thus covering more sensing tasks with higher utility. Moreover, as illustrated in Fig. 6.13a, the utility in real-world is always lower than that of the theoretical results for GD, *RTW-alg*, RTWwo/w, and RTWwo/wt. That is because that the wind, direction change, and acceleration/deceleration of drones raise the real energy consumption in the field experiments, thus undermining the sensing utility with the energy cost constraint.

In the end, we evaluate the energy consumption of *RTW-alg* by employing the energy utilization rate, *i.e.*, the ratio of the real energy consumption to the drone battery capacity. As illustrated in Fig. 6.13b, the energy utilization rates of *RTW-alg*, RTWwo/w, RTWwo/wt, GD, and RTWwo/s are 96.7%, 95.1%, 93.8%, 56.4%, and 24.5%, respectively. Consequently, *RTW-alg* can achieve the highest energy utilization rate with the route-time-weight joint optimization.

Summary

The field experiments indicate that components of the route-time-weight joint optimization in RTW-alg have their exclusive contribution in promoting the sensing and delivery utility with the limited energy budget. In addition, in comparison with RTWwo/s (i.e., the original package delivery without crowdsensing), RTW-alg

jointly optimizes route selection, sensing time, and delivery weight, thus raising the
sensing and delivery utility by 124.7% and the energy utilization rate by 72.2%.

6.6   Discussions and Future Works

6.6.1   Generalizing Drone Route Model

Similar to current works [9, 12], we assume a finite number of feasible drone routes $\mathcal{J}$
, which are constructed based on the privacy and security policies and the physical
environments of the cities [53]. For simplicity of introduction, we assume that each
DG has the same number of routes, namely, J. Nevertheless, our model can be
generalized by simple modifications to the more comprehensive assumption that
different DGs have different numbers of candidate routes. Specifically, we associate
the routing sets of all the DGs into a joint set, using $\eta_{ij} = 0(1)$ to indicate whether
route J is for DG i. With this modification, our method can be adapted to this general
model. We will further investigate a more complex model in the future, where
several routes overlap each other; that is, a subset of sensing tasks is covered by
more than one route.

6.6.2   Incentives Behind Drone Sharing

Recently, the sharing economy has been emerging, since it can extremely reduce the
cost and improve the efficiency of resource utilization, such as ride sharing (such as
Uber and DiDi) [23] and parking space sharing [54]. Drone sharing is emerging with
great promise in the sharing economy, as the number of deployed drones increases
[10]. Therefore, the reuse of delivery drones for crowdsensing is necessary and
helpful to achieve large-scale urban crowdsensing at a low cost. A fundamental
assumption for re-utilizing available drones (*e.g.*, delivery drones) is that there are
sufficient incentives [55], like sufficient monetary compensations [23, 44, 56]. Therefore, it is very important to design specific incentive mechanisms for the reuse of
drones, which will be investigated in our future work, *e.g.*, how to design the
monetary compensation on the basis of the sensing quality and the additional
drone energy consumption; how to guarantee the rationality of individuals, which
is very significant to incentivize the drone sharing; how to guarantee the truthfulness
of each participant [45] and privacy protection [57] in MVCS.

6.6.3 Impacts of Delivery Delay

Because most package delivery businesses are delay-sensitive, the delivery delay is indeed a significant factor in the delivery of drones. Nevertheless, the battery capacity of drone is very restricted that also extremely limits its delivery time. For example, the battery capacity of most existing drones supports flight for not greater than an hour [2]. Therefore, in the majority of cases, the limitation on the energy consumption of the drones also guarantees a satisfactory delivery delay. In addition, if urgent delivery is required in some specific cases (*e.g.*, the delivery of medical supply [1]), our model can be simply spread by adding a new limitation on route selection and the sensing time allocation, *i.e.*, $\forall i \in \mathcal{I}, \forall j \in \mathcal{J}, x_{ij} \left(\sum_{k \in \mathcal{K}_j} t_{ij}^k + \frac{d_{ij}}{v} \right) \le T_{ij}$,

where T_{ij} represents the delivery delay limit of the delivery drone of DG i on route j. Moreover, our approach can be fitted to the new model by simple extensions, e.g., adding a new upper bound $(T_{ij} - \sum_{k' \in \mathcal{K}_j / \{k\}} \hat{t}_{ij}^{k'}(\mathbf{x}) - \frac{d_{ij}}{v})$ on the allocated sensing time in Eq. (6.13). In the future, considering the delivery delay, we will conduct more theoretical analysis and experiments to estimate our method's performance.

6.6.4 Factors in Sensing Utility

In this chapter, we adopt the non-decreasing function of sensing time as the sensing utility function for two following reasons: (1) In many crowdsensing applications, the sensing time is one of the most important contributors to sensing utility, such as crowd surveillance [5], environmental monitoring [7], and wireless data acquisition [42]. Since we do not focus on the sensing utility function design, we only consider the main factor, *i.e.*, the sensing time. (2) In most cases, the sensing task is the requirement for specific data. The longer a drone spends sensing on a task, the more sensing data it can receive, which increases the sensing utility. Nevertheless, the sensing utility always has an upper limit beyond which the utility does not increase even with more sensing time. For instance, when using drones for data collection in IoT, the utility defined as the amount of data collected is proportional to the sensing time and constrained by the maximum amount of data collected and the storage space of the sensing device [11, 12]. Thus, it is reasonable to set the sensing utility as a non-decreasing function of the sensing time.

   In addition to the sensing time, several other factors may affect the sensing utility. First, the distance between drones and sensing targets might have an effect on the sensing utility. For example, when utilizing the drone's camera to monitor traffic and crowd, the distance (between the camera and the object) can significantly affect the quality of image and the sensing utility [58]. Second, the physical environment may introduce more complex factors. For example, wind may have an effect on the drone's stability, thereby reducing the sensing quality [7, 30].

6.6.5 Impact of Sensors and Battery Weight

Firstly, we discuss the impact of the weight of the equipped sensors on the drones' energy consumption, primarily involving two cases. For one thing, many current delivery drones are already equipped with various kinds of sensors, enabling many sensing applications without additional sensing hardware [35]. Therefore, in this case, we do not need to take into account the weight's influence of the sensors on the drones' energy cost. For another, when sensing events require additional sensors, drones equipped with various additional sensors will have a heavier weight and higher energy consumption than normal delivery drones. As equipped sensors have the same effect on the drones' energy cost as the delivery packages [2], according to Eqs. (6.1) and (6.2), our energy consumption model can be extended to fit the equipped sensors' weight easily as follows $P^{\mathrm{h}}(w_{ij}) = \rho_0^{\mathrm{h}} + \rho_1^{\mathrm{h}}(w_{ij} + w_{\mathrm{s}})$; $P^{\mathrm{f}}(w_{ij}) = \rho_0^{\mathrm{f}} + \rho_1^{\mathrm{f}}(w_{ij} + w_{\mathrm{s}})$, where w_{s} indicates equipped sensors' weight.

Secondly, in this work, we do not take into account the effect of different battery weights on energy consumption; its reasonable assumption is that the drones with the same battery capacity (weight) have different available energy, due to battery charging insufficiency and deterioration. In addition, our model can be extended by considering the effect of the battery weight. Specifically, we utilize $\rho_{0i}^{\mathrm{h}}, \rho_{1i}^{\mathrm{h}}, \rho_{0i}^{\mathrm{f}}$, and ρ_{1i}^{f} to denote the power model parameters that depend on not only the factors in Eqs. (6.1) and (6.2), but also the battery weight of the drone. Therefore, we can extend our model by building new power models as $P^{\mathrm{h}}(w_{ij}) = \rho_{0i}^{\mathrm{h}} + \rho_{1i}^{\mathrm{h}}(w_{ij} + w_{\mathrm{s}})$, $P^{\mathrm{f}}(w_{ij}) = \rho_{0i}^{\mathrm{f}} + \rho_{1i}^{\mathrm{f}}(w_{ij} + w_{\mathrm{s}})$, $0 \le w_{ij} \le \overline{w}$. In future, we will further investigate how to construct more experiments in different batteries.

6.7 Conclusion

Unlike current works based on dedicated drones, we study the reuse of existing delivery drones in urban crowdsensing. Particularly, we model the energy cost of delivery drones on the basis of practical experiments. And then, based on this model, we present the route-time-weight joint optimization problem, which is a non-convex MINLP NP-hard problem. To solve this complex problem, we put forward the near-optimal algorithms that achieve $\frac{1}{4+\epsilon}$-approximation rate and the convergence guarantees for the fixed and adjustable delivery weights, respectively. Extensive trace-based simulations, field experiments, and practical applications validate the guaranteed performance of the presented algorithms.

References

1. MarketsandMarkets Research, Drone package delivery market (2019), https://www. marketsandmarkets.com/Market-Reports/drone-package-delivery-market-10580366.html. Accessed 2019
2. K. Dorling, J. Heinrichs, G.G. Messier, et al., Vehicle routing problems for drone delivery. IEEE Trans. Syst. Man Cybernet. Syst. **47**(1), 70–85 (2016)
3. Nikkei, Jd.com makes drone deliveries as coronavirus cuts off usual modes (2020), https://asia. nikkei.com/Spotlight/Coronavirus/JD.com-makes-drone-deliveries-as-coronavirus-cuts-off-usual-modes. Accessed 2020
4. CNBC, Amazon wins FAA approval for prime air drone delivery fleet (2020), https://www. cnbc.com/2020/08/31/amazon-prime-now-drone-delivery-fleet-gets-faa-approval.html. Accessed 2020
5. N.H. Motlagh, M. Bagaa, T. Taleb, UAV-based IoT platform: a crowd surveillance use case. IEEE Commun. Mag. **55**(2), 128–134 (2017)
6. M.T. Rashid, D.Y. Zhang, D. Wang, Socialdrone: an integrated social media and drone sensing system for reliable disaster response. Paper presented at IEEE INFOCOM 2020-IEEE Conference on Computer Communications, 06-09 July 2020
7. Y. Yang, Z. Hu, K. Bian, et al., ImgSensingNet: UAV vision guided aerial-ground air quality sensing system. Paper presented at IEEE INFOCOM 2019-IEEE Conference on Computer Communications, 29 April 2019–02 May 2019
8. Baidu map (2020), http://api.map.baidu.com/lbsapi/getpoint/index.html. Accessed 2020
9. A. Trotta, F.D. Andreagiovanni, M. Di Felice, et al., When UAVs ride a bus: towards energy-efficient city-scale video surveillance. Paper presented at IEEE infocom 2018-ieee conference on computer communications, 16–19 April 2018
10. Medium, Droneshare in review (2017), https://medium.com/nestegg/droneshare-in-review-d9bf4dcc8052. Accessed 2017
11. F. Shan, J. Luo, R. Xiong, et al., Looking before crossing: an optimal algorithm to minimize UAV energy by speed scheduling with a practical flight energy model. Paper presented at IEEE INFOCOM 2020-IEEE Conference on Computer Communications, 06–09 July 2020
12. Z. Zhou, J. Feng, B. Gu, et al., When mobile crowd sensing meets UAV: energy-efficient task assignment and route planning. IEEE Trans. Commun. **66**(11), 5526–5538 (2018)
13. J. Zhang, Z. Li, W. Xu, et al., Minimizing the number of deployed UAVs for delay-bounded data collection of IoT devices. Paper presented at IEEE INFOCOM 2021-IEEE Conference on Computer Communications, 10–13 May 2021
14. C. Dong, Y. Shen, Y. Qu, et al., UAVs as an intelligent service: boosting edge intelligence for air-ground integrated networks. IEEE Netw. **35**(4), 167–175 (2021)
15. M. Moradi, K. Sundaresan, E. Chai, et al., SkyCore: moving core to the edge for untethered and reliable UAV-based LTE networks. Paper presented at Proceedings of the 24th Annual International Conference on Mobile Computing and Networking, 29 October–2 November 2018
16. V. Iyer, M. Kim, S. Xue, et al., Airdropping sensor networks from drones and insects. Paper presented at Proceedings of the 26th Annual International Conference on Mobile Computing and Networking, 2–25 September 2020
17. M. Karaliopoulos, I. Koutsopoulos, L. Spiliopoulos, Optimal user choice engineering in mobile crowdsensing with bounded rational users. Paper presented at IEEE INFOCOM 2019-IEEE Conference on Computer Communications, 29 April 2019-02 May 2019
18. J. Li, Y. Zhu, Y. Hua, et al., Crowdsourcing sensing to smartphones: a randomized auction approach. IEEE Trans. Mob. Comput. **16**(10), 2764–2777 (2017)
19. M. Xiao, J. Wu, L. Huang, et al., Multi-task assignment for crowdsensing in mobile social networks. Paper presented at 2015 IEEE Conference on Computer Communications (INFOCOM), 6 April 2015–01 May 2015

20. Z. Feng, Y. Zhu, Q. Zhang, et al., TRAC: truthful auction for location-aware collaborative sensing in mobile crowdsourcing. Paper presented at IEEE INFOCOM 2014-IEEE Conference on Computer Communications, 27 April 2014–02 May 2014
21. J.L.Z. Cai, M. Yan, Y. Li, Using crowdsourced data in location-based social networks to explore influence maximization. Paper presented at IEEE INFOCOM 2016-The 35th Annual IEEE International Conference on Computer Communications, 10–14 April 2016
22. H. Zhao, M. Xiao, J. Wu, et al., Differentially private unknown worker recruitment for mobile crowdsensing using multi-armed bandits. IEEE Trans. Mob. Comput. **20**(9), 2779–2794 (2020)
23. S. Xu, X. Chen, X. Pi, et al., ilocus: incentivizing vehicle mobility to optimize sensing distribution in crowd sensing. IEEE Trans. Mob. Comput. **19**(8), 1831–1847 (2019)
24. Z. Wang, J. Zhao, J. Hu, et al., Towards personalized task-oriented worker recruitment in mobile crowdsensing. IEEE Trans. Mob. Comput. **20**(5), 2080–2093 (2020)
25. C.H. Liu, Z. Dai, Y. Zhao, et al., Distributed and energy-efficient mobile crowdsensing with charging stations by deep reinforcement learning. IEEE Trans. Mob. Comput. **20**(1), 130–146 (2019)
26. Z. He, J. Cao, X. Liu, High quality participant recruitment in vehicle-based crowdsourcing using predictable mobility. Paper presented at 2015 IEEE Conference on Computer Communications (INFOCOM), 26 April 2015–01 May 2015
27. X. Zhu, Y. Luo, A. Liu, et al., A deep learning-based mobile crowdsensing scheme by predicting vehicle mobility. IEEE Trans. Intell. Transp. Syst. **22**(7), 4648–4659 (2020)
28. M. Xiao, G. Gao, J. Wu, et al., Privacy-preserving user recruitment protocol for mobile crowdsensing. IEEE/ACM Trans. Networking **28**(2), 519–532 (2020)
29. G. Fan, H. Jin, Q. Liu, et al., Joint scheduling and incentive mechanism for spatio-temporal vehicular crowd sensing. IEEE Trans. Mob. Comput. **20**(4), 1449–1464 (2019)
30. Y. Zeng, J. Xu, R. Zhang, Energy minimization for wireless communication with rotary-wing UAV. IEEE Trans. Wirel. Commun. **18**(4), 2329–2345 (2019)
31. C.H. Liu, C. Piao, J. Tang, Energy-efficient UAV crowdsensing with multiple charging stations by deep learning. Paper presented at IEEE INFOCOM 2020-IEEE Conference on Computer Communications, 06–09 July 2020
32. L. Bertizzolo, S. D'oro, L. Ferranti, et al., SwarmControl: an automated distributed control framework for self-optimizing drone networks. Paper presented at IEEE INFOCOM 2020-IEEE Conference on Computer Communications, 06–09 July 2020
33. T. Kimura, M. Ogura, Distributed collaborative 3D-deployment of UAV base stations for on-demand coverage. Paper presented at IEEE INFOCOM 2020-IEEE conference on computer communications, 06–09 July 2020
34. S. Piao, Z. Ba, L. Su, et al., Automating CSI measurement with UAVs: from problem formulation to energy-optimal solution. Paper presented at IEEE INFOCOM 2019-IEEE Conference on Computer Communications, 29 April 2019–02 May 2019
35. Y. Pan, S. Li, Q. Chen, et al., Efficient schedule of energy-constrained UAV using crowdsourced buses in last-mile parcel delivery. Proc. ACM Int. Mob. Wear. Ubiq. Technol. **5**(1), 1–23 (2021)
36. H. Huang, A.V. Savkin, C. Huang, Round trip routing for energy-efficient drone delivery based on a public transportation network. IEEE Trans. Transport. Electrific. **6**(3), 1368–1376 (2020)
37. X. Wang, L. Duan, Dynamic pricing and capacity allocation of UAV-provided mobile services. Paper presented at IEEE INFOCOM 2019-IEEE Conference on Computer Communications, 29 April 2019–02 May 2019
38. D. Zhao, X.Y. Li, H. Ma, Budget-feasible online incentive mechanisms for crowdsourcing tasks truthfully. IEEE/ACM Trans. Networking **24**(2), 647–661 (2014)
39. T. Wu, P. Yang, H. Dai, et al., Collaborated tasks-driven mobile charging and scheduling: a near optimal result. Paper presented at IEEE INFOCOM 2019-IEEE Conference on Computer Communications, 29 April 2019–02 May 2019
40. Z. Cai, Z. Duan, W. Li, Exploiting multi-dimensional task diversity in distributed auctions for mobile crowdsensing. IEEE Trans. Mob. Comput. **20**(8), 2576–2591 (2020)

41. L. Chiaraviglio, F. D'Andreagiovanni, W. Liu, et al., Multi-area throughput and energy optimization of UAV-aided cellular networks powered by solar panels and grid. IEEE Trans. Mob. Comput. **20**(7), 2427–2444 (2020)
42. J. Gong, T.H. Chang, C. Shen, et al., Flight time minimization of UAV for data collection over wireless sensor networks. IEEE J. Select. Areas Commun. **36**(9), 1942–1954 (2018)
43. M. Mozaffari, W. Saad, M. Bennis, et al., Mobile unmanned aerial vehicles (UAVs) for energy-efficient Internet of Things communications. IEEE Trans. Wirel. Commun. **16**(11), 7574–7589 (2017)
44. Y. Wei, Y. Zhu, H. Zhu, et al., Truthful online double auctions for dynamic mobile crowdsourcing. Paper presented at 2015 IEEE Conference on Computer Communications (INFOCOM), 26 April 2015–01 May 2015
45. Z. Duan, W. Li, X. Zheng, et al., Mutual-preference driven truthful auction mechanism in mobile crowdsensing. Paper presented at IEEE 39th International Conference on Distributed Computing Systems (ICDCS), 07–10 July 2019
46. S. Martello, P. Toth, *Knapsack Problems: Algorithms and Computer Implementations* (John Wiley & Sons, Inc, New York, NY, 1990)
47. C. Xiang, Z. Zhang, Y. Qu, et al., Edge computing-empowered large-scale traffic data recovery leveraging low-rank theory. IEEE Trans. Netw. Sci. Eng. **7**(4), 2205–2218 (2020)
48. J. Lee, V.S. Mirrokni, V. Nagarajan, et al., Maximizing nonmonotone submodular functions under matroid or knapsack constraints. SIAM J. Discret. Math. **23**(4), 2053–2078 (2010)
49. J.G. Oxley, *Matroid Theory* (Oxford University Press, New York, NY, 1992)
50. Y. Wu, Y. Wang, G. Cao, Photo crowdsourcing for area coverage in resource constrained environments. Paper presented at IEEE INFOCOM 2017-IEEE Conference on Computer Communications, 01–04 May 2017
51. Y. Yang, Z. Zheng, K. Bian, et al., Real-time profiling of fine-grained air quality index distribution using UAV sensing. IEEE Intern. Things J. **5**(1), 186–198 (2018)
52. Ardupilot, Mission planner home (2019), https://ardupilot.org/planner/. Accessed 2019
53. Marzocchi O, Privacy and Data Protection Implications of the Civil Use of Drones (2015)
54. X. Zhu, S. Wang, B. Guo, et al., Sparking: a win-win data-driven contract parking sharing system. Paper presented at Adjunct Proceedings of the 2020 ACM International Joint Conference on Pervasive and Ubiquitous Computing and Proceedings of the 2020 ACM International Symposium on Wearable Computers, 12–17 September 2020
55. Y. Lin, Z. Cai, X. Wang, et al., Multi-round incentive mechanism for cold start-enabled mobile crowdsensing. IEEE Trans. Veh. Technol. **70**(1), 993–1007 (2021)
56. C. Xiang, S. He, K.G. Shin, et al., Incentivizing platform–user interactions for crowdsensing. IEEE Intern. Things J. **8**(10), 8314–8327 (2020)
57. S. Zhu, Z. Cai, H. Hu, et al., zkCrowd: a hybrid blockchain-based crowdsourcing platform. IEEE Trans. Indus. Inform. **16**(6), 4196–4205 (2019)
58. N. Damera-Venkata, T.D. Kite, W.S. Geisler, et al., Image quality assessment based on a degradation model. IEEE Trans. Image Process. **9**(4), 636–650 (2000)

Part III
Open Issues and Conclusions

Chapter 7
Open Issues

7.1 Exploring New Urban Applications

In this monograph, we present three-dimensional applications of urban sensing by utilizing crowdsensing data, including urban pollution monitoring, traffic volume prediction, and urban airborne sensing. In the future, we will explore new urban sensing applications, such as illegal on-road vehicle parking detection and wireless sensor data collection.

- **Illegal on-road vehicle parking detection.** With the increasing number of vehicles used, the illegal on-road vehicle parking is more and more popular in cities due to highly limited parking spaces. It harms city management, such as aggravating traffic jams, increasing air pollution, and incurring traffic accidents. As a result, it is greatly important to construct the illegal on-road vehicle parking detection system for large-scale cities. However, traditional methods mainly utilize fixed sensors and police patrols, rendering high costs and low coverage in large-scale cities. To this end, as illustrated in Fig. 7.1, we will leverage massive vehicular crowdsensing data (such as drones and vehicles) to detect the illegal on-road vehicle parking events accurately.
- **Wireless sensor data collection.** In recent years, Unmanned Aerial Vehicles (UAVs), have been widely used in wireless communication (*e.g.*, 5 G and 6 G) [1], followed by a proliferation of new applications, such as drone-based LTE communication [2, 3] and drone-provided mobile communication service [4]. A promising application is wireless data collection from ground sensors (GSs) [5–7], since three-dimensional mobility enables drones to easily approach GSs and establish line-of-sight (LoS) air-ground communication links with a high data rate [8, 9], as shown in Fig. 7.2. Hence, in the future, we will explore the re-utilization of delivery drones for the wireless sensor data collection on the way of delivery, thereby decreasing the deployment and maintenance cost greatly.

© The Author(s), under exclusive license to Springer Nature Singapore Pte Ltd. 2023
C. Xiang et al., *Multi-dimensional Urban Sensing Using Crowdsensing Data*, Data
Analytics, https://doi.org/10.1007/978-981-19-9006-9_7

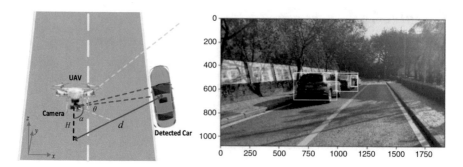

Fig. 7.1 Illegal on-road vehicle parking detection using crowdsensing data of drones and vehicles

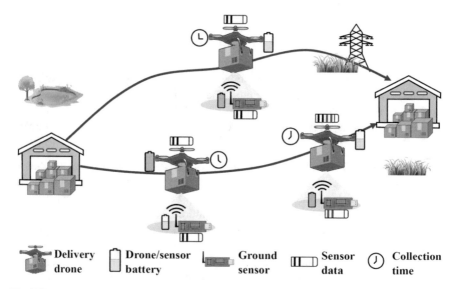

Fig. 7.2 Wireless sensor data collection using UAVs

7.2   Utilizing More Crowdsensing Data

With the rapid growth of cities and the increasing maturity of sensor technology, various sensors are deployed in ubiquitous devices, thereby making more sensing data available. In the future, we will explore utilizing different kinds of crowdsensing data for urban sensing. It mainly consists of smart building sensor data and vehicular sensor data as follows.

- **Smart building sensor data**: There are many different kinds of sensor data in smart buildings. For example, as shown in Table 7.1, the sensors deployed in the building of University of Technology Sydney are classified into three categories, including smart cameras, internal environment sensors, and rooftop weather station sensors. The internal environment sensors are comprised of the

Table 7.1 Different kinds of sensor data in smart building

Category	Data type	Measurement	Detection range	Accuracy (%)
Smart cameras	Images	Number of persons	1/6 s	1
	Video	Streaming surveillance	25/30 fps	1
Internal environment	Temperature	Indoor air temperature	−20 to 60 °C	1
	Air pollutants	Air pollution gases	1–30 ppm	1
	Carbon dioxide	CO_2 concentration	350–1000 ppm	1
	O_2	O_2 concentration	0–30%	1
Rooftop weather station	Air temperature	Outdoor temperature	−40 to 125 °C	1
	Rain gauge	Total rainfall	0–1000 mm	5
	Solar radiation	Sunlight strength	1–1000 W/m^2	5
	Air quality	AQI index	1–500	1

temperature sensor, the air pollutant sensor, the carbon dioxide sensor, and the oxygen sensor. The rooftop weather station sensors include the outdoor temperature sensor, the rain gauge sensor, the solar radiation sensor, and the outdoor air quality sensor. We can exploit these sensor data for different urban sensing applications. For example, we can use smart cameras and internal environment sensors to measure the building occupancy and carbon dioxide concentration. And then, we utilize these sensor data to build the human carbon dioxide emission model.

- **Vehicular sensor data**: The CNN News reported that "the car's sensing data will be more valuable than the car itself" [10]. It is because the ubiquitous vehicles are equipped with plenty of on-board sensors. For example, many vehicles are installed with 60–100 sensors, such as the steering sensor, the fuel level sensor, the wheel speed sensor, the accelerator pedal angle sensor, the tire pressure sensor, and the rear camera. We can utilize the numerous vehicular sensing data to enable many different kinds of urban sensing applications [11, 12], such as self-driving training [13], Pothole Patrol detection [14], turns map construction [15], and air pollution monitoring [16].

7.3   Concerning Privacy Protection

With crowdsensing data being widely used in a variety of smart city applications, privacy protection has become an unavoidable issue. At the individual level, personal information can be easily acquired through data recovery, reconstruction, correlation, and association. For instance, user trajectories can be easily inferred from datasets of urban car hailing applications [17]. At the collective (group) level, privacy leakage through crowdsensing data can have serious impacts on commercial confidentiality, public credibility, and even national security [18]. For example, urban recommendation systems rely on group preferences to recommend Point of Interest to consumers. Such group information is valuable but sensitive, as many malicious third-party would covet it.

We have acknowledged the significance of privacy protection in each work of this monograph. For example, in BuildSenSys, the data provider ensures the anonymity of the building datasets, including occupancy data and environmental data. Therefore, these data will not jeopardize occupants' privacy, as no personal information can be traced back to a single individual. Indeed, existing studies have built different tools and aggregation methods to enhance the anonymity of crowdsensing data. Reference [19] gives an insight into privacy protection techniques in crowdsensing data, including identity privacy preservation, data privacy preservation, attribute privacy preservation, and decentralized privacy preservation.

In the big data era, with more and more sensors exploited for urban sensing, privacy protection remains an open issue, attracting continuous efforts from both the research community and industrial counterparts. In scenarios of urban sensing, the ultimate goal is to preserve individual-level and collective-level privacy without compromising data utility for smart city applications.

References

1. Y. Zeng, Q. Wu, R. Zhang, Accessing from the sky: a tutorial on UAV communications for 5G and beyond. Proc. IEEE **107**(12), 2327–2375 (2019)
2. M. Moradi, K. Sundaresan, E. Chai, et al., SkyCore: moving core to the edge for untethered and reliable UAV-based LTE networks. Paper presented at Proceedings of the 24th Annual International Conference on Mobile Computing and Networking, 29 October 2018–2 November 2018
3. L. Chiaraviglio, F. D'Andreagiovanni, W. Liu, et al., Multi-area throughput and energy optimization of UAV-aided cellular networks powered by solar panels and grid. IEEE Trans. Mob. Comput. **20**(7), 2427–2444 (2020)
4. X. Wang, L. Duan, Economic analysis of unmanned aerial vehicle (UAV) provided mobile services. IEEE Trans. Mob. Comput. **20**(5), 1804–1816 (2020)
5. M. Mozaffari, W. Saad, M. Bennis, et al., A tutorial on UAVs for wireless networks: applications, challenges, and open problems. IEEE Commun. Surv. Tutor. **21**(3), 2334–2360 (2019)
6. J. Gong, T.H. Chang, C. Shen, et al., Flight time minimization of UAV for data collection over wireless sensor networks. IEEE J. Select. Areas Commun. **36**(9), 1942–1954 (2018)
7. C. Luo, M.N. Satpute, D. Li, et al., Fine-grained trajectory optimization of multiple UAVs for efficient data gathering from WSNs. IEEE/ACM Trans. Networking **29**(1), 162–175 (2020)
8. K.K. Nguyen, T.Q. Duong, T. Do-Duy, et al., 3D UAV trajectory and data collection optimisation via deep reinforcement learning. IEEE Trans. Commun. **70**(4), 2358–2371 (2022)
9. F. Shan, J. Luo, R. Xiong, et al., Looking before crossing: an optimal algorithm to minimize UAV energy by speed scheduling with a practical flight energy model. Paper presented at IEEE INFOCOM 2020-IEEE Conference on Computer Communications, 06–09 July 2020
10. CNN, Your car's data may soon be more valuable than the car itself (2017), https://money.cnn.com/2017/02/07/technology/car-data-value/index.html. Accessed 2017

11. G. Gao, M. Xiao, J. Wu, et al., Truthful incentive mechanism for nondeterministic crowdsensing with vehicles. IEEE Trans. Mob. Comput. **17**(12), 2982–2997 (2018)
12. Z. He, J. Cao, X. Liu, High quality participant recruitment in vehicle-based crowdsourcing using predictable mobility. Paper presented at 2015 IEEE Conference on Computer Communications (INFOCOM), 26 April 2015–01 May 2015
13. L. Liu, H. Li, J. Liu, et al., Bigroad: scaling road data acquisition for dependable self-driving. Paper presented at Proceedings of the 15th Annual International Conference on Mobile Systems, Applications, and Services, 19–23 June 2017
14. J. Eriksson, L. Girod, B. Hull, et al., The pothole patrol: using a mobile sensor network for road surface monitoring. Paper presented at Proceedings of the 6th international conference on Mobile systems, applications, and services, 17–20 June 2008
15. D. Chen, K.G. Shin, Turnsmap: enhancing driving safety at intersections with mobile crowdsensing and deep learning. Proc. ACM Int. Mob. Wear. Ubiq. Technol. **3**(3), 1–22 (2019)
16. X. Chen, S. Xu, X. Liu, et al., Adaptive hybrid model-enabled sensing system (HMSS) for mobile fine-grained air pollution estimation. IEEE Trans. Mob. Comput. **21**, 1927 (2022)
17. Medium, Droneshare in review (2017), https://medium.com/nestegg/droneshare-in-review-d9bf4dcc8052. Accessed 2020
18. K. Zhang, J. Ni, K. Yang, et al., Security and privacy in smart city applications: challenges and solutions. IEEE Commun. Mag. **55**(1), 122–129 (2017)
19. Y. Wang, Z. Yan, W. Feng, et al., Privacy protection in mobile crowd sensing: a survey. World Wide Web **23**(1), 421–452 (2020)

Chapter 8
Conclusions

In this monograph, we have introduced the latest research about urban crowdsensing. Specifically, in Part I, we focused on utilizing crowdsensing to sense the smart city in terms of fundamental issues of three key dimensions, including user incentivization, task recommendation, and data transmission.

- In Chap. 1, we have designed and evaluated a novel PB-based incentive mechanism, called *Picasso*, which consists of two main components. First, we have proposed a PB description method in 3D expressive space with AND, XOR, and OR, achieving a good trade-off among expressiveness, computational complexity, and description efficiency. Second, we have designed schemes for constant-factor approximation in optimal task allocation and strategy-proof in payment with computational efficiency by decomposing and recombining task dependency graph of PB. Both the theoretical analysis and trace-based case studies have validated the above essential properties of *Picasso*.

- In Chap. 2, motivated by the user studies and the large-scale vehicle dataset analysis, we have proposed LSTRec, a new Task Recommendation model that combines short-term and long-term profits, trying to resurrect the MOVE-CS market. Behind it is a spatial-temporal differentiation-aware task recommendation scheme, which involves RNN-based pick-up heatmap prediction, the differentiation-aware sensing reward design, and the submodularity-based task recommendation algorithm. Simulation results have shown that LSTRec can ensure positive profits for drivers and a near-optimal profit for the platform, thus reviving MOVE-CS potentially.

- In Chap. 3, we have proposed *GTR*, an edge computing-empowered traffic data recovery system leveraging low-rank theory. First, we conducted experimental explorations based on a large-scale traffic dataset. The results uncovered the serious issue of missing traffic data and revealed its spatio-temporal correlations. Inspired by these observations, we proposed a sub-optimal edge node deployment algorithm with a performance guarantee and an accurate traffic data recovery scheme based on the low-rank theory. Extensive theoretical analyses and

© The Author(s), under exclusive license to Springer Nature Singapore Pte Ltd. 2023
C. Xiang et al., *Multi-dimensional Urban Sensing Using Crowdsensing Data*, Data Analytics, https://doi.org/10.1007/978-981-19-9006-9_8

traces-based evaluations demonstrated that *GTR* outperformed five baseline methods in both the edge node deployment and traffic recovery.

Moreover, in Part II, we put forward three kinds of urban sensing applications leveraging crowdsensing data, including urban pollution monitoring, traffic volume prediction, and urban airborne sensing.

- In Chap. 4, we proposed an EM-based iterative truthful-source identification method, identifying the low-level radiation sources accurately and robustly based on inaccurate crowd-sensing measurements. The sensor efficiency of users and the truthful probability of sources were iterated to be estimated alternatively, gradually increasing the likelihood values of crowd-sensing measurements. The experimental results and theoretical analysis demonstrated that our method could achieve a maximum likelihood, where the truthful probability estimations of sources were optimal. Thus, we can accurately identify the truthful radiation sources based on inaccurate crowd-sensing measurements.
- In Chap. 5, we have proposed BuildSenSys, a building sensing data-based traffic volume prediction system with cross-domain learning. We have performed a wide experimental analysis on building-traffic correlations by applying datasets from multiple sources in the real world. They have shown that building data is hugely related to traffic data. Then, we have put forward a cross-domain learning-based RNN with cross-domain and temporal attention mechanisms to identify building-traffic correlations for accurate traffic prediction cooperatively. Additionally, we have implemented a prototype system of BuildSenSys and conducted many experiments. It has been validated that BuildSenSys outperforms seven baseline methods by up to 65.3% in terms of the prediction accuracy. We believe that this work can pave a new path for the reuse of building sensing data for traffic sensing and prediction, thus revealing an interconnection between smart buildings and intelligent transportation.
- In Chap. 6, we answered the question of when drones deliver packages from the warehouses to the service stations, how could they perform the sensing tasks under the energy capacities? Distinguished from existing works on dedicated drones, we investigated the re-utilization of available delivery drones in urban crowdsensing. In particular, we build the energy cost model of delivery drones based on real-world experiments. Then, based on this model, we formulated the route-time-weight joint optimization problem, which is a non-convex MINLP NP-hard problem. To address this complex problem, we proposed near-optimal algorithms, achieving $\frac{1}{4+\epsilon}$-approximation ratio and the convergence guarantee when the delivery weight of each route is fixed and adjustable, respectively. Extensive trace-based simulations, field experiments, and real-world applications validated the guaranteed performance of the proposed algorithms.

Finally, in Part III, we present three important open issues, *i.e.*, exploring new urban applications, utilizing more crowdsensing data, and accounting for privacy protection. To sum up, this book focuses on "multi-dimensional urban sensing using crowdsensing data." It helps readers comprehend how to collect and exploit the crowdsensing data for diverse urban applications.

Printed in the United States
by Baker & Taylor Publisher Services